eating
&
drinking

an A-Z of great food and drink combinations

eating
& drinking

fiona beckett

illustrations by jessie tattersall

Eating & Drinking
by Fiona Beckett

First published in Great Britain
in 2000 by Mitchell Beazley,
an imprint of Octopus Publishing
Group Ltd, 2–4 Heron Quays,
London E14 4JB

ISBN 1 84000 232 8

A CIP catalogue record for this book is
available from the British Library

Commissioning Editor: Margaret Little
Art Director: Rita Wuthrich
Executive Art Editor: Tracy Killick
Designer: Sarah Williams
Editor: Stephen Guise
Index: Angie Hipkin

Typeset in Franklin Gothic
Printed and bound by Toppan in China

Contents

Introduction

The French and Italians do it without thinking. The Californians have elevated it into a science. But for most of us the business of deciding what to drink with our meals remains a bit of a hit-and-miss affair.

It all used to be so easy. If it was beef or lamb you drank **claret**. With fish you'd never dream of drinking anything other than **Chablis** or **Muscadet**. But the world has moved on from the simple, straightforward food of 30 years ago: in an average week you could easily encounter half a dozen different cuisines and be confronted with hundreds of different wines from all over the globe.

It's utterly understandable under these circumstances that we should give up even trying to work out what goes with what and, instead, take the view that anything goes. Of course, there's nothing to stop you drinking **claret** with oysters or **Lambrusco** with lamb chops, any more than there is to prevent you spreading marmalade on your kippers or sprinkling Parmesan on your cornflakes. Ultimately there's nothing to stop you drinking the same wine with everything if you want.

But many people who love food are keen to explore the myriad different flavours the world of wine, beer and spirits has to offer and experience the buzz you get from discovering a great match. It's not so much a question of: can you drink 'x' with 'y'? Of course you can: no one's stopping you. But there might be something you'd enjoy even more. And if you're taking the trouble to cook for other people, it's well worth taking time to work out what will best show off your food.

This book covers not only wine but other alcoholic drinks as well. Spirits generally don't get a look in because they're considered too strong to drink with food, but it's fun to bring them in where appropriate. And it's high time beer was hauled out of the dark ages and given the recognition it deserves: beer actually works better than wine with some dishes.

You shouldn't feel pressured to go along with any food and drink combination because it's considered a perfect match. Oysters, for example, are great with **Guinness**, but if you don't like **Guinness** – or oysters for that matter – then it's not going to work for you.

Everyone's taste buds differ and you'll find as many opinions about the ideal match as you do about the best way to cook certain recipes. The combinations recommended in these pages are those that work for me and have given my family and friends pleasure. I hope you enjoy them too.

How to use this book

The main part of this book is an **A-Z of food and drink** containing drink suggestions for a range of popular ingredients and dishes. Inevitably they won't cover every single dish on the planet, but I hope you'll find most of things here that you enjoy eating. What I've left out are dishes that aren't fashionable any more (the kind of restaurant dishes you used to find in the '60s and '70s); or that you very rarely come across (woodcock, snipe); or that are simply unappetising (snake, tapioca pudding); or foods you're extremely unlikely to pair with any kind of alcoholic drink, such as pot noodles, porridge, or faggots.

If you don't immediately find the dish you're looking for, check under the entry for the **main ingredient** or other key ingredients in the recipe. If you draw a blank there, try under the different national cuisines that are listed. Take, for example, 'enchilladas', which are not listed as a separate entry. You'll find some useful advice under 'chicken' and under 'chillies'. But your best bet would be to look under 'Mexican food'.

If even this fails – and I hope it won't – think of the *style* of the dish and try to find a similar type of recipe. A dish of pork with cream and mushrooms, for example, would suit the same kind of wine as 'chicken with a creamy sauce'. If the advice you find for two different ingredients appears to conflict, work out which one of them is dominant.

If you can't decide which is the most important influence on flavour, go for something that can cope with the lot. Consult the list of **Ten food-friendly wines** on page 14. What you come up with may not be a *great* match but it'll rub along.

Wines and beers can vary quite considerably – as can recipes – and there may be one or two suggestions here that for a variety of reasons won't quite work for you. Sometimes the dish can turn out hotter, sharper, sweeter or saltier than usual. Also, don't rule out that if you're drinking wine it might be corked, in which case it'll taste musty, or it might be faulty in some other way.

Finally, just because I've mentioned certain wines or beers it doesn't mean that others of a similar style won't work well. If I suggest that a dish, roast lamb for example, goes well with **medium-bodied red wines**, you could probably drink most medium-bodied reds with it. The **Wine and beer styles** section contains a listing of most of the popular wines and beers that come under each of the main wine and beer styles, so do experiment with other bottles.

Some ground rules

I hesitate to use the word 'rule' because you shouldn't feel fettered by them, but here's some basic advice that works.

1. Forget most of the rules you've heard of
All that 'red-wine-with-meat', 'white-wine-with-fish' stuff doesn't make sense these days. But two bits of advice that still do are: drink **dry** before **sweet** wines and **lighter** wines before more **full-bodied** ones (just as you don't eat dessert before your main course or steak before your soup).

2. You can't match wine to chicken
Well, actually you can, but how often do you eat chicken plain and unadorned? More often it's cooked in a sauce or marinade and that's what should dictate your choice of wine. There's a world of difference between chicken in a delicate creamy sauce and a Thai green chicken curry. That of course applies to other basic dishes and ingredients too.

3. Light dishes suit light wines – richly flavoured dishes need more robust wines
You probably do this instinctively anyway, but you need a **lighter** wine with dishes that are served cold or lightly cooked than you do with dishes that are hot, roasted, seared, char-grilled or served in rich sauces. You don't want what you drink to overwhelm the food or to be swamped by it.

4. See what else is on the plate

Strongly flavoured vegetables such as onions and red cabbage, sharply flavoured chutneys and spicy salsas can all affect the taste of your wine. That's not necessarily a reason to choose a different type of wine, but you might need a **more full-bodied** example to cope (a **full fruity Chilean Merlot**, for example, rather than a **light Italian** version).

5. Respect tradition – but not slavishly

Countries such as France and Italy have been putting the same wines and dishes together for years. That's not to say that other wines might not go equally well, but if you know what works, hey, why struggle to find one?

6. Follow the logic of the recipe

If a dish or recipe suggests an appropriate drink: go for it. If a dish is cooked in wine, beer or cider it generally makes sense to drink the same or a similar bottle with it. If you're serving a chocolate dessert with raspberries or cherries, it's a natural progression to serve a **sweet red wine** or **fruit-flavoured beer** alongside the dish.

7. Sweet dishes need sweeter wines

If you have a dessert that's sweeter than your wine it can make it taste unpleasantly sharp. Go for a wine that's sweeter than your pud: a **fortified wine** such as **sherry** or **port** if need be.

Eating out

If there's one thing that makes your heart sink in a restaurant, it's being handed the wine list. It's bad enough having to choose something to drink with two different dishes, but what if you're ordering for a party of eight or ten? Given the number of ingredients on most plates these days, it could easily result in 50-odd different flavours to contend with. So, is finding a wine to match a forlorn hope?

If you're looking for one of those combinations that make the earth move, the answer is probably 'yes'. But there are a number of food-friendly wines (*see* page 14) that will accommodate a whole range of flavours. On the whole, wines from the **new world** (countries such as **Australia** and **Chile**) cope better with the bold flavours of modern food. They're also more consistent. But it depends on the restaurant. If you're eating Italian, go for an **Italian** wine. In Italy or any other wine producing country it always makes sense to drink local. But many restaurants these days serve dishes that incorporate a number of different ethnic influences. What then?

If it's the kind of restaurant that has a specialist wine waiter, don't be afraid to ask for advice, and don't regard this as a cop out. They'll probably relish the opportunity to exercise a bit of creative matchmaking skill on your behalf. If you're worried they'll sting you with a more expensive wine than you can afford, tell them what you're prepared to pay.

Wines by the glass can be a great boon, particularly if there are only a couple of you and you don't want to buy two different bottles. Or you could order a couple of half bottles, though the selection in most restaurants is generally not as good.

If there's no one to turn to for expert advice, think about the flavours in the dish you've chosen. Sometimes you get a clue from the description – 'Salad Niçoise', for instance, might lead you towards a **Provençal rosé** – but otherwise run your eye over the ingredients.

Menu examples

Wild mushroom, artichoke, anchovy and goat's cheese tart
There are four strong flavours in this tart that would overwhelm
anything a bit subtle. On the other hand it's a starter, so you might
not want to kick off with a powerful red. Goat's cheese is the clue –
it goes brilliantly with **Sauvignon Blanc** and the rest of the ingredients
should follow suit.

Baked fillet of cod with basil mash and smoked bacon *jus*
Cod might suggest white, but this is a strongly flavoured dish.
The cod is baked and accompanied by a savoury bacon gravy. A **red**
is just as good as a white. Go for a **Merlot** or a **Pinot Noir**.

Roast chicken with wild mushrooms, pasta and Madeira sauce
If you concentrate on the chicken you might think this is a light dish,
but 'Madeira' should flash a warning light that the sauce is going to
be rich and could take a **full-bodied red** such as a **Syrah** or **Shiraz**,
or a strong **Belgian beer**.

**Grilled fillet of beef with noodles, Chinese cabbage and
soy dressing**
The classic beef and claret combination is going to struggle a bit
given the oriental twist on this dish. A **softer fruitier red**, such as
a **Chilean Merlot**, would work better.

**Fresh raspberries glazed with almond cream served with
lemon curd ice cream**
Raspberries might suggest a sweet red, but you've also got the tart
lemon influence of the ice cream, which is likely to be the stronger of
the two flavours. Go for a **Late-Harvest wine** – **Riesling** generally
works well with lemon.

Ten food-friendly wines

Unoaked Chardonnay

A more flexible friend than some of the big oaky monsters that can overwhelm lighter dishes. A useful partner for chicken, salmon and lighter pork dishes.

Sauvignon Blanc

Particularly good with fish, salads and spicy southeast Asian dishes.

Australian Riesling

Again, a good candidate for spicy food, particularly fish, chicken and pork.

Australian Sémillon

And another.

Pinot Blanc from Alsace

Not dissimilar to Chardonnay (and works with the same sort of dishes), but marks you out as a bit of a wine buff.

Pinot Grigio

The quality of this Italian grape variety can vary, but at its best it's great with antipasti, pasta dishes, fish and chicken dishes. There's also a version called **Pinot Gris** that is fuller and richer. Look in the **Alsace**, **California** and **New Zealand** sections of the wine list.

Albariño

Something of a cult wine at the moment. A luscious **dry Spanish white** that's particularly good with fish. Works well with pasta and rice dishes too.

Pinot Noir

Can vary depending on where it's grown (it's most famous incarnation is in Burgundy) but generally a **lightish fruity red** that goes as well with fish as it does with lighter meats.

Merlot

Especially from **Chile**. Crowd-pleasing **soft red** that works with a wide range of foods from pizza to steak.

Dry rosé

Deserves to be more widely recognised for its versatility. Obvious candidate for salads and charcuterie but can also work with mildly spiced dishes like paella. Great summer drinking.

Eating in

The big advantage of eating in – or out of doors in your garden – is that everyone's eating the same food. This means that you only have to pick *one* drink to complement *one* set of flavours.

The way you play it depends how formally the meal is structured. If you're having a slap-up three-course dinner party, serve a different bottle with each course. If it's a more informal affair with a range of dishes (for example, if you were cooking Mexican or middle eastern food), put two or three different bottles on the table and let everyone help themselves.

Any wine or aperitif you serve before the meal kicks off can usually be carried through to the first course. Then switch to another wine for the main course. It's common to have red wine at this stage, but remember to leave enough white wine on hand for guests who prefer it.

If you're having cheese you can either serve it straight after the main course as the French do and carry on drinking the same wine. Or you can serve it in the traditional way at the end of the meal with a glass of sweet wine or port (see page 35). If you like you can also serve **dessert wine** as a substitute for a pudding if you haven't time to make one. Just lay on a few really delicious biscuits or dried fruit and nuts and serve it well chilled.

Nine Fine Aperitifs
- **Chilled fino** or **manzanilla sherry**
- **German** or **Australian Riesling**
- **Viognier**
- **Champagne** or **sparkling wine**
- **Kir** or **kir royale**
- **Gin and tonic** (with lots of ice and lemon)
- **White port**
- **Wheat beer**
- **Fruit beer**

The downside, of course, is that the more wines you serve the more you're likely to consume. You should normally allow half to two-thirds of a bottle a head – depending on how many of the guests are likely to be drinking. If you serve a wider selection of wines, you need to allow closer to a bottle each.

For parties of more than ten people, stick to two or three wines – a **white**, a **red** and maybe a **sparkling wine** or **fruit cup**. With large numbers there's no point in trying to be unduly clever about matching the food. Just go for simple crowd pleasers that work well with everything. You can hardly go wrong with **Chardonnay** and **Merlot** though stick to ones that are light and fruity,

A bit of psychology

Which wine or beer to choose depends on the type of food you're serving (there's plenty of advice on that in the main part of the book) but also who's sitting round your table. Just as you instinctively choose food you think your guests will appreciate, it's thoughtful to pick wine they're likely to enjoy. If I were having elderly relatives round for a traditional Sunday lunch for example, I'd go for **Chablis** and **claret**. If a whole crowd of my kids' backpacking friends came round for a barbecue I'd choose something offbeat like **Argentinian Malbec**, **Uruguayan Tannat** or a **Moroccan red** and a good supply of **beer**.

Six Foods that Flatter Wine
Simply roast meat and game – most good red wines
Luxury shellfish (scallops, langoustines, lobster) – good **white burgundy** and **new world Chardonnay**
Mushrooms – **older reds** especially **Pinot Noir**
Truffles – ditto
Parmesan – the best cheese to serve with **older reds**
Apple or pear tarts – show off fine **dessert wines**

You also need to be aware of the seasons. Unless you're a real red wine maniac, don't carry on serving hefty oaky reds all through the summer, particularly on boiling hot days. But when it comes to winter and you've got a ribsticking casserole in front of you it doesn't make sense to be sipping a light flowery German Riesling.

Special occasions

If you've got a very special bottle or celebration you might want to work the food round the wine. **Champagne** is actually more flexible than you might think and is just as good a partner for food as many white wines. Although it's seen as an aperitif it goes terrifically well with fish, crispy deep fried foods, and delicate Chinese and Japanese dishes. Older, more mature reds also need careful handling if you're not to overpower their fragile delicate flavours. Simply roast meat or game is the safest option.

Of course, wine is not essential. I personally don't like mixing wine and spirits, so if you kick off with a cocktail or fruit punch (as I might with a spicy Thai or Caribbean meal) offer beer as well as wine. In fact, sometimes you can do without wine at all. With a Russian-style brunch of blinis (tiny pancakes topped with smoked salmon, caviar or lumpfish roe), **iced vodka shots** and a good **premium lager** would be ideal.

Finally don't forget that **coffee** and **tea** are not just drinks to round off the meal but can accompany food in their own right. **Herbal** and **green teas** are fantastic with Chinese, Japanese and Vietnamese food, and coffee is a great partner for anything chocolatey – particularly when it's strong and black.

Wine and beer styles

Not all the wine and beer recommendations in this book are specific. Sometimes a dish goes with a whole group of drinks such as **lager** or **full-bodies red wines**. In case you're unfamiliar with some of the descriptions I'm using, here's a list of the most common wines and beers in each style together with a few food suggestions.

Wines

CRISP FRESH FRUITY WHITES

Includes: **Sancerre** and other **Sauvignon Blancs**, **dry Italian whites** like **Pinot Grigio**, **Soave** and **Frascati**, **Chablis**, **Muscadet**, **Vin de Pays des Côtes de Gascogne** and other inexpensive **French whites**, **Rueda**, inexpensive **white Rioja**, **Vinho Verde**, **Greek whites**. Good with: fish, salads, pasta and antipasti, stir-fries, dishes flavoured with lemon or lime, garlic, chilli and coriander, summery food in general.

SMOOTH DRY WHITES

Includes: **unoaked Chardonnay**, **Sémillon**, **Chenin Blanc**, **Pinot Blanc**, **Albariño**, **Roussanne**, basic **Bourgogne Blanc** and other inexpensive **white burgundies**. Good with: salmon, chicken, turkey, pork and veal especially in light creamy sauces, fishcakes, eggs, quiches.

FULL-FLAVOURED OAKY WHITES

Includes: **oaked** or **Reserve Chardonnays** (especially from **California**), expensive **white burgundies** like **Meursault**. Good with: richly flavoured chicken, fish and shellfish dishes (especially lobster), buttery sauces.

AROMATIC, SPICY or FLOWERY WHITES

Includes: **Riesling**, **Viognier**, **Gewürztraminer**, **Pinot Gris**, **dry Muscat**, **Torrontes** (most wines from **Alsace**, **Austria** and **Germany** come into this category). Good with: spicy oriental (particularly Thai and Vietnamese) and fusion food (dishes with an oriental influence – sometimes called Pacific Rim), mild curries. Also good for drinking on their own.

LIGHT FRUITY REDS

Includes: basic **red burgundy** and other inexpensive **Pinot Noirs**, **Beaujolais** and other wines made from the **Gamay** grape, **Côtes du Rhône**, simple **French *vin de pays***, **Valpolicella**, **Montepulciano d'Abruzzo** and other **light Italian reds**, inexpensive **Australian** and **South African reds**. Good with: pasta, pizza, cold meats and pâtés, grilled chicken, salmon and tuna, tomato-based sauces.

SMOOTH MEDIUM-BODIED REDS

Includes: most **Merlot**, moderately priced **Cabernet Sauvignon**, **claret**, **Chianti**, **Rioja**, more expensive **red burgundies**. Good with: simply grilled and roast meat and game, roast or char-grilled vegetables, baked pasta dishes, mushrooms, cheese.

RICH FULL-BODIED REDS

Includes: **Australian Shiraz**, more expensive **Cabernets** or **Cabernet blends**, **Argentine Malbec**, **South African Pinotage**, **Zinfandel**, **Grenache**, top **Italian reds** such as **Barolo**, **Châteauneuf-du-Pape**, **traditional southern French reds** such as **Fitou** and **Corbières**, pricier **Spanish** and **Portuguese reds**. Good with: steak, rich braises and casseroles, barbecued ribs, spicy meat dishes, chillies, winter food.

ROSES

Light and medium dry includes: **Hungarian rosé**, **Portuguese rosé**, **Rosé d'Anjou**, **white Zinfandel**.

Soft and fruity includes: **Pinot Noir rosé**, **Merlot rosé**, **Bordeaux rosé**, **Bergerac rosé**.

Rustic includes: **Spanish *rosado*** (especially from **Navarra**), **Provençal** and **southern French rosé**, **Syrah rosé**.

Intensely fruity includes: **Australian** and **Chilean rosé**, **Cabernet Sauvignon rosé**.

Good with: **lighter rosés** – cold meats, salads, picnics; **more robust rosés** – Mediterranean, spicy and barbecued foods.

Dessert wines

LIGHT AND FIZZY

Asti and **Moscato d'Asti**, **Clairette de Die**. Good with: fresh fruit, fruit salads, light lemon flavoured puddings, pavlovas.

LIGHT AND SWEET

German Auslese and inexpensive **Beerenauslese Rieslings**. **Late-Harvest Riesling**. Good with: apple- and lemon-flavoured desserts.

SAUTERNES-STYLE

Sauternes, **Barsac**, **Cadillac**, **Loupiac**, **Monbazillac** and other **sweet wines** from **Bordeaux**, **Late-Harvest Sémillons**. Good with: fruit tarts (especially apple, pear, apricot and strawberry), crème brûlée, blue cheeses.

RICH AND SWEET

Southern french Muscats such as **Muscat de Beaumes-de-Venise**, **Moscatel de Valencia**, **Orange Muscat**, **Australian Liqueur Muscat**, **Tokaji**, **Vin Santo**. Good with: orange-, caramel- and toffee-flavoured desserts, mince pies, Christmas pudding, blue cheeses.

INTENSELY SWEET

German and **Austrian Beerenauslese**, **Trockenbeerenauslese** and **Eiswein**. Best sipped on their own.

SWEET REDS

Port (*see* below), **Californian Black Muscats**, **Recioto**, **Greek Mavrodaphne**. Good with: chocolate-, raspberry- or cherry-flavoured desserts, pears or peaches in red wine.

Fortified wines (port, sherry and Madeira)

CRISP AND DRY

Fino and **manzanilla sherry**, **Sercial Madeira**. Good with: olives, nuts, tapas, tortilla.

LIGHT AND SWEET

Pale cream sherry, **white port**, basic **tawny port**. Good with: melon, mild creamy cheeses.

RICH AND NUTTY

Amontillado and **dry oloroso sherry**, **five-** and **ten-year-old Madeira**, **ten-** and **20-year-old tawny port**. Good with: caramel, toffee, nut flavoured puddings and hard cheeses.

SWEET AND RAISINY

Sweet oloroso sherry, **malmsey Madeira**, **Australian Liqueur Muscat**. Good with: fruit cake, nuts, or on its own.

RICH RED AND BRAMBLY

Ruby, **vintage character**, **late-bottled vintage** and **vintage ports**, **fortified southern French wines** such as **Banyuls** and **Rivesaltes**. Good with: chocolate-, raspberry- and cherry-flavoured desserts, blue cheese.

Beers

LIGHT DRY CRISP BEERS

Includes: **lager**, **pilsner**, **wheat beers**, **pale ales**, **summer beers**. Good with: fish, salads, deep fried foods, spicy or oriental dishes.

FRUITY HOPPY BEERS

Includes: **English bitter**, **American amber ales**, **IPA**. Good with: cold meats, sandwiches, cheese, chicken and pork dishes, mild curries.

DARK MALTY BEERS

Includes: **stout** and **porter**, **nut brown ales**, **Trappist beers** and **winter ales**. Good with: ribsticking casseroles and braises, chocolate, cheese.

SUPER-STRONG BEERS (6% PLUS)

Includes: many **Belgian** and **northern French beers**, **vintage ales**. Good with: robustly flavoured garlicky dishes, steak, cheese.

FLAVOURED BEERS

Includes: **fruit beers** (good with: salads, brie-type cheeses, desserts), **honey beers** (salads, chicken), **ginger-flavoured beers** (crab, stir-fries), **smoked beers** (smoked fish, bacon).

A-Z of food & drink

Aioli

Super-garlicky Provençal mayonnaise that works best with traditional **southern French dry whites** or **rosés** – from **Provence** if you want to do the whole Peter Mayle bit (**Bandol** if you can afford it). And **Spanish Albariño** works well, as does **Australian Verdelho**.

Afro-Caribbean

A spicy style of cooking that tends to go better with **beer** or **rum-based cocktails** – such as **rum punch**, **daiquiris** or **mojitos** – than wine. To carry through the Caribbean theme, serve a **Jamaican lager** such as **Red Stripe**. (*See also* Jerk chicken.)

Almonds

Salted almonds are the classic accompaniment for **fino** or **manzanilla sherry**. With almond or frangipane tarts go for a **sweet Loire white** such as **Coteaux du Layon**. For almond cake with lemon or orange pick an **Australian Late-Harvest** or **botrytis Riesling**. With macaroons, a **five-** or **ten-year-old Madeira** or **oloroso sherry**.

Anchovies

Can give dishes a really salty tang that goes better with **whites** and **rosés** than reds (though red works fine with pizza). With Mediterranean dishes, such as *anchoiade* (anchovy and garlic paste) and *bagna cauda* (anchovy and garlic dip), drink a **southern French** or **dry Italian white**, inexpensive **Sauvignon Blanc** or a **French** or **Spanish rosé**. **Manzanilla sherry** is also good. (*See also* Salads.)

Antipasti (Italian-style cold meats and vegetables)

Why stray outside Italy? **Dry Italian whites** such as **Pinot Grigio**, **Soave**, **Frascati**, **Orvieto** and **Verdicchio** are just made for this type of food. Or a **light red** such as **Montepulciano d'Abruzzo** or **Valpolicella**.

Apples

Apple desserts Light mousses, parfaits and sorbets: **Prosecco, Moscato d'Asti, German Spätlese Riesling** and **Australian Riesling**. Traditional apple pies and puddings: **Californian** or **Chilean Gewurztraminer** can work if the pudding is not too sweet or heavy; otherwise stick to custard. French apple tart is a classic partner for fine **dessert wines** such as **Sauternes, Coteaux du Layon** and other **dessert wines from the Loire**, or a **botrytis Sémillon** (see also Tarte Tatin). Baked apples: **sweet oloroso sherry, Liqueur Muscat** or a **vintage** or **festive ale**.

Apples in savoury dishes **Cider** is the obvious choice, but **softer oaked Sauvignon Blancs** – from **California, Germany** or **Alsace** – or **Australian Rieslings** and **Chenin Blanc** also work well. (See also Chicken, Pork, Pheasant.)

Apricot tart

Great with a **southern French Muscat** such as **Muscat de Beaumes-de-Venise** or **Muscat de Rivesaltes**, or **Hungarian Tokaji**.

Artichokes

Globe artichokes Tough on any wine. You can just get away with a **rustic earthy white** such as **southern French Terret** or **Italian Verdicchio** if you dress the artichokes with a lemony vinaigrette. A big **Aussie** or **New Zealand Sauvignon Blanc** should also power through. Avoid red wines like the plague: artichokes make them taste metallic. (See Sauces for hollandaise.)

Jerusalem artichokes Most commonly encountered in soup, but occasionally in salads or purées. Best partnered by a **smooth dry white** such as **unoaked Chardonnay** or **Pinot Blanc**.

Asparagus

Not nearly as difficult as it's made out to be. **Sauvignon Blanc** is the star choice, particularly with salads or asparagus served with a vinaigrette or balsamic vinegar. Also **blends of Sémillon and Sauvignon (dry white Bordeaux), dry Muscat** and **wheat beer**. With richer dishes, such as asparagus with melted butter, hollandaise, asparagus quiche or *feuilleté* of asparagus, **unoaked Chardonnay** or **Pinot Blanc** work better. Note: grilling or barbecuing asparagus makes it more wine friendly – you could even drink a **rosé** or **light red**.

Aubergines

Generally incorporated in rich spicy Mediterranean or Middle Eastern dishes, often with tomatoes and sometimes with cheese (*see* Moussaka). Choose a **full-bodied red** to match: wines from the **Rhône**, **Languedoc-Roussillon**, **Portugal**, **Spain** and **Morocco** all fit the bill, as do the up-and-coming **new Greek reds**. Aubergine purée or dip goes better with a **dry southern French white** or **rosé**.

Avocados

Don't have much flavour of their own but are often partnered with rich or flavourful ingredients. Served with a vinaigrette or salad, they're generally best with a **crisp dry white** (**Italian** in the case of avocado, tomato and mozzarella salad). Stuffed with prawns or crab, in a cocktail or slightly spicy sauce, they need a wine with a bit more character such as a **New Zealand Sauvignon Blanc** or an **Australian sparkling Chardonnay**. Delicately flavoured dishes such as avocado mousse or soup work with a **neutral white** such as **Chablis** or **Pinot Blanc** (*see also* Guacamole).

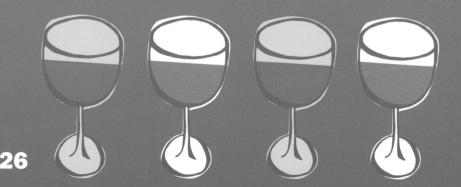

Bacon

Doesn't have a strong enough flavour to interfere with any wine unless it's particularly smoky (in which case try a **smoked beer**). Bacon and egg pie, for instance, would be fine with a **light Chardonnay**. More substantial dishes such as boiled bacon and cabbage or bacon roly poly are terrific with **Guinness** or a good **British bitter**. Bacon and eggs are surprisingly good with **claret**.

Balsamic vinegar

Intensely concentrated sweet-sour seasoning that tends to flatten lighter wines. **Fruity reds** tend to work better than whites. Good **Valpolicella**, **Dolcetto**, less expensive **Australian Shiraz** and **Cabernet/Shiraz**, and other **fruity Cabernets** (from **Chile** for example) should all cope well.

Balti

See Indian.

Bakewell tart

Belgian cherry- or **raspberry-flavoured fruit beer; sparkling Aussie red; basic ruby port** or **cherry brandy**.

Banoffee pie (and other banana-flavoured desserts)

Rich sticky toffee-flavoured **Australian Liqueur Muscat** works brilliantly with almost all banana desserts – even bananas cooked in rum (rum is too strong to drink with it). If you find this too sweet, go for a **Tokaji**, **Madeira** or **ten-year-old tawny port**. (*See also* Tarte Tatin.)

Barbecued ribs

Big jammy reds are called for. **Zinfandel** is a particularly good choice. **Australian** or **South African Shiraz**, **Australian** or **Chilean Cabernet Sauvignon** and **Argentinian Malbec** would all be fine too. So would **Bourbon-based cocktails**, such as **mint julep**.

Basil

An integral part of Mediterranean cooking – particularly French and Italian – basil is seldom seen without the company of tomatoes, which influence your wine choice as much as the herb itself. With salads and pasta dishes, go for **dry Italian whites** such as **Soave** and **Bianco di Custoza**, or a **light Chardonnay** or **Sauvignon Blanc**. With more robust dishes, choose a gutsy **southern French** or **Italian red** such as a **Sangiovese**. (*See also* Pesto, Tomatoes.)

Beans

Generally incorporated in substantial rustic dishes, such as cassoulet, that need gutsy **full-bodied wines** to match. **Southern French reds** such as **Fitou**, **Costières de Nîmes**, **Pic St-Loup**, and **Côtes du Roussillon** are all suitable, as are inexpensive **Spanish**, **Portuguese** and **southern Italian reds**. **French** and **Spanish rosés** are also good, particularly with bean salads. Boston Baked Beans, with their rich, sweet, treacly sauce, would be better with a **Shiraz** or **Grenache**, or a **Scotch Ale**. (*See also* Cassoulet; for black bean sauce *see* Chinese.)

Beef

Simply roast or grilled beef The ideal opportunity to show off a really good **red**, though it goes particularly well with **red Bordeaux**, **Cabernet**, **Merlot** (and **Cabernet/Merlot blends**), **Shiraz** and substantial reds such as **Châteauneuf-du-Pape**. If you're drinking a relatively young or intensely fruity wine I would serve the beef rare or char-grilled. Medium-rare or well-cooked beef suits a softer red such as a **mature claret** or **Rioja** – particularly if served with old-fashioned gravy. (*See also* Burgers, Steak.)

Beef braised in beer *Carbonnade Flamande* and beef and ale pie, for example, can be drunk with a strong **Belgian beer** such as **Chimay**, **Orval** or **Duvel**. If you use Guinness in the recipe, serve **stout** or **porter**.

Beef braised in wine *Boeuf Bourguignonne* and *Boeuf en daube* for example: you would traditionally drink the same type of wine that you used for cooking. However, there's no harm in cooking with an inexpensive wine (a **basic red Burgundy**, say) and serving a more substantial one (such as **Volnay**). More **full-bodied reds** such as **Bandol**, **Barolo**, **Cornas**, **Madiran**, **St-Joseph** and **Australian Shiraz** also fit the bill.

Boiled beef, salt beef and cold roast beef A decent **Beaujolais** (such as a **Morgon** or **Moulin-à-Vent**) or a **Merlot**. With the Italian dish *Bollito misto* go for a good **Valpolicella** or young **Barbera**. With salt-beef sandwiches a **light lager**.

Beef stroganoff A good **village wine** from the **Rhône** such as **Cairanne**, **Vacqueyras** or **Lirac**, or an inexpensive **red Bordeaux**. **Vintage rosé Champagne** if you're feeling daring.

Beef Wellington and *Boeuf en croute* **Red Bordeaux**, especially **St-Emilion** and **Pomerol**, or a top **Chilean Merlot**. Côte-Rôtie from the **Rhône** if you can run to it.

Beef *teriyaki* and stir-fried beef Fruity medium-bodied Australian **Shiraz**, **Grenache**, or **Zinfandel**.

Beef stew with dumplings A simple **fruity red** such as **Côtes du Rhône**, inexpensive **Spanish** or **Portuguese red**, or a **traditional British ale** or **cider**.

Beetroot

Has a robust earthy slightly sweet flavour (particularly when baked) that's best matched by a **fruity young red** such as **Californian** or **New Zealand Pinot Noir**, or a **Chilean Cabernet** or **Merlot**. With beetroot *risotto* try a **Dolcetto**. Avoid pickled beetroot with decent wine. (*See also* Borscht.)

Blackberry and apple pie (or crumble)

Really good with a **Californian Black Muscat**, such as **Elysium**, or a **young Rivesaltes** from the **south of France**.

Blackcurrants

Because of their sharpness, blackcurrants are often well sweetened and need particularly sweet wines to cope. With tarts and crumbles try a **German Beerenauslese Riesling**. With blackcurrant fools and mousses, which are lighter and creamier, go for an **Asti** or **Moscato d'Asti**.

Black pudding

A few years ago you wouldn't have dreamt of drinking anything other than **bitter**; now it's fashionable you're more likely to drink wine. A **rustic French country red** might be the obvious choice, but **whites** also work curiously well, particularly if you're serving the black pudding with apples (try an **Alsace Riesling** or **cider**) or asparagus (try **Sauvignon Blanc**).

Blinis (pancakes with smoked fish and caviar or lumpfish roe)

Iced vodka or **Champagne**. If you're serving lumpfish roe you could get away with **Cava**.

Borscht (Russian beetroot soup)

Vodka, or a **German** or **Czech pilsner**, such as **Budweiser Budvar**.

Bouillabaisse (Provençal fish soup)

A **southern French white** – white Châteauneuf-du-Pape** or **Lirac** would be especially good – or a **Provençal**, **Languedoc** or **Spanish rosé**.

Brandade (purée of salt cod, potato cream and garlic)

Traditionally made with salt cod, though sometimes other fish such as smoked haddock are given the same treatment. **Dry southern French whites** such as **Picpoul de Pinet** or **white Côtes du Rhône** go with the classic version. With smoked haddock *brandade* try a **light Chardonnay**.

Bread and butter pudding

Lighter than many traditional British puddings, bread and butter pudding will happily partner a range of inexpensive dessert wines, such as **Moscatel de Valencia**, **Muscat de Rivesaltes**, **Premières Côtes du Bordeaux** or **Late-Harvest Sémillon**.

Brie

See Cheese.

Broccoli

Although it has a slightly bitter flavour it's not so dominant as to affect your wine choice. If it's in a quiche or pasta bake, try a **light Hungarian** or **southern French Chardonnay**. If it's stir-fried with soy, garlic or chilli, go for a basic **Australian red**.

Brownies

Sometimes creep into the dessert course these days. To be honest, **coffee** (particularly **espresso**) beats any wine option, though a decent **bourbon** such as **Maker's Mark** is pretty good.

Bruschetta

Any inexpensive **Italian red** or **white** would do – **Sicily** provides some of the cheapest.

Bubble and squeak

A glass of **sparkling cider** if you're having bubble and squeak on its own or with bacon or ham. **Sparkling Shiraz** if you eat it, as we do at home, with cold turkey.

Burgers

There's no reason why you can't treat real burgers like steak when it comes to wine. Seriously good **claret** works as long as the burger isn't smothered in too much gunk. Otherwise, stick to a large fattening **milkshake**.

Cabbage

Plain buttered cabbage doesn't have a big impact on a dish, but cooked for any length of time it develops a slightly sharp, pickled flavour that's better with **beer** than wine: **Czech** or **German pils** and **British pale ales** are both good. (See also Choucroute.)

Red cabbage Often served with pork, duck or goose, red cabbage suits **Italian reds** such as **Barbera** and **Dolcetto**, or a robust **Romanian Pinot Noir**.

Caesar salad

The parmesan in this dish makes **Chardonnay** a good choice, but **Sauvignon Blanc** and **dry rosé** work as well. **Wheat beers**, **pale ales** and **honey beers** are also particularly good.

Cajun

A traditional style of cooking from the southern states of America that has given its name to a spicy style of seasoning. Suits **zesty Chilean** or **South African Sauvignon Blanc** or ripe jammy reds such as **Zinfandel**. Alternatively, try a **light lager**.

Calamares

See Squid.

Calves liver

A delicately flavoured dish that goes well with **lighter red burgundies** such as **Savigny-** or **Chorey-lès-Beaune**, or a **Californian Pinot Noir**. Or go for a **Chianti** or **Sangiovese**.

Camembert

See Cheese.

Cannelloni

With meat and tomato sauce: an inexpensive **Chianti** or **Sangiovese**. With spinach and ricotta: a **Valpolicella** or **Sicilian red**, or, if you prefer to drink white, a **Frascati** or **Sicilian white**.

Cantucci & cantuccini

Alternative names for the little crunchy almond biscuits that are served with the **Italian** wine **Vin Santo**. But you could equally well serve them with the slightly less expensive **Passito di Pantelleria** or **Tokaji**.

Capers

Tend to go in tandem with strongly flavoured Mediterranean ingredients such as anchovies, garlic and olives. Best with a **dry southern French** or **Italian white**, or a **strong dry rosé**.

Carpaccio (raw marinated beef fillet)

Traditionally served with a red wine such as **Chianti**, but a **dry white** such as **Gavi** or **Lugana** goes equally well. So – if you're feeling extravagant – does **vintage rosé Champagne**. **Champagne** and **sparkling wine** also work well with salmon carpaccio.

Caribbean

See Afro-Caribbean.

Carrots

Carrots have a natural sweetness that is intensified by cooking but rarely overwhelms the ingredients they accompany (braised beef and carrots for example). With carrot soup, **cider** is a natural (if the soup is flavoured with coriander try a **wheat beer**). **Colombard**, **Semillon** or **Semillon/Chardonnay**, and **basic Côtes du Rhône** also work well.

Cassoulet

A robust bean, pork, lamb and duck stew from the southwest of France. **Gutsy local reds** such as **Corbières**, **Cahors** and **Madiran** are the traditional accompaniments, but if you find them a bit heavy try a **dry French** or **Spanish rosé**. A **northern French bière de garde** such as **Jenlain** would also be good.

Cauliflower cheese

An inexpensive **soft fruity French**, **Spanish** or **Portuguese red**, **Côtes du Rhône**, or **Hungarian** or **southern French Merlot**. **Chardonnay** if you prefer to drink **white**. Or a **fruity pale** or **amber ale**.

Caviar

The world divides into people who think **iced vodka** is the only thing to drink with caviar and those who wouldn't touch anything but **Champagne**. I'm firmly in the Champagne camp: there's just something quite magical about the fusion of eggs and bubbles.

Ceviche (raw fish marinaded in lime juice)

Chilean Sauvignon Blanc has the right Latin American feel and enough intensity to cope with the pungent flavours of this dish. **New Zealand** or **South African Sauvignon** would be an alternative, or try one of the new very sharp **lemony Greek whites**.

Charcuterie (cold meats, cured sausage and pâtés)

In France you wouldn't think twice about what to drink: it would be the **local red** or **rosé**. **Beaujolais** is particularly good with charcuterie but go for **Villages** quality rather than basic Beaujolais or Beaujolais Nouveau. Other **Gamay-based wines** work well too.

Cheese

Cheese and wine is far from the perfect match it's made out to be. **Dry white wines** and **dessert wines** often go just as well as reds, particularly if they're young and oaky. Even apparently mild cheeses, such as brie, can clash horribly, especially if you let them get too ripe and runny.

The mistake most people make is to have too many different types of cheese, which makes a good match more difficult. If you're serving a carefully chosen wine it's better to pick a really good cheese that will go with it rather than five or six, one of which is bound to clash.

Alternatively, if you want to have a range of different cheeses choose a simple inexpensive wine to accompany them: **new world reds**, especially **Cabernet** and **Merlot**, tend to cope reasonably well, so do **mature oak-aged Spanish reds** such as **Rioja** and **Valdepeñas** and **southern Italian reds** such as **Copertino** and **Salice Salentino**. But I would still avoid including very strong or pungent cheeses, like Münster and Danish Blue, unless you have exactly the right wine to match them.

Mild hard cheeses Classic English cheeses, such as Caerphilly, Wensleydale, mild Cheddar and Cheshire, pair well with **English dry white wines**, **Sauvignon Blanc**, **dry cider** and **pale ales**. Slightly waxy cheeses (such as Jarslberg, Emmenthal, Edam and Gouda) work with **soft fruity reds** such as **Merlot** or **Zinfandel**, or a **lager**.

Tangy hard cheeses Mature Cheddar, farmhouse Lancashire, red Leicester and double Gloucester, for example, are particularly good with **traditional English bitter**. Or go for a **southern Italian** or **mature French** or **Spanish red**, a **tawny port** or a **dry amontillado sherry**.

Soft white-rinded cheeses Brie or Camembert for example: tricky with wine, though a **soft fruity Merlot** or **Pinot Noir** should cope. But your best bet is a **fruit-flavoured beer** such as **Kriek (Belgian cherry beer)** or **Framboise (raspberry flavoured beer)**. **Sparkling cider** is good too.

Goat's cheeses **Sancerre**, **Pouilly-Fumé** and other **Sauvignon Blancs** from the **Loire** are outstandingly good with young goat's cheese. More mature cheeses or grilled goat's cheese can benefit from **more powerful Sauvignons** (such as those from **New Zealand**), or try an **English dry white** made from **Bacchus**.

Sheep's cheeses These can be quite salty so it helps to have a wine with a touch of sweetness, such as a **Late-Harvest** or **Auslese Riesling**. Otherwise go for a **southern French** or **mature Spanish red** such as a **Valdepeñas** or **Rioja Reserva**. Pecorino is heaven with **Poire William**.

Rich creamy cheeses Vacherin or Explorateur for example: a **powerful red burgundy** or **Californian**, **New Zealand** or **Oregon Pinot Noir**. **Chablis** is the traditional match for Chaource.

Pungent cheeses Münster, Pont L'Eveque and other washed-rind cheeses: **Gewürztraminer** and Münster is a classic combination, otherwise this type of cheese is tricky. A **ten-year-old tawny port** or **Madeira** is probably your best bet or a **strong Belgian ale** such as **Chimay** or **Orval**.

Smoked cheeses A wine with a touch of sweetness, such as **Morio Muskat**, or a drink that is smoky itself, such as **smoked beer** or an **Island malt whisky** such as **Lagavulin** or **Talisker**.

Blue cheeses These work well with **sweet wines**: the most famous combination being Roquefort and **Sauternes**; you can pull the same trick with cheaper wines such as **French** or **Greek Muscats**, or less well-known wines from the **Bordeaux** region such as **Saussignac** or **Monbazillac**. **Late-bottled vintage** and **tawny port** work with traditional English blues such as stilton and with Italian blues such as Dolcellate and Gorgonzola – or you could try a **sweet red** such as **Recioto**.

Flavoured cheeses Garlic: a **Sauvignon Blanc** or **Vin de Pays des Côtes de Gascogne**. Fruit-flavoured cheeses: go with the flavour of the fruit. With an orange-flavoured cheese try an **Orange Muscat** or an **orange-flavoured liqueur**; with pineapple-flavoured cheese, a **Late-Harvest Semillon**.

Cooked cheese dishes *See* Fondues, Pasta, Omelettes, Quiches, Soufflés.

Cheesecake

A particularly rich dessert that needs a bit of sharpness to set it off, which is why it's often combined with lemon or blackcurrants and other fruits. **Raspberry-** or **cherry-flavoured beers** are great with plain or raspberry-flavoured cheesecake. With lemon cheesecake go for a **Beerenauslese** or **Late-Harvest Riesling** or **light sparkling Moscato d'Asti**. With orange cheesecake try a **Californian Orange Muscat**. With blackcurrant-topped cheesecake a **Californian Black Muscat**.

Cherries

With fresh cherries cooked in a pie, or the classic French dish *Clafoutis* (a sort of cherry toad in the hole), try a **light dessert wine** such as **Coteaux du Layon** or a **cherry-flavoured beer**. Bottled or macerated cherries already cooked or preserved in alcohol go well with **late-bottled vintage port** or **Rivesaltes** from the **south of France**. (*See also* Duck.)

Chestnuts

Rich dense and sweet, chestnut-flavoured desserts go with similar wines to chocolate, particularly **Black** and **Orange Muscat**. In savoury dishes, chestnuts also add richness. Try an **Argentinian Syrah**, **Australian Shiraz** or a **Syrah-based wine** from the **Rhône**.

Chicken

Given that chicken can be cooked in so many different ways, the advice on wine labels 'drink with chicken' isn't terribly helpful. The only useful generalisation is that it's a light meat and is therefore easily overwhelmed by full-bodied reds – or whites for that matter. Remember that supermarket dishes tend to be milder than home-made versions.

Simple roast chicken Perfect for showing off a good red or white wine, particularly **red** or **white burgundy** or their **new world** equivalents: **Californian** or **New Zealand Pinot Noir**, or good-quality **Chardonnay**.

Deep-fried or southern-fried chicken Needs a wine with a touch of sharpness: **Sauvignon Blanc**, a **light citrussy Chardonnay** from, for example, **southern France** or **Chile**, or a **Sauvignon/Chardonnay blend**. **Beaujolais**, **Gamay de Touraine** and **Teroldego** are reds that will also work. Or try a **light lager**.

Char-grilled or barbecued chicken This usually has some sort of marinade to stop it drying out, so be guided by the ingredients in that. Inexpensive **Aussie Chardonnays** and **Shiraz** are a safe bet, particularly if you're basting with a barbecue sauce.

Chicken in a creamy sauce **Chardonnay** is the obvious choice thanks to its own slightly creamy texture, but a good **Riesling** – particularly from **Alsace** – or **Viognier** can provide an attractive contrast. **Alsace, New Zealand** or **Californian Pinot Gris** is also good as is a *blanc de blancs* **Champagne** or **Australian sparkling wine**.

Chicken with cheese sauce or in a pasta bake Calls for a **light red** such as a **Côtes du Rhône**, **Merlot** or inexpensive **Sangiovese**, or a **light Chardonnay**. Also good with **bitter** or **amber**, **golden** or **blonde** beers. These drinks would also work with chicken *cordon bleu*.

Chicken pies and casseroles **Pale ale** or **cider** – particularly if the chicken is cooked in cider. Alternatively try a **lightly oaked** or **unoaked Chardonnay**.

Mediterranean-style chicken dishes with tomatoes and garlic **Robust southern French reds**, such as **Côtes du Roussillon**, **Minervois**, **Faugeres** or **Vin de Pays d'Oc Syrah**, or an inexpensive **Shiraz**, **young Rioja**, **Sicilian red** or **dry rosé**.

Chicken Kiev **Vin de Pays d'Oc** or **Chilean Chardonnay**, **Sauvignon Blanc** or **lager**.

Chicken cooked with wine Drink a similar type of wine to that used in the cooking of the dish. **Robust reds** such as **Gigondas** if you're cooking with **Côtes du Rhône**; **Alsace Riesling** with *coq au Riesling* and so on (*see also* Coq au vin).

Sweet and sour or fruity chicken dishes With honey and orange, say: **southeastern Australian Chardonnay** and **Semillon/Chardonnay**, **Australian Semillon** and **Australian** or **South African Colombard**, all of which have a touch of sweetness – as do **Australian dry Rieslings** and **dry Muscat** from the **south of France**. **Very soft fruity reds** such as **Merlot** or **Tarrango** from **Australia** work too. Or try a **honey beer**.

Chicken stir-fries and Asian-inspired dishes with lime and coriander **Sauvignon Blanc** and other **crisp lemony whites** such as **Vin de Pays des Côtes de Gascogne**; or a **lager** or **pilsner** (*see also* Thai green chicken curry).

Spicy or curried chicken Mild dishes such as chicken Korma: **crisp dry whites** and **rosés**; or **lager**. Moderately hot dishes such as chicken tikka masala: **Australian Semillon/Chardonnay** or **Cabernet/Shiraz**; **pale ale** or **IPA**. (*See also* Indian.)

Chicken salads and smoked chicken Light citrussy Chardonnays, **Sauvignon Blanc**, **Australian Riesling**. Alternatively try **wheat beers** such as **Hoegaarden**, or even **Pimms**.

Chicken livers

There's a touch of bitterness about chicken livers that needs a corresponding touch of sweetness in any wine you choose. Chicken liver pâté works well with **soft reds** such as **Merlot**, but is also demon with **dry amontillado sherry** or **Madeira** (*see also* Crostini). Creamier chicken-liver parfait is particularly delicious with **Sauternes** and other **similar wines from the Bordeaux region**, or with a **slightly spicy white** such as **Alsace Pinot Gris**. With chopped liver try a **Californian Sauvignon Blanc**. In warm salads, chicken livers work well with **light reds** such as **Pinot Noir** or **Hungarian Merlot**.

Chickpeas

Often incorporated into spicy Indian, Spanish or Moroccan (*see* entries) dishes that are best with **dry rosés** or **young fruity reds**. Lighter Middle Eastern dishes such as felafel or hummus are good with **crisp lemony Greek whites** or **Sauvignon Blanc**.

Chillies

It's not so much the taste that causes problems with chillies as the heat. New world wines – particularly **Sauvignon Blanc** and jammy reds such as **Cabernet Sauvignon** and **Shiraz** – cope better than classic European ones. This type of red also goes well with the flavour of smoked chillies that you find in southwest American and Tex Mex cooking.

Chilli con carne

Chilean or **Australian Cabernet Sauvignon** fits the bill perfectly. Or try a **fruity Zinfandel**; or a **Mexican** or **Spanish lager**.

Chinese

Many Chinese dishes have a degree of sweetness, which can be quite a challenge. The most successful wines overall are **fruity rosés**, or **light fruity reds** such as **Beaujolais** or **Australian Tarrango**. **Pils** is preferable to most Chinese beers. Or you could, of course, drink **China tea**.

Delicately flavoured dishes Dim sum, scallops, soups, light chicken dishes, stir-fries and noodle dishes: **German** or **Alsace Riesling**, **Californian Sauvignon Blanc**, **Muscadet**, **Beaujolais**, **Bordeaux rosé**, **Champagne** or **sparkling wine**, or **chilled fino sherry**.

Deep-fried dishes Wontons, spring rolls, prawn toasts, and soft-shell crabs: **Sauvignon Blanc**, **Champagne** or **sparkling wine**.

Sweet and sour dishes Australian **Semillon/Chardonnay**, **Colombard**, **Torrontes**, **Gewürztraminer**, **Irsai Oliver**, or **white Zinfandel**.

Meaty or spicy dishes Spare ribs, beef with oyster or black bean sauce: **fruity reds** such as **Zinfandel**, **Ruby Cabernet**, **Australian Shiraz/Cabernet** and **Chilean Merlot**. If you're having beef with black bean sauce, try a **porter** and **nut brown ale**. Crispy duck and Peking duck are both particularly good with **Pinot Noir**.

Chocolate

Chocolate is held to be difficult because it doesn't go with traditional sweet wines such as Sauternes. But there are many other wines with which it rubs along quite happily. **Sweet reds** are generally a better bet than sweet whites, which makes sense when you think how delicious raspberries and cherries are with chocolate. And by the same logic, **orange-flavoured dessert wines** tend to work well too. (*See also* Ice cream, Profiteroles.)

Light chocolate desserts Mousses made with white and milk chocolate for example: **sparkling Moscato d'Asti** is particularly good, though other inexpensive **Muscats** such as **Brown Brothers Orange Muscat** go well too. **Raspberry** and **cherry beers** can be sensational.

Rich chocolate desserts Dark chocolate mousses, *petits pots au chocolat*, chocolate marquise, profiteroles and chocolate roulade for example: **Californian Orange, Black Muscat**, or **Mavrodaphne of Patras (sweet Greek red)**. With Black Forest gâteau try a **Recioto (sweet Italian red)** or **raspberry liqueur**.

Very rich chocolate desserts Warm Valrhona chocolate cake, chocolate nemesis or puds with hot rich chocolate sauces: **French *vin doux naturels*** such as **Rivesaltes, Banyuls** and **Maury; vintage character port**, or **Australian Liqueur Muscat. Porter** is surprisingly good too – try it!

Chocolate cake Devil's food cake or sachertorte for example: best with **coffee** (preferably black).

Chocolate truffles and other hand-made chocolates **Cognac** and **cigars**.

Chorizo

This gutsy paprika-flavoured sausage adds a spicy character to many Spanish dishes – including fish. It goes particularly well with the **Spanish white**, **Albariño**, and with inexpensive **Spanish reds** such as **Toro** and other **Tempranillo-based wines**. Or, if you're eating it as a *tapa*, with a glass of **fino** or **manzanilla sherry**.

Choucroute

A substantial Alsace dish of cabbage and smoked meats that is almost always drunk with the **local Riesling**, or a **light French lager**.

Chowder

A thick, creamy American-style soup generally based on cod, clams or smoked haddock. Serve an inexpensive **Bulgarian**, **Hungarian** or **Vin de Pays d'Oc Chardonnay**, or one from **New York state**.

Christmas cake

An excuse to sneak an extra glass of **port**. **Sweet oloroso sherry**, **Malmsey Madeira** and **Australian Liqueur Muscat** are also great.

Christmas pudding

Tokaji is particularly good, but **southern French Muscats** such as **Muscat de Beaumes-de-Venise** or **Spanish Moscatel de Valencia** work well too. If you don't want anything too rich, try a glass of **Moscato d'Asti**.

Chutneys

The intense sweet and sour flavours of chutneys and pickles are very tough on wine. If they're hot and sour it's even worse. **Beer** usually copes better than wine but don't waste a decent bottle either way.

Cinnamon

See Spices and seasonings.

Clams

Popular ingredient of Italian pasta dishes such as *Spaghetti alla Vongole*. Clams go well with basic **dry Italian whites** such as **Pinot Grigio**. Other **dry whites** such as **Muscadet** and **Vinho Verde** also work. With a tomato and garlic sauce try a robust **Sicilian** or inexpensive **Portuguese red**. (*See also* Chowder.)

Cockles

In England or Wales, where cockles tend to be soused in vinegar, they're best accompanied by a half of **best bitter**. As part of a classic *plateau de fruits de mer* you can't beat a **crisp Muscadet**.

Cod

With cod in parsley sauce drink a **lightish Chardonnay**. Roast cod with pancetta and lentils could take a **light red** such as a **Bourgeuil** from the **Loire**. With deep-fried cod in a beer batter it's got to be a **traditional pale** or **brown ale** – or at the very least **lager**. (*See also* Salt cod.)

Coffee-flavoured cakes & desserts

You'd think it would be too similar but most coffee-flavoured cakes taste best with coffee, particularly **black coffee**. Otherwise, go for an **Australian Liqueur Muscat** or **sweet oloroso sherry**.

Coq au vin (chicken cooked in red wine)

Serve a slightly more full-bodied wine than that you've used to cook the dish. Red burgundy is traditional but I actually prefer **Languedoc** or **Rhône reds** such as **Gigondas** or a really good **Beaujolais** such as a **Morgon**. (*See also* Chicken.)

Coriander

If you've got fresh coriander in a recipe you've generally got lime, garlic and chillies too. That calls for something **lively** and **lemony** such as a **Vin de Pays des Côtes de Gascogne** or a **Sauvignon Blanc**. (*See also* Indian, Lebanese, Turkish.)

Corn on the cob

See Sweetcorn.

Corned beef hash

An inexpensive **fruity red** such as **Zinfandel** or **Pinotage**. If you're serving it up for brunch, try a good strong **Bloody Mary**. **Lager** is also an option or, better still, an **amber ale** such as **Anchor Liberty**.

Cornish pasties

Go native and drink **scrumpy** – or **cider** at the very least.

Cottage pie

Comfort food that needs a comforting drink to match. No, not cocoa! More like a **half of bitter** or a **Bulgarian Cabernet Sauvignon** – nothing too fancy.

Courgettes (and courgette flowers)

Baked with tomatoes and cheese: a **light Italian red** such as a **Montepulciano d'Abruzzo** or a good **Valpolicella**. Courgette flowers have a particularly delicate flavour that needs to be set off by an equally subtle and delicate white: an **Arneis**, **Gavi** or **Cortese del Piemonte** would be ideal. Otherwise go for a decent **Soave**.

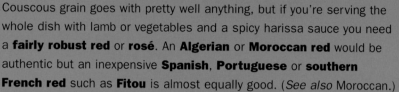

Couscous

Couscous grain goes with pretty well anything, but if you're serving the whole dish with lamb or vegetables and a spicy harissa sauce you need a **fairly robust red** or **rosé**. An **Algerian** or **Moroccan red** would be authentic but an inexpensive **Spanish**, **Portuguese** or **southern French red** such as **Fitou** is almost equally good. (*See also* Moroccan.)

Crab

Simply dressed fresh crab Fantastic with **Chablis** or other good **white burgundies** such as **Puligny-Montrachet**. It also goes well with **Sancerre** and **German Kabinett Riesling** or **Pinot Blanc**.

Rich cooked crab dishes Crab tart, crab soufflé and crab bisque, for example, are candidates for **Chardonnay**; with crab bisque you could also try a **dry fino sherry** or **Roussanne**. Crab with linguine calls for a good **Italian Soave**.

Spicy crab dishes Crab cakes or Asian-style crab salads, for example, work well with **Sauvignon Blanc**, **Viognier** and **Australian** or **New Zealand Riesling**, or a **ginger-flavoured beer**. (*See also* Chinese, Thai.)

Cream cakes & gâteaux

Something naughty but nice, such as **Champagne**. Or, if you're not feeling quite that naughty, **Australian sparkling Chardonnay** or **Moscato fizz**.

Crème brûlée

A good excuse to show off an expensive **Sauternes** or **Barsac** (although a less expensive **sweet Bordeaux** would work equally well). If it's infused with ginger or lemongrass try a **Beerenauslese** or **Late-Harvest Riesling**. Coffee-flavoured crème brûlée is nice with **Orange Muscat**.

Crème caramel

Cream sherry – **pale** or **dark** – is curiously good. Otherwise try a **Tokaji** or an **Australian Liqueur Muscat**.

Crêpes

See Pancakes.

Croque monsieur (fried cheese and ham sandwich)

Classic brasserie fare that calls for a **light French** or **Alsace lager**, or **basic *vin blanc*** or ***rouge***. With *croque madame*, which includes an egg, you could drink a **light Chardonnay** or **Pinot Blanc**.

Crostini (toasted slices of ciabatta with different toppings)

Crostini are often handed round at the start of a meal, so, although the flavours can be robust (chicken liver, say), you don't want too powerful a wine. **Italian whites** such as **Soave** or **Frascati** work well, or try **light Italian reds**, such as **Valpolicella**, **Barbera** or **Dolcetto**; or a **Merlot**.

Crudités

Can either refer to raw vegetables served with dips or the classic French starter salads of grated carrot, celeriac remoulade and beetroot. Either way, **crisp dry French whites** and **rosés** will work, or an inexpensive **French Sauvignon Blanc** such as **Sauvignon de Touraine**. Alternatively, try **French** or **Alsace lager**.

Cucumber

Cucumber has a delicate flavour that's easy to swamp: with an iced cucumber soup, for example, go for a **smooth dry neutral white** such as **Soave**. Scandinavian-style salads with cream and dill suit a **light Hungarian** or **Bulgarian Chardonnay**; or a **Pilsner**. **Sauvignon Blanc** is better for Greek-style cucumber salads with yoghurt and mint. Cucumber sandwiches? **Iced tea**, **Pimms** or **home-made lemonade**.

Curry

The idea of 'curry' is a bit out of date (*see* Indian), but dishes that use curry powder or paste, such as curried eggs and coronation chicken, still survive. **Aussie Chardonnay**, **Semillon/Chardonnay** or **Colombard** should ride to the rescue. **Viognier** if the sauce is particularly delicate.

Dates

Dates are often incorporated in sticky-toffee-type puddings, so drink a sticky-toffee-type wine – an **Australian Liqueur Muscat** or **sweet oloroso sherry** such as **Matusalem** – to match.

Dill

A strongly flavoured herb that has a particularly affinity with **Sauvignon Blanc** and which is also very good with **lager** or **pils**.

Dim sum

See Chinese.

Dolmades

Stuffed vine leaves with a distinctly tart flavour that needs to be offset by an equally **sharp Greek** or **Cyprus white** (*see* Greek).

Doner kebabs

Lager might be the drink that comes to mind, but an inexpensive **crisp lemony white** such as **Vin de Pays du Gers** is actually much nicer.

Dover sole

See Sole.

Duck

Duck is often paired
with tart fruit to offset
its potential fattiness, so fruity
wines tend to go with it too. The one that
almost always works is **Pinot Noir** –a good excuse for drinking **top
red burgundy** or **Californian Pinot**. Other strong candidates are
St-Emilion and **Pomerol**; **Italian reds** such as **Barbera**, **Barolo** and
Valpolicella Ripasso; good **Beaujolais**; and the **Lebanese** wine
Chateau Musar. **White wines** from **Alsace** can be particularly good
too. (For crispy duck *see* Chinese.)

Duck with fruit-based sauces
With apples: **German Kabinett** or **Alsace Riesling**.
Duck *a l'orange*: **German Spätlese** or **dry Auslese Riesling**, **Alsace
Pinot Gris**, **Aussie Semillon** or **Shiraz**. With cherries: **Chilean Merlot**,
Dolcetto, **Valpolicella Ripasso**, or a **Belgian cherry-flavoured beer**.

Duck with olives
A good **Côtes du Rhône** or **Gigondas**, or a
Languedoc red such as **Corbières**.

Duck glazed with honey
Demi-sec (**medium-dry**)
Vouvray, **Spätlese Riesling**, or **Californian Viognier**.

Duck confit (slow cooked in fat)
A **robust southern French red**
such as **Costières de Nîmes**, **Pic St-Loup** or **Madiran**, or **Shiraz**.

Duck pâté
A **rich sweetish white** such as an **Alsace Pinot Gris** or
Gewurztraminer or **German Spätlese Riesling**. With a smooth elegant
parfait you could even get away with a **Sauternes** (*see also* Foie gras).

Smoked duck
Be daring and try a **raspberry-** or **cherry-flavoured
beer**. Or a **fruity red** such as **Valpolicella** or **Merlot**.

E el

Smoked eel, which often crops up in starter salads in fashionable restaurants these days, goes well with **Alsace, Australian** or **German (Kabinett) Rieslings** or **light citrussy Chardonnays**,from **Chile** for example. If you're a jellied-eel addict you probably wouldn't drink anything other than tea.

Eggs

It's the mouth-coating effect of runny egg yolk that's supposed to be the problem here. There's a happy solution: **Champagne** or other **sparkling wines** (particularly with scrambled eggs, eggs benedict and other eggy brunch dishes). Other wines that go well with most egg dishes, including quiches and eggs florentine, are **lighter Chardonnays** (particularly inexpensive **white burgundy**), **Alsace Pinot Blanc** and **Soave**. (*See also* Omelettes, Quiches, Soufflés, Mayonnaise, Meringues.)

A few egg dishes suit **red** wines. Bacon and egg is excellent with inexpensive **claret**; the classic French dish *oeufs en meurette* (eggs cooked in red wine) goes well with **robust Rhône reds** such as **Gigondas**; and egg dishes with tomato, such as *huevos rancheros*, work with cheap **Spanish** or **Argentinian reds**.

Elderflower fritters

Not a dish you'd think demands to be accompanied by wine, but **well-chilled Moscato d'Asti** is brilliant.

Empanadas

South America's answer to the Cornish pasty, only smaller and spicier. Drink an **Argentinian** or **Chilean white**, especially **Sauvignon Blanc** or **basic Argentinian** or **Spanish red**. Or a **Pisco Sour** (Chilean brandy cocktail).

Endive

Confusingly, the word endive refers both to a slightly bitter curly type of lettuce (*see* Salads), and to what we called chicory, which is the more interesting of the two from a wine (or beer) point of view. When braised chicory develops a bitter-sweet flavour that goes best with **Belgian ales** or oddball whites such as **Jurançon Sec**, **Roussanne** or **white Côtes du Rhône**. In a gratin with ham and cheese go for a **light Chardonnay**, a **Pinot Blanc** or a **light Belgian beer** (such as **Leffe Blonde**).

Escabeche (fried fish soused in a hot spicy marinade)

The hot-sour flavours of this dish, which is common to Mediterranean and Caribbean cooking (where it's known as Escovitch), work best with a sharply flavoured **Muscadet** or **Sauvignon Blanc**. Or **lager**.

Fajitas

Whether they're made of beef or chicken, these Mexican-style pancakes with onions and pepper tend to be quite spicy, so hit them with a **big fruity red** such as a **Chilean Cabernet Sauvignon** or **Zinfandel**.

Felafel (spiced chickpea patties)

Classic Middle Eastern street food that needs a **crisp refreshing white** or **rosé** to wash it down. Try **white Côtes du Rhône** or a cheap **Spanish** or **Portuguese white**, or **Spanish** *rosado*.

Fennel

Fennel is common in Italian dishes and tends to work well with **Italian dry whites** such as **Frascati**, **Orvieto** and **Verdicchio**. Braised or baked with cheese, you could also partner it with a **light Italian Chardonnay**. It's also good with **wheat beer**.

Figs

Fresh or roast figs are fantastic with **Californian Black Muscat**. Poached in red wine, they need a slightly more intensely flavoured **sweet red** such as **Rivesaltes** or the ridiculously inexpensive **Greek Mavrodaphne of Patras**. Dried figs are perfect with **sweet figgy oloroso sherry**.

Fish

When to drink white and when to drink red? I always drink **dry whites** with fresh shellfish, seafood salads, plainly grilled fish and oily fish such as sardines and mackerel. With spicier fish dishes, such as steamed fish with ginger, garlic and spring onions, I choose **zestier whites** such as **Sauvignon Blanc**. With fish pies or fish in rich creamy sauces I go for **smooth dry whites** such as **Chardonnay**.

Reds come into their own with more robustly cooked fish dishes such as seared or barbecued salmon or tuna, roast fish such as cod or monkfish and fish with strongly flavoured tomato-based sauces. And I would always drink **red** with a fish dish that has been cooked in red wine. (*See also* individual fish such as Cod, Salmon, Pâtés, Sauces, Soups, Terrines.)

Fish and chips and other fried fish Perfect with a **crisp lemony white** – just like a squeeze of lemon. **Sauvignon Blanc** is an obvious choice, but **simple French whites** such as **Vin de Pays du Gers** or **Vin de Pays des Côtes de Gascogne** will do just as well. **Champagne** or cheap **sparkling wine** such as **Cava** is surprisingly good, particularly with the children's fish fingers! If the fish is fried in a beer batter, drink a **traditional pale** or **brown ale**. **Lager** and **wheat beer** are also good too.

Fish cakes Old-fashioned fish cakes made with white fish are good with a **crisp white** such as **Muscadet**. If they're spiced, like Thai crab cakes, go for a **Sauvignon Blanc**. Salmon fish cakes are better with **Chardonnay**.

Fish pie **Chardonnay** is a safe bet – which type depends on the pie. With a basic fish pie topped with mashed potato go for an inexpensive **Hungarian** or **Bulgarian Chardonnay**. With a more elaborate pie, topped with pastry and luxurious ingredients such as prawns and scallops, you could drink a good **white burgundy** or **Australian unoaked Chardonnay**.

Smoked fish Can be delicate (such as smoked trout or eel) or quite oily (such as mackerel): **Riesling** is generally a good choice with delicately flavoured fish; while **fino sherry** and **malt whisky** can help you out with the more awkward customers. Good **Czech** or **German pilsner** and **wheat beer** work too.

Foie gras

Foie gras and **Sauternes** is reckoned to be one of the all-time great matches – it is, but not everyone enjoys such a rich sweet start to a meal. Less intense alternatives are **dry Muscat** from the **south of France** or **Gewurztraminer** from **Alsace**. If it's served fashionably seared with an apple sauce, you could try a **German Spätlese**.

Fondues

Cheese fondues **Crisp dry white wines** work best – **Chasselas** from **Switzerland** if you want to be authentic. Otherwise **Sauvignon Blanc** is a good choice; or an **ice-cold lager**.

Meat fondues Trickier as they have a range of different sauces. A **soft fruity red**, such as good **Beaujolais** or **Merlot**, or even **Shiraz**, should do the trick.

Frankfurters

See Sausages.

French

French wine: it would be quite perverse to drink anything else. The French would go one step further and drink only the wine of the region (except perhaps for Champagne). Clearly, you wouldn't drink the same wine with the cream- and dairy-dominated dishes of Normandy and the tomato- and garlic-infused dishes of Provence.

Most of the French dishes that you're likely to come across or make at home – such as crème caramel, cassoulet and coq au vin – you'll find elsewhere in this book. Other dishes, such as frogs' legs or *boudin blanc*, you're unlikely to encounter unless you're travelling in France and I'd always suggest that you drink the local wine with them.

Frittata

See Omelettes.

Fruit salad

Goes particularly well with frothy **sparkling Moscato d'Asti** or **Asti**. Or a **Beerenauslese** or **Late-Harvest Riesling**.

Game pie

Good old-fashioned British cooking, so bring out the classics. With a hot pie, serve a *cru bourgeois* **claret**, a **substantial red burgundy** such as a **Pommard**, a **Ribera del Duero** or an **old Australian Shiraz** if you can lay your hands on one. With a cold pie, go for a good **Beaujolais**, or a good **fruity ale**; or, if you are feeling wildly extravagant, a **vintage rosé Champagne**.

Gammon

Remember gammon with pineapple? Well you can get a similar effect by drinking an **Australian Semillon** or **Marsanne**.

Garlic

Garlic finds its way into practically everything these days so it's really only super-garlicky dishes such as Chicken Kiev and garlic prawns or snails you have to take special account of. **Sharply flavoured whites** such as **Sauvignon Blanc**, and **more citrussy Chardonnays** such as **Chilean**, or **Vin de Pays d'Oc Chardonnay** cope best, though **simple French *vin de pays*** are good with garlicky pâtés and garlic sausage. With garlic soup drink **Albariño**. Note: uncooked or quickly cooked garlic is much tougher on wine than slowly cooked or roast garlic, so spare your best bottles. (*See also* Aioli, Chicken Kiev.)

Gazpacho

A Spanish soup, so drink **Spanish** wine. **Crisp dry whites** such as **Rueda**, **unoaked white Rioja** and **Sauvignon Blanc** work best, or **well-chilled fino sherry**. With fashionable white gazpacho, try an **Albariño**.

German

Curiously, German food doesn't travel, so unless you visit Germany you're unlikely to get to sample it. Much of the food has a delicacy you wouldn't suspect from the more substantial pork-based dishes for which the country is known. For example, Germany boasts delicate creamy sauces to accompany trout, and some extremely good asparagus. The grape to understand is **Riesling**, which is made in an incredibly diverse range of styles: from dry (**Kabinett**) to ultra-sweet (**Trockenbeerenauslese**). There is also an amazing selection of **German beers** that are well worth getting acquainted with, particularly the **wheat beers**.

Ginger

Often used in oriental dishes, fresh ginger goes with **Sauvignon Blanc**, and **spicy whites** such as **Riesling** and **Gewurztraminer**, and you could also try **ginger-flavoured beers** (*see also* Chinese, Thai). Ginger-flavoured puddings can be quite tricky. If crystallised ginger is involved choose a **sweet sherry** or **Australian Liqueur Muscat**.

Gnocchi

Has to be **Italian** really. Light, but not too weedy: a decent-quality **white Pinot Bianco**, **Pinot Grigio** or **Soave**, or a good **Valpolicella**. **Merlot** is fine too.

Goat's cheese

See Cheese.

Goose

Goose can be partnered by wines very similar to those you'd pick for duck, but as it's often served at Christmas you might want to push the boat out a bit. **Aromatic whites**, such as **German Spätlese Riesling** or **Alsace Gewurztraminer**, work well, particularly if the goose is served with apple sauce. Otherwise choose a **classic red burgundy**; a **German Spätburgunder**; a **Pinot Noir** from **California**, **Oregon** or **New Zealand**; a **Barolo** or **Barbaresco**; a **Loire red** such as **Saumur-Champigny** or a **Cabernet Franc**.

Gooseberry pies & tarts

Gooseberry desserts are fantastic with floral grapey **Muscats**: **Muscat de Rivesaltes** or **Beaumes-de-Venise** for gooseberry pies and crumbles; **Moscato d'Asti** for gooseberry fool. (*See also* Mackerel.)

Gougère (cheese-flavoured choux pastry)

The classic pre-dinner nibble with a glass of **Chablis**, but other inexpensive **white burgundies**, such as **Mâcon-Villages**, or other **French Chardonnay** would be good too.

Goulash

A rich spicy dish that needs a **spicy red** to match. **Hungarian Kekfrankos** or **Austrian Blaufränkisch** for authenticity, but **Spanish Tempranillo** and most **Syrah/Shiraz-based** wines work as well. **Czech lager** is also tempting.

Granita

Like sorbets, these are very hard to match with wine. A **matching liqueur** is your best bet: **lemon-flavoured liqueur** with lemon granita; **Kahlua** with coffee-flavoured granita; **Campari** with orange- and Campari-flavoured granita, and so on.

Grapefruit

Grilled grapefruit with medium-dry sherry was a '70s classic but you seldom see it these days. Pink grapefruit sometimes pops up in salads and tends to go well with **very ripe Sauvignons**, such as those from **New Zealand** or **Chile**, or **New Zealand Gewürztraminer**. Grapefruit sorbet is best eaten on its own.

Gratin dauphinoise

If you serve this rich creamy garlic-flavoured potato dish with a grill or roast you need go for a **medium-** or **full-bodied red** rather than a light one – preferably **French**.

Gravadlax

You need something with a touch of sweetness to deal with the mustard sauce. *Demi-sec* **Vouvray**; **Kabinett** or **Spätlese Riesling** from the **Mosel**; **dry cider** and **wheat beer** all work. Spirits can be surprisingly good: try **iced vodka** or **malt whisky** cut with a splash of water.

Greek

There didn't use to be many inspiring options with Greek food until the recent renaissance of the Greek wine industry. Now *mezze*-type starters of hummus, taramasalata, dolmades and tzatsiki go perfectly with the new **ultra-dry lemony Greek whites**, which also suit grilled fish and marinated lamb dishes such as kebabs (or try an inexpensive **Sauvignon Blanc**). With richer spicier dishes, such as sausages or moussaka, try one of the excellent new **Greek reds**, or a **spicy Rhône**, **Portuguese** or **southern Italian red**. Sweet Greek pastries with syrup and nuts go perfectly with **Greek** or inexpensive **southern French Muscats**.

Grouse

A rare delicacy these days, so drink something wantonly extravagant such as **Chambolle-Musigny**, **Côte-Rôtie** or the priciest **claret** your finances will permit. **Fraoch**, a **Scottish heather ale** would also be appropriate.

Guacamole (spicy avocado dip)

Zesty Chilean or **South African Sauvignon Blanc**. Or a **Mexican beer**.

Guineafowl

By and large, works with the same kind of wines as chicken, though it generally has more flavour. Often served simply roast, so basically any **medium-bodied red**, though not too overpowering or oaky. I'd go for a **two-** or **three-year-old Gigondas** or **Crozes-Hermitage**, or a sexy supple **Italian red** such as **aged Vino Nobile de Montepulciano**.

Gumbo (spicy soupy Creole stew with chicken, prawns and okra)

Needs a **Chilean** or **South African Sauvignon Blanc**; or a **beer**.

Haddock

Fresh haddock goes with the same kind of wines as cod (*see* Cod). Smoked haddock is particularly good with **lighter French** and **Italian Chardonnays**, such as **Vin de Pays d'Oc Chardonnay**, **Pinot Blanc** and **Soave**. (*See also* Kedgeree.)

Haggis

A wee dram of **whisky**, preferably an **Island malt**. For fun you might like to track down the **Australian Bobbie Burns Shiraz** – though if you're drinking wine almost any **Shiraz** would do.

Halibut

An opportunity to show off a **Premier Cru Chablis** or other **fine white burgundy**. If it's smoked, treat it as smoked haddock (*see* Haddock).

Hake

Hake is particularly prized in Spain a **Spanish** wine seems appropriate. I'd pick **Albariño**, which can cope with the piquancy of the *salsa verde* that often accompanies the fish. Or try a **traditional white Rioja**.

Ham

Every country has its own kind of ham, from mild sweet York ham to the intensely flavoured acorn-fed Spanish Pata Negra. (*See also* Bacon, Gammon, Melon.)

Milder boiled or cooked hams Particularly good with **unoaked Chardonnay** (**Chablis** in the case of the classically French *jambon persille*), **Semillon** and **Semillon/Chardonnay**, and **light fruity reds** such as **Beaujolais-Villages** or **Merlot**. Mild hams also go extremely well with **fruity pale ales**, **honey ales** and **cider**.

Air-dried hams Parma, Serrano, Bayonne and Pata Negra, for example, are slightly more delicate but can also be quite salty; **simple crisp dry whites** and **rosés** are generally the best option, preferably from the same country or region as the ham. **Manzanilla** and **fino sherries** are particularly good with Spanish hams.

Hare

Hare produces intensely rich dishes that provide a good excuse to wheel out a massive great red: an **Amarone**, **Barolo** or **Chianti** in the case of the famous Italian dish *Parpardelle con Lepre* (pasta with hare sauce); a big **Syrah**, **Shiraz** or **Zinfandel** with a casserole such as jugged hare. **Strong Belgian ales** such as **Chimay** or **Orval** will also cope.

Harissa

This hot spicy pepper sauce is an integral part of North African dishes such as couscous, but increasingly pops up as an ingredient on fashionable menus elsewhere. With fish dishes try a **Sauvignon Blanc**; with meat dishes a **robust southern French red** such as **Fitou**, **St-Chinian**, **Collioure**; or **Jumilla** from **Spain**.

Hazelnuts

Hazelnuts have a great affinity with chocolate, so wines that go with chocolate often work with hazelnut desserts too. If you're feeling adventurous you could try a **chocolate stout**. Hazelnut-flavoured shortbread and biscuits are particularly good with **amontillado sherry** and **sweet Madeira**.

Herbs

Herbs are rarely dominant enough to determine your wine choice but can have an important influence in terms of the overall feel of a dish.

Mild herbs The classic French *fines herbes* (parsley, chervil, chives and tarragon) are often added to egg dishes or delicate cream or butter sauces. **Light Chardonnay** tends to work best, although with a herb-based salad you might prefer a classic **Sauvignon Blanc** such as **Sancerre**.

61

Mediterranean herbs Thyme, marjoram, oregano and *herbes de Provence* go best with **slightly herby southern French reds** such as **Corbières**, **Minervois**, **Côtes du Roussillon**, or with **Rioja**.

Strongly flavoured herbs Basil, coriander, dill, mint, rosemary and sage have very distinct personalities and uses (*see* individual entries).

Herrings

Herrings are not a natural with wine, though fried in oatmeal they're pleasant enough with a **dry white** such as **Muscadet**, or even with **pale ale** or **cider**. Pickled herrings are much better with a good **lager**, or with **vodka** or **aquavit**.

Hollandaise sauce

See Sauces.

Honey

Honey-flavoured beer works with dishes that aren't too sweet: a salad with a honey dressing say. Recipes such as duck or chicken with a honey glaze go well with **Viognier** or a **basic Aussie red**. **Muscat** works best with honey-flavoured desserts: **Muscat de Beaumes-de-Venise** or other **southern French** or **Greek Muscats** with honey drizzled over roast peaches, Greek yoghurt or soft cheese. **Australian Liqueur Muscat** with honey cake (assuming you have a seriously sweet tooth). Try **Earl Grey** or **jasmine tea** if you haven't.

Horseradish

Fresh horseradish is not a seasoning to use lavishly if you value your wine. Commercial sauces are less harsh, but still suggest **new world Cabernet Sauvignon** rather than fragile old claret with your Sunday roast.

Hummus

See Greek.

ce cream & iced parfaits

The iciness of ice cream makes most dessert wines taste thin and weedy, so if you're eating it on its own it's better to go for something seriously sweet and sticky. Vanilla, toffee, caramel and nutty-flavoured ice creams are fantastic with **Australian Liqueur Muscat**, **ultra sweet sherries** (**PX** if you can get hold of it, otherwise **Matusalem**) and **malmsey Madeira**. With flavoured ice creams try to find a matching **liqueur**. Don't worry so much about desserts that include a scoop of ice cream as the overall flavour of the pudding is more important.

Indian

The big myth about Indian food is that lager is the only thing you can drink with it. In fact, there are plenty of wines, and beers, that are better. The tricky bit – which is common to Asian cuisines – is that several different types of dish are served together, so it's more useful to think about how hot the meal is overall rather than individual recipes. If it's a combination of mild and moderately hot dishes go for wines that suit the hotter ones.

Mild dishes Pakoras and onion bhajis, biryanis, dishes with yoghurt and cream such as kormas,and tandoori chicken for example: **crisp dry whites** such as **Vin de Pays des Côtes de Gascogne**, **rosés**, **off-dry whites** such as the **modern dry German Rieslings**, **Viognier**, or **Hungarian** or **Chilean Gewurztraminer**. Dishes with cream and butter chicken go well with **Chardonnay**. And, of course, **lager** (**Kingfisher** or **Cobra** if you want to be authentic) or **pale ale**.

Moderately hot dishes Chicken tikka masala, rogan josh and baltis for example: **new world whites**, especially **Aussie Semillon/Chardonnay** and **jammy Aussie reds** such as **Cabernet/Shiraz**. **Pale ale** or an **IPA** (rather than lager) if you prefer beer.

Hot dishes Vindaloo for example: almost impossible to pair with wine, but really big macho reds (13.5 per cent plus) such as **Australian Shiraz**, **Zinfandel** and **South African Pinotage** can cope. Otherwise drink **lager** or **lassi**.

Indian desserts **Spiced tea** is the best option I think. But **sweet Muscats** such as **Moscatel de Valencia** or **Greek Muscat** would be delicious too.

Irish stew

Irish beer, what else? **Guinness** or **Murphy's** if you like stout; **Caffrey's** or **Kilkenny** if you prefer something milder.

Italian

Italian food is so popular we probably all eat it at least once a week, not necessarily with Italian wines. But as with France, there are many regional variations and partnerships of wine and food that have stood the test of time, many of which you'll find elsewhere on these pages.

If you're not used to Italian wines you may find them a bit sharp and even characterless compared to, say, Australian or Chilean wines, and the quality can vary alarmingly. With well-known names such as **Valpolicella** it's better to avoid cheaper bottles. Wines that offer particularly good value are lesser-known **dry Italian whites** such as **Bianco di Custoza**, **Orvieto**, **Verdicchio**, and **Vernaccia di San Gimignano** and **robust Southern Italian reds** such as **Negroamaro**, **Primitivo** and **Salice Salentino**. (*See also* Antipasti, Pasta, Pizza, Ravioli, Risottos.)

Jambalaya

A spicy New Orleans spin on paella that includes prawns, chicken and ham or smoky sausage. **Sauvignon Blanc** would be a suitable white, **Spanish Tempranillo** a good red. But I'd probably go for a **lager** or a **Harvey Wallbanger**.

Japanese

Includes a wide range of flavours, from clean fishy dishes such as sushi to strong meaty dishes such as Teriyaki and miso soup. **Sake** is the traditional accompaniment, but the Japanese are great **whisky** lovers too. You can also get hold of **Japanese beers** such as **Asahi** and **Sapporo**. (*See also* Noodles, Sashimi, Sushi, Tempura.)

Jellies

Wine with jelly might sound a bit weird but **sparkling wines** are just what you need: **Moscato d'Asti** in the case of light fruit jellies; **Champagne** or a similar **dry sparkling wine** with jellied seafood or vegetable terrines. Sweet jellies that accompany savoury dishes, such as redcurrant jelly with lamb, point to a **fruitier than usual red** – a **Chilean Merlot** for example.

Jerk chicken or pork

Rum punch is a natural with this spicy Caribbean-style dish, but if you're not in the mood to party an inexpensive **Zinfandel** or **Ruby Cabernet** will do nicely. Or a bottle of **Red Stripe**.

Jewish

The sweet-sour salty and pickled flavours of many traditional Jewish dishes such as gefilte fish are not naturals with wine, but **softer Sauvignon Blancs**, **dry Rieslings** and **lighter Chardonnays** are reasonably flexible choices. There are now plenty of **kosher wines** available. (*See also* Cheesecake, Chicken livers, Herrings, Pastrami, Salt beef, Smoked salmon.)

Jus

Jus is what chefs call gravy these days. It means an intensely flavoured reduction of wine and cooking juices, which tends to steer you towards a **full-bodied** rather than a light **red**.

Kangaroo

It has to be **Australian Shiraz** really, doesn't it? Or at least some kind of big bouncing **Aussie red**.

Kebabs

Almost anything can be speared on a kebab skewer so it's hard to generalise; the fact that it is most likely to be grilled or barbecued means a reasonably **robust wine** is called for. The classic combination of lamb, onions and peppers goes well with **Sauvignon Blanc**, which is also what I'd choose for most fish-based kebabs. Otherwise go for an inexpensive **Australian**, **Chilean** or **South African red**. With fruit kebabs, drink an inexpensive **Muscat** or **Asti**.

Kedgeree

Amazingly good with *blanc de blancs* **Champagne**, **Australian sparkling wine** or **Buck's Fizz**. **Wheat beer** and **pale ale** are also very good.

Keylime pie

A **sweet Riesling** is the best bet for this creamy lime-flavoured tart. Given that it's a classic American dessert, it would be appropriate to drink a **Californian** wine, but an **Aussie** one would do just as well.

Kidneys

The delicate flavour of veal or lambs' kidneys is easily overwhelmed, so go for **light-** or **medium-bodied**, rather than full-bodied, **reds**. **Italian reds** such as **Chianti** and **Barbera**; and **Spanish reds** such as **Rioja** and **Valdepeñas** go well; and most **Pinot Noirs** are good. With kidneys cooked in red wine you can afford something more robust such as **Vacqueyras**, **Cairanne** or **Côtes du Roussillon-Villages**.

Kippers

Tea is about the only sane thing to drink with kippers. With kipper pâté you could get away with a **powerful New Zealand Sauvignon Blanc** or an **island malt whisky**.

Laksa

As with most soups or soupy stews, this fashionable Malaysian dish tastes better on its own or possibly with a **light beer**.

Lamb

Simply roasted lamb Good with a wide range of **medium-bodied reds**, and is one of the classic dishes to show off a **mature red Bordeaux** or **Rioja** (as long as you don't swamp the meat in mint sauce). **Italian reds** such as **Chianti Classico** also go well, as does almost any kind of **Cabernet Sauvignon** or **Cabernet Franc**.

Grilled lamb Goes particularly well with **southern French reds** such as **Corbières**, **Minervois** and **Côtes du Roussillon** (and other reds mentioned above). You could also try **Sauvignon Blanc** and **Greek whites** – particularly if the lamb has been marinated in oil, garlic and lemon juice.

Braised lamb shanks **Full-bodied reds** from the **Rhône**, such as **Crozes-Hermitage** and **Gigondas**, or a gutsy **Australian** or **Argentinian Shiraz**.

Middle Eastern-style lamb spiced with cumin and coriander A **Greek**, **Moroccan** or **Portuguese red**. The same type of wine will go with spicy sausages and meatballs. For lamb kormas and curries *see* Indian)

See also Irish stew, Shepherd's pie.

Lancashire hotpot

A **traditional British**, preferably **Lancashire**, **ale** – or at least not a Yorkshire one.

Langoustines

The delicate sweetness of these upwardly mobile prawns provides a perfect excuse for a good **white burgundy** or expensive **new world Chardonnay**. **Puligny-** or **Chassagne-Montrachet** for preference; **St-Véran** if the budget's a bit tight.

Lasagne

There are many variations these days on the classic meat and cheese lasagne: roast vegetables, chicken and mushroom, and even fish. On the whole, stick to **Italian** wines as their slight sharpness cuts through the richness of this dish. A **Puglian** or **Sicilian red** with vegetable or meat-based lasagne; a **light Italian Chardonnay** with chicken or fish.

Lebanese

Lebanese food follows the typical Middle Eastern pattern of *mezze* before grilled meat. **Greek** wines fit the bill better than Lebanese, with the outstanding exception of the famous **Chateau Musar**. **Dry rosés** also go well with Lebanese food, particularly those from **Navarra**.

Leeks

Leeks have a delicate sweetness that makes them a natural with **cider**, which goes particularly well with leek-based soups and chicken and leek pie. **Vin de Pays d'Oc Chardonnay** is a good match for leek quiches. Served cold with a vinaigrette dressing, leeks are better with a **crisp dry white** such as **Muscadet**.

Lemon

Lemon – and lemon rind in particular – has an incredibly powerful flavour that dominates dishes in which it's a major ingredient, though cream can modify the effect. Sweet lemon dishes tend to go well with wines made from the **Riesling** grape; savoury ones with **Sauvignon Blanc** and other **crisp dry whites**. Note: adding a squeeze of lemon to a dish can make a wine taste less bitter and oaky – this way you can make **Chardonnay** partner simple fish dishes.

Light lemon desserts Lemon mousse and lemon soufflé for example: **Asti**, **Late-Harvest** or **botrytis Riesling**.

Rich lemon desserts Lemon syllabub, lemon posset, lemon meringue pie and lemon tart, for example, go well with **Late-Harvest Rieslings**, but the wine needs to be intensely sweet in the case of very sharply flavoured lemon tarts: a **German** or **Austrian Trockenbeerenauslese** would be ideal.

Lemon ice creams and sorbets Tricky unless they are just a part of the dessert. If they dominate, a **lemon-flavoured liqueur** would be the best bet.

Hot lemon puddings Lemon surprise pudding and lemon sponge pudding for example: **Sauternes** and similar **dessert wines** from **Bordeaux** work reasonably well, but wine never seems quite right with this type of dessert.

69

Savoury dishes with lemon **Dry Italian whites** such as **Verdicchio** work well if the lemon flavour is not too overpowering – *spaghetti al limone* for instance. With dishes with a more pronounced lemon flavour, such as chicken with preserved lemons, try an **Australian Sauvignon Blanc**.

Lemongrass

Common to Thai and Thai-style dishes, lemongrass has a delicate lemon flavour that suits **Australian Riesling** and **Sauvignon Blanc**.

Lentils

Lentil dishes tend to be quite rustic and substantial and suit equally characterful wines. Inexpensive **French reds** such as **Côtes du Ventoux** or **Côtes du Roussillon** tend to work well, particularly with chunky lentil and bacon soups. Puy lentils, which sometimes accompany roast fish such as cod, are a bit more delicate and can take a **reasonably full-bodied white** such as an **Albariño** or **Australian Verdelho**. With lentil salads try a **basic *vin de pays*** – **white**, **red** or **rosé** – or a **Spanish white** such as **Rueda**.

Lime

Lime-flavoured dishes, on the whole, suit the same kind of wines that match lemony ones, though lime's slightly sharper flavour sometimes calls for more powerfully flavoured wines. **Aussie Riesling** and **Verdelho** and **New Zealand Sauvignon Blanc** are good matches for savoury dishes, as is **lager** (unsurpisingly, when you think of lager and lime). (*See also* Keylime pie.)

Liver

With simply grilled or panfried calves' liver it's best not to have too powerful a wine: **Rioja**, **claret**, **Merlot** and **Italian reds** such as **Chianti** tend to work best. If you add a rich onion gravy, go for a **Shiraz**; or even a good old-fashioned **porter** or **nut brown ale**. (*See also* Chicken livers.)

Lobster

The two wines that are made for lobster dishes are good **white burgundy** and **Champagne**, or their top **Australian, Californian** or **New Zealand** counterparts. If you're pushing the boat out with the lobster you might as well splash out on the wine too.

Lobster salad and cold lobster dishes Ideally a **Puligny-** or **Chassagne-Montrachet** or **non-vintage Champagne**. With lobster mayonnaise you could also drink a **Pouilly-Fumé** or **Sancerre**.

Grilled lobster, lobster ravioli and lobster bisque **Meursault** or **vintage Champagne**.

Richly sauced lobster dishes *Lobster a L'Americaine* and lobster thermidor for example: a top quality **Californian, Australian** or **New Zealand Chardonnay**.

Spiced lobster dishes **New Zealand Sauvignon Blanc, Viognier** or **Champagne**, providing the dish isn't too spicy.

Lychees

Wines made from **Gewürztraminer** are supposed to taste of lychees. Test the theory out for yourself with a **Vendange Tardive (Late-Harvest) Gewurztraminer** from **Alsace**.

acaroni cheese

White wine works as well as **red** with macaroni cheese. Nothing grand: an inexpensive **Hungarian** or **Bulgarian Chardonnay** or a **Chilean white** would do. Or go for a **Chilean red** or **Merlot**. **Draught bitter** is good too.

Mackerel

Mackerel can be very oily, particularly when it's smoked, so you need a **sharply flavoured white** to compensate. **Muscadet** is good, especially with simply grilled mackerel; **Sauvignon Blanc** if the dish is given an oriental twist. As mackerel is sometimes served with gooseberry sauce you could also try a **gooseberry-flavoured beer** such as **Grozet** or (easier to track down) a **wheat beer** such as **Hoegaarden**.

Mango

Mango's lush ripe flavour is mirrored by cheaper **Australian Chardonnays** and **Semillon/Chardonnays**, which go perfectly with chicken, duck or prawn salads with mango and mango salsas. Mango fool or ice cream needs quite a **rich sweet white**: again, go Down Under for an **Aussie Late-Harvest Riesling**.

Marinades

Marinades have more of an influence on what you drink than the food you're marinading. They can add a touch of sweetness (orange or honey), sharpness (lemon or lime), or spiciness (garlic, chilli or barbecue), so it's hard to generalise, other than to say that **new world** (particularly **Australian** and **Chilean**) **wines** stand up better than traditional European ones. Look under the main marinade ingredients.

Mascarpone

This super-creamy Italian cheese is generally offset by lemon, lime or red fruits such as strawberries, but still needs quite a powerful dessert wine to cope – preferably **Italian**. Try a **Recioto di Soave** or **Passito di Pantelleria** if you can get hold of them. Or a **Late-Harvest Riesling**.

Mayonnaise

Bottled mayonnaise doesn't have much influence on a dish. Home-made mayonnaise, which is richer and eggier, can be more tricky. A **citrussy Chardonnay** from **Chile**, for example, or a blend of **Chardonnay** and **Sauvignon** is about the best bet. (*See also* Aioli.)

Meatloaf & meatballs

Basically, any inexpensive **red** you enjoy or one that is going cheap at the supermarket at the time (ideally both). I prefer something gutsy, such as a **Fitou**, though with spaghetti and meatballs you might want to go for a **Sangiovese** or **southern Italian red**. (*See also* Beef, Lamb.)

Melon

Varies considerably in ripeness and sweetness. Honeydew melon is good with **Moscato d'Asti**, or if you're eating it with parma ham, a **dry Muscat**. Ultra-ripe ogen or charentais melons can take a **sweetish white port**, or a **pale cream sherry** or **Montilla**.

Merguez

See Sausages.

Meringues

Sweet fizzy Asti and **Moscato d'Asti** are magic with airy meringues, particularly if they're combined with summer fruits or lemon. If there's cream involved you could also drink a **Sauternes** or **Sauternes-style** wine such as **Monbazillac** or **Saussignac**. Rich caramelly brown-sugar meringues are good with a glass of **Orange Muscat**. (*See* Pavlova.)

Mexican

Margaritas, **Mexican beer** and **fruity red wines**, in that order. There are a few Mexican wines around but on the whole **Chilean** ones (especially **Cabernet Sauvignon** and **Carmenere**) are much better; **Chilean Sauvignon Blancs** go particularly well with avocado-based dishes. **Bloody Marys** are also good with Mexican food – a bit like liquid salsa. (*See also* Ceviche, Chilli con carne, Fajitas, Guacamole.)

Mince pies & mincemeat tarts

Both go really well with inexpensive **Greek** and **southern French Muscats** such as **Muscat de Rivesaltes**, **Muscat de Frontignan** and **St-Jean-de-Minervois**. Or with **five-year-old Madeira** or **late-bottled vintage port**.

Minestrone

Heinz minestrone: **Sicilian red** or **white**. River Café summer minestrone: **Arneis**, **Gavi** or **Cortese del Piemonte**. River Café winter minestrone: **Barbera**. (*See also* Soups.)

Mint

There's something quite minty about **Cabernet Sauvignon**, which is one of the reasons it works well with lamb (though avoid sousing the meat with mint sauce, which is a killer). Mint is also widely used in Greek or Middle Eastern food, where it tastes good with **sharp dry lemony whites**, such as **Greek whites** or **Portuguese Vinho Verde**.

Monkfish

Generally roasted, often with pancetta, monkfish can easily take a **light red** such as **Chinon** or **Pinot Noir**, but it also works with a good **Chardonnay** – from **Australia** or **California** – or one of the stylish new **Marsanne**, **Roussanne** and **Viognier blends** from the **Languedoc**.

Moroccan

Moroccan reds go well with couscous and tagines made from beef or lamb but you could easily substitute a **Portuguese red** or **Southern French red** such as **Fitou** or **Corbières**. Fish and chicken tagines with olives and preserved lemons are better with **crisp dry whites** such as **Sauvignon Blanc**. These whites also work well with Moroccan starter salads, as does **dry rosé**. **Mint tea** is a must to finish.

Moules marinières

Muscadet is the classic choice, but any **basic dry French white** such as **Picpoul de Pinet** or **Terret** will do.

Moussaka

Choose a **gutsy Greek**, **Portuguese**, or **southern Italian red** such as **Primitivo** or **Negroamaro**. Or, if you like beer, an **amber ale**.

Mushrooms

One of the best ingredients for showing off a good **red burgundy** or **Pinot Noir** – mushrooms are generally wine friendly.

Raw or marinated mushrooms and mushroom salads **Dry Italian whites** such as **Verdicchio** and **Pinot Grigio**.

Grilled or baked with garlic and parsley **Full-bodied reds** such as **Shiraz**, **Zinfandel**, **southern French reds** such as **Fitou** and **Corbières**, or **Portuguese reds**. And **Pale ales**.

Mushrooms in creamy sauces, pancakes, pasta dishes or quiches **Soft fruity reds** such as **Merlot** or **Pinot Noir**, or **smooth dry whites** such as **Chardonnay**; or **Soave** or **Lugana**. **Belgian ales** such as **Chimay** are stunning with creamy mushrooms on toast.

Wild mushrooms An expensive delicacy that deserves a decent bottle. **Red burgundy** or **Pinot Noir** if the sauce is **dark and rich**; a **Barolo** or **Chianti** if the dish is Italian. A good **white burgundy**, **Chardonnay** or **Pinot Gris** will partner lighter creamier dishes.

Oyster/shitake mushrooms Generally incorporated into stir-fries or orientally inspired dishes. Try an **Australian Riesling** or **Verdelho**.

Mushroom risotto A **light Italian red** such as **Barbera d'Asti** or a **Pinot Noir**. And **vintage rosé Champagne** is wicked.

Mushroom soup Mild creamy mushroom soup: inexpensive **Chardonnay**. A more intensely flavoured soup with mustard or spinach: a **light red** such as **Merlot**, **Pinot Noir**, or **Saumur-Champigny**.

Mussels

Belgian beers are just the best thing to drink with mussels. **Wheat beers** such as **Hoegaarden** with *moules frites* or spicy dishes with coriander, ginger and chilli. **Strong ales** such as **Leffe Blonde** or **Duvel** with stuffed mussels, or recipes with tomato and garlic. Wine-wise: **crisp dry whites** such as **Muscadet** and **Sauvignon Blanc** work best overall, except with creamy dishes such as *moules bonne femme*, which are better with a **light Chardonnay**. With mussel and saffron soup or *mouclade*: go for an **Albariño**, **southern French white**, or **Californian Viognier**.

Mustard

Hot English mustard is best avoided with wine, but Dijon and grain mustards are fine. French country dishes such as rabbit and kidneys with mustard sauce go well with **Chablis** and other inexpensive **white** and **red burgundies**, but other **soft reds** such as **Merlot**, **Rioja** and **Zinfandel** are good too. **Cider** also goes very well with mustardy dishes.

N

achos

Pint of **lager**, natch.

Nectarines

See Peaches.

Noodles

Although many pastas are, strictly speaking, noodles, most of the noodle dishes you come across derive from Far Eastern countries such as Japan, Malaysia and Thailand. Many are slurpy, soupy dishes such as *laksa*, which don't really go with either wine or beer. Otherwise, their hot, sour and spicy flavours tend to work best with **fruity modern whites** such as **Sauvignon Blanc**, **Australian Riesling** and **Verdelho**, or **lager**.

Nuts

There's a great affinity between nuts and **sherry** (and to a lesser extent **Madeira** and **tawny port**). Salted nuts go with **dry fino** and **amontillado sherries**; nut-flavoured desserts with **sweeter oloroso sherry** and also **Australian Liqueur Muscat**. (*See also* Almonds, Hazelnuts, Walnuts, and Pecan pie.)

Savoury dishes (such as nut burgers or roasts) go with wide range of **medium-** to **full-bodied reds**, though I'd personally go for a **southern French red** such as **Costières de Nîmes** or **Pic St-Loup**. Or, appropriately enough, a **nut brown ale**.

O lives

A **bone-dry well-chilled fino** or **manzanilla sherry** is ideal, but if you don't like sherry try a **crisp dry white**. If the olives are marinated with oil, herbs and spices make it a powerful one: say, a **zesty Chilean Sauvignon Blanc**. (*See also* Tapenade.)

Omelettes

Like other egg dishes, most omelettes go with **Chardonnay** and **Pinot Blanc**. **Light Hungarian**, **Bulgarian** and **French Chardonnays** in the case of more delicate fillings; more powerful (though not too oaky) **Australian** or **Chilean Chardonnays** with richer fillings such as crab, lobster or smoked haddock (**Champagne** is also good with these luxury fillings).

More substantial or highly seasoned omelettes with wild mushrooms, chicken livers or roast vegetables, or rustic omelettes, such as *omelette paysanne*, are good with a **light fruity red** such as a **Côtes du Rhône-Villages** or inexpensive **French red vin de pays**. (*See also* Tortilla.)

Onions

Raw onion's coarse flavour presents a tough challenge for any wine – best avoided if you plan to drink something special.

Onion confit/marmalade Slow-cooked onions have an intense sweetness that points in the direction of a **ripe soft fruity red** such as a **Chilean Cabernet** or **Merlot**, or **Australian Cabernet/Shiraz**.

Onion soup French onion soup: a simple **French vin blanc** or **white vin de pays** has the right bistro feel, though a carafe of **rouge** wouldn't go amiss; I prefer **beer** – **Leffe Blonde** where possible. Creamy onion soup: an inexpensive **white burgundy** such as **Bourgogne Blanc**, **Vin de Pays d'Oc Chardonnay** or **Alsace Pinot Blanc**.

Onion tart A speciality of the Alsace region of France that goes brilliantly well with **Alsace Riesling**. Otherwise try any **smooth dry white** such as a **light Chardonnay** or **Pinot Blanc**.

Oranges

Orange-flavoured desserts Although Orange Muscat sounds like the ideal answer when serving orange-flavoured desserts, it's too similar in flavour to work really well. A **botrytis** or **Beerenauslese Riesling** or **Late-Harvest Semillon** is generally a better match. **Spanish Moscatel de Valencia** goes well with fresh-flavoured orange desserts such as caramelised oranges or Moroccan-style orange fruit salads.

Savoury dishes with orange Chicken or salmon with an orange sauce, for example, and orange-based salad dressings: try a **Australian Semillon**, **Semillon/Chardonnay** or **Colombard**.

Organic food

See Vegetarian & organic food.

Ostrich

It has to be **South African**. **Pinotage** for ostrich steaks or burgers. A **Cape medium dry** (they're not allowed to call it sherry) with air-dried ostrich or biltong.

Oxtail

Almost any **full-bodied red**. A **big Zinfandel** would be my favourite. Braised oxtail (if you can get your hands on some) should be rich dark and sticky, and needs a weighty wine to match.

Oysters

Raw oysters **Chablis**, **Champagne** and **Guinness** are the classic matches with raw oysters and all work brilliantly well. But that doesn't mean other less expensive wines aren't as good. **Crisp dry whites** such as **Muscadet** or **Picpoul de Pinet** also go well, as do most **Sauvignon Blancs** and **sparkling wines** from **Australia**, **New Zealand** and **California**. If you care about your wine, don't add too much lemon or tabasco. And do avoid spirits, which can make oysters indigestible.

Cooked oysters Oysters cooked in a creamy sauce or soup lose that strong seaweedy flavour and can be treated more like normal seafood. A good-quality **white burgundy**, **Californian Chardonnay** or **Champagne** is the best bet. **Sparkling wine** is also great with deep-fried oysters.

Paella

I reckon that nothing goes better with paella than **rosé** – preferably a **rosado** from **Navarra**. If you prefer, drink an inexpensive **Spanish white** such as **Rueda** or a **modern white Rioja**.

Pancakes

Sweet pancakes With lemon and sugar: **Asti** or **Moscato d'Asti**. With orange (*crepes suzette*): **Asti** or **Tokaji**. With golden or maple syrup: **Australian Liqueur Muscat** (though it makes for a bit of a sugar overload unless you've got an exceptionally sweet tooth).

Savoury pancakes With cheese, ham or eggs: **French sparkling cider** (particularly if you're having buckwheat pancakes), or inexpensive **Chardonnay**. With spinach: **Italian** or **southern French Chardonnay**, or **Soave**. With mushrooms: **Pinot Noir**, or an inexpensive **Merlot**.

Pancetta

See Bacon.

Panettone

A festive Italian cake that makes great bread and butter pudding. Sip a **southern French** or **Italian Muscat** such as **Muscat de Rivesaltes** or **Passito di Pantelleria**.

Panna cotta

This simple creamy Italian dessert is often served with fruit for contrast, and you'll need to take account of that (*see* individual fruit entries). Otherwise, drink almost any dessert wine you enjoy: I'd go for a **Recioto di Soave** or **Orange Muscat**.

Parma ham & prosciutto

When served as part of an antipasti or with artichokes try a **dry Italian white** such as **Frascati** or **Orvieto**. With melon you need a wine with touch of sweetness: such as a **dry Muscat** (not as much of a contradiction in terms as it sounds). (*See also* Ham, Melon.)

Parmesan

See Cheese.

Parsnips

Parsnips have a natural sweetness that is accentuated if they're roasted with honey. Match that by picking a wine with some obvious fruit such as a **Merlot** or an **Aussie Chardonnay**, or go for a **honey-flavoured beer**. Spiced or curried parsnip soup works well with a **full-flavoured white** such as **Viognier** or **Roussanne**.

Partridge

See Pheasant.

Passionfruit

There's something particularly decadent about passionfruit: spoil yourself with an expensive **Austrian Ausbruch** or **Trockenbeerenauslese Riesling**. Or **Aussie botrytis Riesling** if you can't find an Austrian one.

Pasta

As you might imagine it doesn't make any difference what shape of pasta you're dealing with: what counts is the flavour of the sauce. There are too many to mention, but here are the main types you're likely to come across.

With baby vegetables (primavera) or herbs (verdura) A **fruity Frascati** or **aromatic Arneis**; or **Sauvignon Blanc**.

Creamy sauces *Carbonara* or smoked salmon for example: **Soave, Bianco di Custoza, Pinot Bianco, Sicilian whites** and **lighter Chardonnay** or **Chardonnay blends**.

Cheese sauces Four cheese or Gorgonzola for example: **crisp dry whites** such as **Verdicchio, light Chardonnays**, or **light reds** such as **Barbera d'Asti** or **Merlot**.

Tomato sauces Fresh tomato with basil: **crisp dry whites** such as **Pinot Grigio** or **Verdicchio**. Cooked tomato and garlic (*napoletana*): **Montepulciano d'Abruzzo** or a **light Sicilian red**.

Seafood S*paghetti alle vongole*, spaghetti with mussels, and linguine with crab for example: **crisp dry whites** such as **Frascati, Verdicchio, Vernaccia di San Gimignano, Muscadet**. Crab can take a **fuller white** such as a **Soave** or **light Chardonnay**.

Meat Bolognese, spaghetti with meatballs or sausage-based sauces: **Sicilian** and **Puglian reds** (especially **Primitivo**), **Sangiovese**, **Rosso di Montalcino**, and **Zinfandel**.

Mushroom **Soave, Bianco di Custoza, Lugana** or **Chardonnay**, or a **light Merlot** or **Pinot Noir**.

Pesto I prefer **dry whites** with green pesto (**Soave, Bianco di Custoza, Sicilian whites, lighter Chardonnays**); **light reds** (**Montepulciano d'Abruzzo, Sangiovese, Merlot**) with red pesto. It's a colour thing as much as anything.

Spicy sauces *Arabbiatta*, *aglio olio e peperoncini*o (garlic, oil and chilli) and *Puttanesca* (anchovies, capers and olives) for example. *Aglio olio e peperonciono* is good with either a **sharply flavoured white** (**Pinot Grigio**) or a **light fruity red** (**Valpolicella, Beaujolais**). For the other dishes go for a **gutsy red**: a **Primitivo** or **Sicilian red**, **Valpolicella Ripasso** or **Zinfandel**.

With beans or lentils *Pasta e Fagioli* for example: **earthy whites** (**Orvieto, Vernaccia di San Gimignano**), or **rustic reds** from **Sicily, Sardinia** or **the south of France**.

Baked pasta dishes With chicken, serve **Soave** or **Chardonnay**; with meat or vegetables, **Chianti, Sangiovese** or **Merlot** (*see also* Cannelloni, Lasagne).

Stuffed pasta These usually have quite a light filling, such as spinach and ricotta, so **dry whites** tend to go better than reds: for preference, **Soave** or a **light Chardonnay**. (*See also* Ravioli.)

Pasta salads **Crisp dry whites** such as **Pinot Grigio, Soave** and **Orvieto** usually work, but it depends on the dressing (*see* Salads).

Pastrami

Classic deli fare. A **Bud**, or other **American lager**.

Pâté

Smooth pâtés and parfaits Surprisingly good with **off-dry whites**, particularly **dry Muscat**, **Pinot Gris** or **Gewurztraminer** from **Alsace**; and even with **sweet wines** such as **Sauternes** or **Monbazillac**. But if that seems an odd start to a meal, try a **fruity Australian Semillon**, **Semillon/Chardonnay** or **Marsanne**.

Rough rustic pâtés and terrines Good with **Beaujolais-Villages** (and individual '*crus*' such as **Brouilly** and **Morgon**) but almost any **French country red** will do. **Fruity Merlots** and **Australian Shiraz** are also fine. Or go for a **fruity English bitter** or **amber ale**.

Fish pâtés **Sauvignon Blanc** is a safe bet, especially those from **Chile** or **California** (see *also* individual fish entries).

Vegetarian pâtés It depends on the vegetables used, but an **Aussie Chardonnay** will probably do the trick; or a **blonde** or **pale ale**.

Pavlova

Delicious with **bubbly**. **Australian sparkling Chardonnay** has to be the most appropriate choice, but a glass of **Moscato d'Asti**, **Asti Spumante** or **Prosecco** would also do nicely.

Peaches & nectarines

Could have been made for dessert wines. Poached, roast or stuffed baked peaches are a fine match for a good **Sauternes** or **Barsac**, or cheaper equivalents such as **Loupiac**, **Cadillac**, **Saussignac** and **Monbazillac**. Poached in red wine: go for a **sweet red** such as **Recioto**. With peach melba: **Raspberry liqueur topped up with Champagne** or **sparkling wine** – in fact, it's almost worth eating peach melba just to drink this.

Peanut sauces

Reds struggle a bit with peanut sauces, so with dishes such as pork or chicken satay, *gado gado* (cooked vegetables in peanut sauce), or bang bang chicken, I tend to stick to an **Aussie Chardonnay** or **Semillon/Chardonnay**. Or a decent **lager** such as **Tusker** from **Kenya**.

Pears

Pear desserts Pear and almond tart is particularly good with **dessert wines** from the **Loire** such as **Coteaux du Layon**, **sweet** (**Moelleux**) **Vouvray**, **Bonnezeaux** and **Quarts de Chaume**; otherwise try a **Late-Harvest Riesling**. With pears in red wine, try **Southern French** *vin doux naturels* such as **Rivesaltes**, **Maury** and **Banyuls**, or **Mavrodaphne of Patras**. Pears with ice cream and chocolate sauce (Poire Belle Helene) are particularly tricky because of the chocolate sauce but a **Californian Orange Muscat** should work. With pear sorbet try a **Poire William** *eau de vie* from **Alsace**.

Pears in salads or with cheese *See* Roquefort, Salads.

Peas

Peas have a natural sweetness that can make some wines taste quite sharp. A **light citrussy Chardonnay** from **southern France** or **Chile**, or (even better) a **Chardonnay/Sauvignon blend** goes well with chilled pea soup and dishes with a pea purée. *Petits pois à la française* (peas braised with lettuce) are delicious with **Pinot Noir**, especially **mature red burgundy**. Pea and ham soup or dishes with mushy peas: call for an **English bitter** (preferably on draught) or a **dry cider** rather than with wine.

Pecan pie

Australian Liqueur Muscat, **sweet oloroso sherry** and **malmsey Madeira** match pecan pie for toffeed sweetness – overwhelmingly so you may find. A **ten-year-old tawny** or **Madeira** is slightly more restrained.

Peking duck

See Chinese.

Pepper

Shiraz (**Syrah** in France) has a slightly peppery note in it so tends go well with peppery dishes such as steak *au poivre*; but other **big jammy reds** do too. Creamy sauces with green peppercorns respond to a **slightly softer red** such as a **Rioja** or **Tempranillo** from **Navarra**, or a **smooth unoaked Chardonnay**.

Peppers

Raw or stir-fried peppers needn't have too much effect on your choice of wine, although red, yellow and orange peppers are more wine-friendly than the green variety. When grilled, baked or roasted, however, peppers acquire an intense sweetness that needs careful handling.

Chicken, pork or fish with peppers A **fruity southern French** or **Spanish red** such as **Côtes du Roussillon** or **young Tempranillo**.

Peperonata or ratatouille **White** or **red Côtes du Rhône** or **dry rosé**.

Piedmontese peppers or piquillo peppers **Cortese del Piemonte**, **Soave**, **Lugana** or an inexpensive **Hungarian** or **Chilean Sauvignon Blanc**. Spanish *piquillo* peppers often form part of a selection of *tapas*, so a **chilled fino sherry** is ideal.

Piperade (scrambled eggs with peppers) **Navarra rosado** or **Cava**.

Red pepper soup An inexpensive **Viognier** or **modern Languedoc white**.

Stuffed peppers A **southern French red** such as **Minervois** or **Corbières**.

Pesto

See Pasta.

Pheasant

Roast pheasant is a golden opportunity to show off your most prized wines. **Older vintages** of **Bordeaux**, **burgundy**, **Rioja** and **Barolo** work brilliantly, but **younger fruitier reds** are also good: **Chilean Merlot**, **Australian Shiraz** or **Californian Pinot Noir**. It's pretty well up to you. If you serve an apple sauce, or casserole the pheasant with apples, **German Spätlese** and **Alsace Riesling** also work well. As does **Normandy cider**.

Pickles & piccalilli

Sharp-flavoured pickles do little for wine – particularly those that accompany Indian and Japanese meals. **Traditional British ales** just about survive piccalilli.

Pies & pasties

Pies stem from an age when we weren't really wine drinkers and I still think they go better with **beer** or **cider** than wine, with the exception of fish pies. And fruit pies I find infinitely preferable with cream or custard. (*See also* Steak, Pork, Fish, Apple.)

Pigeon

Richly flavoured meat often served fashionably rare with a dark intense *jus* (see *Jus*). **Australian**, **Chilean** or **Californian Cabernet Sauvignons** work well, or go for a spicy **Rhône red** such as **Crozes-Hermitage** or **St-Joseph**. With a warm salad of pigeon, I'd choose a **Pinot Noir**.

Pineapple

Fresh pineapple is tricky unless you go for broke and a **piña colada**. With roast or grilled pineapple, serve an **Australian botrytis** or **Late-Harvest Riesling** or **Semillon**; or alternatively a **Jurançon Moelleux**.

Piri Piri chicken

A **basic Portuguese red** would be the most appropriate choice for this spicy Portuguese chicken dish. But **Zinfandel**, **Pinotage** or any **jammy Aussie red** will do.

Pizza

I stick to **Italian**: inexpensive **Sicilian whites**, **Orvieto** or **Verdicchio** with fishy or vegetarian pizzas; cheap **Chianti** or **Sangiovese** with pepperoni or other meaty pizzas. Or do as the Italians and drink **lager**.

Plaice

Delicately flavoured fish that deserves a decent **dry white**. **Chablis** with grilled plaice; **Chilean** or **South African Sauvignon** if the plaice is deep-fried. A **light French** or **Italian Chardonnay** if the fish is stuffed with prawns or cooked in a creamy sauce.

Plums

French-style plum tarts are good with **sweet Alsace** or **German Rieslings**; poached plums are better with a **sweet red** such as **Mavrodaphne of Patras** or even a **vintage character** or **late-bottled vintage port**. Plum pies and crumbles are, in my view, more enjoyable without wine, though a **damson-** or **plum-flavoured beer** would be worth a try.

Polenta

Has very little flavour of its own, so match the wine to whatever you're eating with it. You might want to make it **Italian** though.

Pork

Like chicken, pork is as well suited to white wine as it is to red: in fact many of the sauces are interchangeable (*see* Chicken). But pork is often combined with fruit, or sweet, or spicy flavourings, making it especially good with **fruity whites** and **soft fruity reds**. (*See also* Bacon, Charcuterie, Gammon, Goulash, Ham, Pâté, Rillettes, Satay, Sausages.)

Roast pork A good **Beaujolais** such as **Fleurie** or **Morgon**, or a **Chilean Merlot**. If the pork is cooked with a sweet apricot stuffing, try **Californian Chardonnay** or **Viognier**. With apple sauce: an **Australian unoaked Chardonnay** or a **dry Vouvray**. With cold roast pork: **unoaked Chilean** or **Vin de Pays d'Oc Chardonnay**, or **South African Chenin Blanc** all go well.

Italian style with garlic, rosemary and fennel An **Orvieto**, **Soave Classico** or a **Pinot Grigio** from the **Alto Adige**.

Pork with apples or pork and apple pie A **dry cider**, or even simple **apple juice**.

Pork pie Traditional British pork pies are best with **pale ale**, **draught bitter** or **scrumpy**.

Sweet pork dishes With honey, apricots or peaches for example: **Australian Semillon**, **Colombard** or **unoaked Chardonnay**, or **Californian Viognier**, and **American amber ales**. Pork with prunes works better with a **demi-sec Vouvray**, or a **mature southern Italian red** such as a **Copertino Riserva**.

Sweet and sour pork and Char siu (barbecue pork) **Australian Sémillon/Chardonnay**, **Tarrango**, or a **full-bodied Chilean** or **Australian rosé**.

Spare ribs As above – unless marinated in a smoky barbecue sauce, in which case drink **Zinfandel**.

Potatoes

Potatoes shouldn't have a great impact on your wine choice, taste-wise at least, but they might suggest a direction to go in. If it's *frites* it's got to be **French** (or **Belgian**). If you're eating great Irish mashed potato dishes such as champ or colcannon you can't beat an **Irish beer**. The only dish you might give a moment's thought to is stuffed baked potatoes: my vote would go to a traditional **English bitter**. (*See also* Gratin dauphinoise.)

Poussin

See Chicken.

Prawns

Rather like chicken, prawns take on the flavour of the sauce or seasoning they're cooked in, but in general taste better with **crisp dry whites** than reds. (*See also* Paella, Pasta, Stir-fries, Indian.)

Prawns in a tomato and garlic sauce Dry southern French whites or rosés.

Char-grilled prawns with garlic and chilli Sauvignon Blanc or Australian Riesling.

Prawn cocktail Champagne, Cava or Babycham.

Profiteroles

Orange Muscat or, if you pour over lashings of hot chocolate sauce, Australian Liqueur Muscat.

Prosciutto

See Parma ham & prosciutto.

Prunes

Prunes are positively sexy these days and deserve respectful treatment on the wine front. Choose a **mature soft red** such as Rioja Reserva, Valdepeñas or the Lebanese wine Chateau Musar for dishes such as pork and rabbit with prunes. Moroccan lamb tagines with prunes go well with Moroccan reds or Chilean Cabernet/Merlot. With prune and armagnac ice cream: try a sweet oloroso sherry or Moscatel.

Puddings

Cream or custard is a much better option than wine with the vast majority of traditional British steamed or baked-suet puddings (though I did once drink a Krug vintage rosé with a steamed ginger sponge and it was fabulous). There are a few exceptions, such as marmalade pudding with Tokaji. (*See also* Bread and butter pudding, Queen of puddings, Rice pudding, Summer pudding.)

Pumpkin

Given that pumpkin pie is the traditional dessert for Thanksgiving, a **Californian Late-Harvest wine** would be an appropriate choice. Or a glass of **sweet sherry**. (*See also* Soups.)

Quail

Pinot Noir – especially **Californian Pinot Noir** – is a reliable choice, but if the dish is very spicy or served with a dark concentrated *jus*, you might want something more robust such as a **Cabernet Sauvignon** or a **Shiraz**. Quails eggs are a bit of a delicacy, so I'd be tempted to accompany them with a glass of **Champagne** – or at least **sparkling wine**.

Queen of puddings

There's often a touch of lemon in this light, airy meringue pudding; go for an **Australian Late-Harvest** or **botrytis Riesling**, or drink a **Moscato d'Asti**.

Quorn

Follow the advice for chicken (*see* Chicken).

Quiches

Unsurprisingly, quiches work with the same wines as eggs: **unoaked Chardonnay** or, in the case of quiche lorraine, **Alsace Pinot Blanc**. (*See also* individual entries for vegetables.)

Quinces

Quinces are so hard they tend to be poached in syrup or an inexpensive **dessert wine** such as **southern French Muscat**. You could drink the same wine, but I'd go for something obscure and exotic such as a **Vendange Tardive Gewurztraminer** from **Alsace**.

Rabbit

Although rabbit meat is delicate, the way it's cooked is often quite robust. Rabbit stews cooked in red wine need a **hearty red** such as a **Fitou**, **Madiran** or **Grenache**. Drink **ale** or **cider** if the rabbit has been cooked in either. Simply roast or grilled rabbit is pretty flexible – almost any **light** to **medium-bodied red** will go – but why not try a good **Beaujolais** or a **Chilean Merlot**. (See Mustard, Prunes.)

Raspberries

Raspberries have an intense flavour – particularly when puréed and sweetened – that can easily overwhelm dessert wines. (*See also* Summer pudding.)

With tarts try **Moscato d'Asti**, or **Muscat de Beaumes-de-Venise**. Raspberry sorbet: **raspberry-flavoured eau de vie** (*Framboise*) from **Alsace**. Raspberry ripple ice cream is great with a **raspberry liqueur** such as **Southbrook Farms Framboise** (pour it over the ice-cream rather than drink it). Desserts with a raspberry coulis: **Framboise topped up with Champagne** or **sparkling wine**. With raspberry-flavoured salad dressings, drink a **Belgian raspberry-flavoured beer**.

Ratatouille

See Peppers.

Ravioli

There's the ravioli you get in tins and the kind of posh ravioli that a smart restaurant serves. With seafood or spinach stuffings, go for a **Soave** or **light Chardonnay** (a **white burgundy** in the case of lobster or crab); with pumpkin ravioli, a **Sicilian Chardonnay**; and with a wild mushroom filling, a **Pinot Noir**. Tinned ravioli? **Southern Italian** or **Sicilian red**. (*See also* Sage.)

Red cabbage

See Cabbage.

Red mullet

Southern French rosé or **Spanish rosado** is particularly good with this Mediterranean fish, or try a **crisp dry white** such as a **Muscadet** or **Picpoul**. You could even drink a **light red**. **Chinon** or **Saumur-Champigny** would be my choice.

Rhubarb

Delicate pale pink poached rhubarb is incredibly good with **dry Champagne**. Other rhubarb puds such as rhubarb fool – and even, at a pinch, rhubarb pie and crumble – go well with **southern French Muscats** or **Spanish Moscatel de Valencia**. **Californian Orange Muscat** is good too. (*See also* Trifle.)

Ribollita (white bean soup)

A characterful **dry Italian white** such as **Orvieto**, or a **Barbera**.

Rice

You wouldn't normally choose a wine to go with rice but there are occasions where it's the star rather than the supporting cast. Dishes such as biryanis and pilaus have quite a delicate taste and texture so you don't want to swamp them. My vote actually goes to inexpensive **sparkling wines** such as **Cava** or **Australian Pinot-Chardonnay**. With more substantial brown rice dishes, go for a **robust red** such as a **Merlot**, **Shiraz** or a **Portuguese red**. (*See also* Kedgeree, Paella, Risotto, Sushi.)

Rice pudding

Hot rice pudding and wine is a bit of a weird combination. Cold rice pud – particularly trendy versions such as rice-pudding brûlée – is a different matter. **Tokaji** goes particularly well, especially if there are apricots or peaches involved. **Sauternes** is good with lemony rice puds. **Californian Black Muscat** or **sweet Recioto della Valpolicella** with red berries.

Risotto

Most risottos go with **dry Italian whites** such as **Soave**, **Bianco di Custoza** or **Lugana**, and with **lighter Chardonnays**, though I would drink an **Australian**, **Californian** or **New Zealand Chardonnay** with richer ingredients such as crab, lobster, butternut squash and pumpkin. And a slightly livelier **Italian white** such as **Verdicchio** or **Frascati** with a risotto *nero* (risotto with squid ink).

Reds are better with risottos with wild mushrooms (try a **Pinot Noir** for example), beetroot (**Dolcetto** or **Cabernet Sauvignon**), or any risotto cooked with red wine (**Valpolicella** or **Barbera**).

Rillettes

The liberal amount of pork, goose or duck fat in *rillettes* needs a bit of acidity to compensate. **Beaujolais**, **basic red burgundy** and **Loire reds** such as **Saumur-Champigny** are all good bets. Or try a **dry rosé**.

Rocket

Adds a slightly peppery character to any salad but not generally enough to influence your wine choice. With a fresh rocket and parmesan salad, drink a **Soave** or **unoaked Chardonnay**.

Roquefort

Sauternes is the classic if you're eating this on its own (*see* Cheese). Crumbled into a salad with pears and walnuts, go for an **Alsace Riesling**.

Rosemary

In general goes well with herby **southern French reds** such as **Corbières**, **Minervois** and **Côtes du Roussillon**, as well as **Italian reds** such as **Chianti**.

Roulades

Light, airy desserts (or occasionally savoury dishes) that need **light bubbly wines**. **Demi-sec Champagne** or **Moscato d'Asti** go well with most sweet roulades. With spinach, mushroom or seafood roulades try **blanc de blancs Champagne** or **sparkling Chardonnay**.

Saffron

Often used in Spanish and other contemporary fish dishes, saffron goes particularly well with **aromatic whites** such as **Albariño** and **Viognier** and **dry** (preferably **Spanish**) **rosé**. (*See also* Paella.)

Sage

Sage has a slightly bitter note so avoid oaky wines. **Unoaked Chardonnay** and **dry Italian whites** such as **Soave**, **Gavi** and **Lugana** tend to work best (particularly with ravioli with butter and sage). **Cider** can be good with traditional British dishes, especially sausages. Note: dried sage is too harsh for anything but the most robust reds.

Salads

Given that salads are by and large light and uncooked, **whites** and **rosés** generally go better than reds – particularly **Sauvignon Blanc** and other **crisp dry whites**, **light citrussy Chardonnays** and **dry Rieslings**. **Lighter beers** such as **lager** are also good.

Some general tips: if one ingredient in a salad is more powerful than the others (for example, blue cheese would be a stronger flavour than pears) match your wine to that ingredient; if the salad dressing is the most dominant flavour match it to the dressing (*see* Salad dressings); if the salad comes from a particular country, such as Greece or Morocco, it makes sense to drink the local wine with it.

Green salad If it's a side salad choose your wine to match the main course. A **light Chardonnay** is a good foil for spinach and bacon salad. (*See also* Caesar salad, Rocket, Watercress.)

Salad selections, layered salads and party salads Often we eat more than one type of salad at a time – particularly at parties or barbecues. Inexpensive **Australian whites** and **reds** and **fruity rosés** will almost always cope, though **lager** is a better match for coleslaw.

Seafood salads Prawns, crab or tuna for example: **dry whites** such as **Muscadet**, **Sancerre** and other **Sauvignon Blancs**. Drink **Chablis**, **white burgundy** or **Australian Verdelho** if there are luxury ingredients involved, such as langoustines, lobster or scallops. With salad Niçoise drink a **crisp dry white** or **southern French rosé**.

Salads with meat Chicken livers, pigeon, duck breasts or rare roast beef for example: go for **light reds** such as **Beaujolais**, **Valpolicella**, or **Loire reds** such as **Chinon**. **Pinot Noir** is particularly good with warm salads. With chicken or ham: try a **light Chardonnay**, or a **fruity bitter** or an **amber ale**.

Salads with cheese A **light Chardonnay**, or **pale ale**. A **dry Riesling** with blue cheese; **Sauvignon Blanc** with goat's or feta cheese (*see also* Cheese). (*See also* Avocado for avocado, mozzarella and tomato salad.)

Salads with fruit Apples or pears: a **fruity Chardonnay** or **Chenin Blanc**, **wheat beers** or **Perry**. With pineapple, mango or papaya: **Australian Semillon, Semillon/Chardonnay** or **Riesling**, or **New Zealand Sauvignon Blanc**. Berries: **Beaujolais**, **Merlot** or **Pinot Noir**, or **raspberry-flavoured beer**.

See also individual salad ingredients: Cucumber, Lentils, Pasta, Tomatoes.

Salad dressings

If you want to flatter a fine wine, try using wine or Japanese rice vinegar rather than vinegar or lemon juice in your salad dressing. (*See also* Mayonnaise.)

Vinaigrette **Crisp dry whites** such as **Sauvignon Blanc**, **Pinot Grigio** and **Verdicchio**; or try **Chardonnay** if the vinaigrette is particularly mustardy or includes nut oil.

Creamy dressings **Unoaked Chardonnay**.

Blue cheese dressing Somewhat tricky. **New Zealand** or **Californian Sauvignon Blanc**, or an **unoaked Chardonnay** should work, but don't expect a great match.

Tangy lime, coriander or garlic dressings **Sauvignon Blanc** or **Australian Verdelho**.

Spicy tomato or barbecue dressings **Merlot** or **Zinfandel**.

Soy sauce-based dressings **Chilean** or **Australian rosé**.

Salami

Rustic Italian whites such as **Orvieto** and **Verdicchio** are good, and **light Italian reds** such as **Valpolicella** or **Bardolino**. Or try a lager such as **Peroni**. (*See also* Antipasti.)

Salmon

Salmon is, for the most part, pretty simple to deal with. Unless the fish is seared, blackened, barbecued or has been cooked with a tomatoey sauce, you can drink **Chardonnay**. Which style of **Chardonnay** you go for depends on the style of the recipe. (*See also* Smoked salmon.)

Cold salmon with mayonnaise or salmon terrines **Vin de Pays d'Oc Chardonnay**, **Chilean Chardonnay** or a **Chardonnay/Sauvignon blend**. If the salmon is wild, good **white burgundy** such as **Premier Cru Chablis** or **Puligny-Montrachet**.

Hot salmon with a hollandaise sauce or beurre blanc Top quality **Chardonnays** from **Australia** or **New Zealand**. Or try a **Meursault**.

Salmon en croute, fish pies with salmon, salmon fishcakes and salmon hash Unoaked Chardonnay, **blanc de blancs Champagne**, **Australian sparkling Chardonnay**, or a **light pale ale**.

Salmon cooked with tomatoes or peppers A **light red** such as **Merlot** or **Sangiovese**.

Seared, blackened or barbecued salmon **Pinot Noir** (particularly **Pinot Noir** from **California** and **New Zealand**), **light Loire reds** such as **Chinon** and **Saumur-Champigny**, or a decent **Beaujolais**. You can even go for **Zinfandel** if you are eating blackened or spice-crusted salmon.

Salsas

Difficult on the face of it, because salsas contain raw onion, but as they are usually served with seared or barbecued foods, **super-fruity wines** are in order. **Lager** and **cocktails** can be even better.

Mexican-style raw tomato salsas Sauvignon Blanc, **light lager**, or a **margarita**. **Chilean Cabernet Sauvignon** if the salsa accompanies something meaty.

Fruit salsas With, for example, mango or chilli: work well with **Aussie Chardonnay**, **Semillon/Chardonnay** or **Verdelho**. Or try **rum punch** or a **daiquiri**.

Salsa verde A tangy Italian parsley, caper and anchovy sauce: with fish, a **modern Italian white**, **Albariño** or **dry rosé**; with boiled meats, a good **Valpolicella**.

Salt

A tip from Californian food and wine expert, Tim Hanni: adding salt to a dish makes an oaky red wine seem softer and less tannic.

Salt beef

See Beef.

Salt cod

Widely used in southern French, Spanish and Portuguese cooking: for example *brandade de morue* (salt cod purée). **Smooth dry whites** such as **Albariño**, **Roussanne** and other **southern French whites** are particularly good. **Dry rosés** work with more robust dishes, such as stews with chickpeas. It's also worth giving **Cava** a whirl.

Samosas

See Indian.

Sandwiches

Beer and sandwiches
is not just a cliché.
Because of the
yeastiness of both,
beer – particularly
traditional British ale –
really does go well with bread.

Sardines

Sharp lemony whites. **Portuguese Vinho Verde** or a **Greek white**
would be ideal. **Hungarian** and **South African Sauvignon Blanc** are
both a good second best.

Sashimi

See Sushi.

Satay

Supermarket satay isn't too much of a
problem because the sauce is comparatively mild. Inexpensive
Aussie whites and **reds** would both work. Authentic satay sauce
needs something more powerful, such as an **Australian Semillon** or
Semillon/Chardonnay. Or **lager**. (*See also* Peanuts.)

Sauces

There isn't a vast array of classical French sauces to get your head
round these days, but there are still too many to list individually.
In the sections overleaf I've concentrated on sauces you pour over
dishes or serve alongside them, rather than those that are part of a
recipe, such as sweet and sour sauce. You'll find a number of these

covered under Chicken and Pasta,
or under their main ingredient:
chocolate, lemon or raspberries,
for example. Note: traditional British
bottled sauces (tomato ketchup, brown
sauce, horseradish and mint sauce) are all
pretty dire with wine. Hot sauces are even
worse: **strong cocktails** such as **Caiprinhas** are
about the only drinks that will cope. (*See also*
Aioli, Chutneys, Salsas, Soy.)

Sauces (savoury)

Apple German Spätlese Riesling or **oaked
Sauvignon Blanc**.

Bearnaise sauce Makes white wine with steak possible:
I'd suggest **Californian Chardonnay**. Or, if you prefer red, a
good **Beaujolais** such as a **Morgon**.

Barbecue sauce Zinfandel, **Shiraz**, or **Chilean Cabernet
Sauvignon** or **Merlot**.

Bechamel and other white sauces With cheese: **Australian** or
southern French Chardonnay. Onion or leek sauce: a
Chardonnay, **pale ale** or **cider** will normally work (though with a
dark onion sauce or gravy you could need a **porter**, **stout** or
southern French red such as **Fitou**). Parsley sauce: **light citrussy
Chardonnay** or **Sauvignon/Chardonnay**.

Butter sauces *Beurre blanc* for example: a **white burgundy**,
Champagne or a **subtly oaked Chardonnay** from **Australia**,
California or **New Zealand**. **New Zealand Sauvignon Blanc** if the
sauce has lemon in it.

Cranberry sauce **Fruity reds** such as **Shiraz**, **Merlot**, good **Beaujolais**, or **robust Rhône reds** such as **Crozes-Hermitage** and **Gigondas**.

Cumberland sauce Good **Beaujolais**, or a **ripe fruity Australian Cabernet/Shiraz**.

Dipping sauces Often sweet and sour in flavour, so a wine with a touch of sweetness, like a **dry Muscat**, helps. (*See also* Thai, Vietnamese.)

Hollandaise sauce **Unoaked Chardonnay**, **Sauvignon/Chardonnay** or **Champagne**.

Rouille **Southern French dry whites**, or go for **French rosés** or **Spanish rosados**. (*See also* Soups for fish soups.)

Tartare sauce **Sauvignon Blanc** or other **lemony whites**; the same advice applies to *sauce ravigote* (a tartare with herbs) and *sauce gribiche* (a tartare with chopped hard boiled eggs).

Sauces (sweet)

Butterscotch and toffee **Australian Liqueur Muscat**, which has a great sticky toffee flavour of its own.

Chocolate *See* Chocolate.

Custard If it's made from Birds powder, forget it; a home-made egg custard can be quite wine-friendly, however, particularly if it's made from a **dessert wine** such as **Sauternes** or **Muscat** – in which case drink the same wine with the dessert.

Sabayon **Sauternes**, **Barsac** or, more modestly, **Monbazillac** or **Premières Côtes de Bordeaux**. Or you could drink a **demi-sec Champagne**.

Sausages

Beer goes better with traditional British or German sausages. **Gutsy red wines** suit the more trendy kind, and recipes involving spicy or garlicky sausages such as paella, jambalaya and cassoulet (*see* individual entries). (*See also* Black pudding, Charcuterie, Chorizo, Salami, Toad in the hole.)

Traditional British sausages Traditional British ales or, in the case of pork and leek sausages, or sausage and apple pie, **cider**. Sausage and chips and sausage sarnies are better with a good strong cup of **tea**.

Sausage and mash with onion gravy Brown ales, **porters** or **Australian Shiraz**.

Garlicky French-style sausages Toulouse sausages for example: **regional French reds** such as **Cahors**, **Madiran** and **Buzet**.

Fish and seafood sausages Try an **unoaked Chardonnay** or **white burgundy**.

Smoked sausages Frankfurters for example: **light French** or **Alsace lager**, **Czech lager** or **German pils** (s*ee also* Choucroute).

Spicy, chilli or barbecue-flavoured sausages Chorizo and merguez for example: good with inexpensive **Spanish**, **Portuguese** or **Moroccan reds**, or **Zinfandel**.

Thai-style sausages Sauvignon Blanc or **lager**.

Sausage casserole A big chunky **southern French red** such as **Fitou** or **Corbières**, **Bulgarian Merlot** or **Cabernet Sauvignon**, or **Australian Shiraz**.

Scallops

In spite of their delicate flavour, scallops are often seared or served with spicy ingredients, which makes a **light red** as suitable as a white – particularly **Californian**, **Oregon** or **New Zealand Pinot Noir**. **Unoaked Chardonnay** and **Pinot Gris** are good all-purpose whites.

Scallops with lime, coriander and lemongrass **New Zealand Sauvignon Blanc**, or **New Zealand** or **Australian Riesling**; **Pinot Noir** if soy or oyster sauce is involved.

Scallops in a creamy sauce or soup *Coquilles St Jacques* for example: a **white burgundy** such as **St-Véran**, good **new world Chardonnay**, **Champagne** or **Aussie sparkling Pinot-Chardonnay**. (*See also* Fish for fish pie.)

Sea bass

As you'll know if you're a Rick Stein fan, sea bass can be cooked in a wide variety of ways: baked whole or filleted, with tomatoes and peppers, or a rich buttery *beurre blanc*. Good generally reliable candidates are **Australian unoaked Chardonnay**, **Verdelho**, **Albariño**, **Californian** or **New Zealand Pinot Gris**; or, if the fish is seared, a **light Californian Pinot Noir**.

Sea bream

Treat as sea bass, above.

Seafood

Shorthand for a mixture of different fish and shellfish. It matters less what they are than the way they're cooked. (*See* Fish for fish pies, Pasta, Risottos, Salads.)

Serrano ham

See Ham.

Shellfish

Elaborate selections of raw shellfish – the classic French *plateau de fruits de mer* – are best suited to **dry whites** such as **Chablis** or **Muscadet**.

Traditional English shellfish such as cockles, winkles and whelks taste better with a **lager** or **pale ale**. (*See also* Crab, Oysters, Prawns, Shrimps.)

Shepherd's pie

Wines that are good with lamb such as **Rioja**, inexpensive **claret**, **Cabernet Sauvignon** and **Merlot** are all in order. But there's no point in being too prissy about it. Any **red** wine you enjoy will do. Or a pint of **best bitter**.

Shrimps (and potted shrimps)

Try a **dry English white** for this very British treat. **German Kabinett Riesling** would be good too and **Chablis** is always a safe bet with shellfish. Or else try a **light British**, **Belgian** or **German wheat beer**. Dried shrimps have a more pungent salty flavour that calls for a stronger **Sauvignon Blanc** or **Australian Riesling**.

Skate

The classic way to cook skate is with 'black' butter (butter that has been allowed to brown), lemon and capers – I'd drink a good **white burgundy**, **Californian** or **New Zealand Chardonnay** or **Sauvignon Blanc**. However, with a more delicately flavoured skate terrine, try **unoaked Chardonnay**, **Semillon/Sauvignon**, **Albariño** or a **blend** of **Marsanne**, **Roussanne** and **Viognier** from the **Languedoc**.

Smoked haddock

See Haddock.

Smoked salmon

The ideal wine (or whisky for that matter) depends on the smoke.

Good quality smoked salmon **Non-vintage** (and especially **blanc de blancs**) **Champagnes**, **Premier Cru Chablis**, **Sancerre**, **Pouilly-Fumé** and **light malt whiskies**.

Cheaper or more heavily smoked salmon A **new world** (especially New Zealand) **Sauvignon Blanc** or **unoaked Chardonnay**, **German Kabinett** or **Australian Riesling**. Or try **Australian**, **New Zealand** or **Californian sparkling wine**. A shot of **lemon-flavoured vodka** is also surprisingly good.

Smoked salmon pâté, mousses and terrines These tend to be made with off-cuts so don't go mad. Inexpensive **bubbly** (**Australian sparkling Chardonnay** or **Cava**), **unoaked Chardonnay**, inexpensive **Sauvignon Blanc** and **crisp dry whites** such as **Vin de Pays des Côtes de Gascogne** and **Vin de Pays du Gers** are all fine. **Champagne** is better with more elaborate terrines.

Hot smoked salmon Tricky – try an **oaky Chardonnay** but, honestly, I think **malt whisky** is better.

See also Eggs, Gravadlax.

Snails

Inexpensive **white French vin de pays**.

Snapper

Usually barbecued, char-grilled or spiced, so take your pick from **light reds**, **crisp dry whites** or **rosé**. **Sauvignon Blanc** or **Spanish rosado** would be my choice. Or a **lager** or **rum punch** if part of a Caribbean feast. (*See also* Afro-caribbean.)

Sole

If you're blowing the budget on Dover sole you might as well go for a classy wine too. **Premier Cru Chablis**, **Puligny-Montrachet** or **Pouilly-Fumé** if it's simply grilled and served with butter, lemon and parsley. **Australian** or **New Zealand Sauvignon Blanc** if it's char-grilled, spiced or served with lime. Similar advice for lemon sole (just scale the price down a bit): **basic Chablis**, inexpensive **white burgundy** or **Vin de Pays d'Oc Chardonnay**.

Sorbets

The whole idea of a sorbet is to create a refreshing end to (or interval in) a meal so, unless it's part of a more fancy dessert, don't worry about wine. What do go well, if you want to create a bit of an effect, are **fruit-flavoured white alcohols** or **eaux de vie**: Poire William with pear sorbet, **framboise** with raspberry sorbet, **lemon-flavoured liqueurs** (the Italians make good ones) with lemon sorbet and so on.

Sorrel

Sorrel has quite a sharp lemony flavour, but is usually used in a creamy sauce with a rich fish such as salmon. **Rich oaked (preferably New Zealand) Sauvignon Blanc** or **unoaked** (preferably **Australian**) **Chardonnay** seem to me the best bets.

Soufflés

A glass of **bubbly** is by far the best choice with a soufflé whatever the flavour might be (if you've taken the trouble to cook one, it's the very least you deserve). My personal preference is a **blanc de blancs** (**all Chardonnay**) or **non-vintage Champagne**, or equivalent (**Australian** or **Californian**) **sparkling wine**, except with rich crab or lobster soufflés, which need the richer flavour of **vintage Champagne**.

Twice-baked soufflés with goat's cheese A **Sancerre** or other **Sauvignon Blanc** from the **Loire**.

Sweet soufflés **Asti** or **demi-sec Champagne** is a safe bet, but an appropriate **liqueur topped up with fizz** can be even more impressive.

Soups

Given that soup is a liquid there's something slightly odd about drinking another liquid with it, so wine tends to go better with more robust chunky soups than with thin ones. In general, I find **neutral dry whites** such as lighter (particularly **Australian** and **Vin de Pays d'Oc**) **Chardonnays**, **Italian whites** such as **Soave** and **Spanish Viura** are the best option, particularly with chicken or vegetable soups. (*See also* under main soup ingredients: Mushroom, for example.)

Consommé **Sherry** is the traditional partner and by far the best bet with meaty consommés: choose an authentic **Spanish-style fino** or **dry amontillado**. Fish consommés with, for example, lobster or crab ravioli: **Chablis** or **Champagne**. Tomato consommé: **Sancerre** or other **Loire Sauvignon Blancs**.

Chicken soup Supposed to be homely and comforting – alcohol seems inappropriate; however... Creamy soups with tarragon suit a **light Chardonnay**. For soups with lemongrass and coconut milk try a **New Zealand Sauvignon Blanc**.

Cold soups **Crisp dry whites** such as **Frascati** or **Verdicchio** (*see also* Cucumber, Gazpacho, Vichysoisse).

Curried soups With just a hint of curry powder (curried parsnip soup, say): a **Roussanne**, **Verdelho** or a **Viognier**. More robust curried soups such as mulligatawny are better with a **pale ale** or **lager**.

Fish soups Crisp dry whites such as **Muscadet**, **Picpoul** or **Verdicchio**, or **dry southern French rosé** or **Spanish rosado**. (*See also* Bouillabaisse, Chowder, Crab, Lobster, Mussels.)

Fruit soups A **matching fruit liqueur topped up with Champagne** or good **new world sparkling wine**. Chilled cherry soup is best with a **cherry-flavoured beer**.

Thick chunky soups Dry southern French rosé or **Spanish rosado**, **Côtes du Rhône** and other inexpensive **French**, **Italian** or **Spanish reds**.

Soups with cheese or ale **Pale ale** or a **fruity bitter**.

Spaghetti bolognese
See Pasta.

Spaghetti carbonara
See Pasta.

Spanish
Apart from the ubiquitous lamb and grilled fish, Spanish cooking is hotter than you'd expect, with ample use of Spain's version of paprika, *pimenton*. Luckily, the country's best known red, **Rioja**, can cope, and other **Spanish reds** such as **Garnacha** and **Tempranillo** are good too. **Albariño** is the best white with fish dishes. (*See also* Chorizo, Gazpacho, Paella, Tapas.)

Spices & seasonings
Although spices can have a major influence on the character of a dish they're rarely used in isolation so it's hard to say what wine goes with, for example, allspice, cardamom or nutmeg. However, a number of them tend to be associated with a particular cuisine or cuisines – such as five spice with Chinese, or cumin with Greek, Turkish, Moroccan or Indian food – so it's worth looking at those entries for suggestions.

In general, though, spiced or spice-crusted dishes tend to steer the choice to **reds** rather than whites: **Pinot Noir** if it's a fish dish; and **Cabernet**, **Shiraz** or **Zinfandel** if it's meat. (*See also* Chilli, Dill, Ginger, Mustard, Salt, Saffron, Pepper, Vanilla.)

Spinach

You only have to think of three or four spinach dishes – eggs florentine, cannelloni, quiche, spinach pancakes – to realise that spinach is most often combined with cheese or eggs. **Lighter Chardonnays** and **dry Italian whites** such as **Soave**, **Bianco di Custoza** and **Lugana** work, though you might want a livelier **Greek white** with a *spanakopitta* (spinach and feta cheese pie). (*See also* Eggs.)

Spring rolls

See Chinese.

Squid

Sauvignon Blanc is the ideal wine for most squid dishes, particularly char-grilled squid or salads. With Greek-style *calamares* you could also drink a **Greek** or **lemony Portuguese white**. Stuffed squid, which is popular throughout the Mediterranean, goes with either a **dry white** or **dry French rosé** or **Spanish rosado**. (*See also* Risottos.)

Steak

Steak basically goes with the same wines as beef (*see* Beef) though there are some steak dishes, such as steak *au poivre* (*see* Pepper) and steak *bearnaise* (*see* Sauces), that point you in a slightly different direction.

Steak tartare

This raw highly seasoned steak dish is quite challenging for any wine. A **vodka Martini** strikes me as a better bet. Or a glass of **pink fizz**.

Steak and kidney pie (or pudding)

A pint of **best bitter**, **stout** or **porter** depending on how dark and rich the gravy is. **Bulgarian Cabernet Sauvignon** if you want to drink wine.

Sticky toffee pudding

For complete sticky toffee overload try an **Australian Liqueur Muscat**.

Stilton

See Cheese.

Stir-fries

Can involve quite powerfully flavoured sauces such as oyster or yellow bean sauce. My vote goes to **light reds** such as **Beaujolais** or **Australian Tarrango**, or a **fruity Chilean** or **Bordeaux rosé**. With lighter stir-fries drink a **crisp fruity white** or a **Riesling**, or simply settle for a **lager**.

Strawberries

Strawberries without sugar or cream Moscato d'Asti or **Clairette de Die**.

Light strawberry mousses, gateaux, meringues and souffles Asti or **demi sec Champagne**, depending how flush you're feeling, how sweet-toothed you are and how sweet the dessert is (your wine should be sweeter than the dessert).

Strawberries with cream or strawberry tarts Sauternes or similar **sweet wines from Bordeaux, Muscat de Beaumes-de-Venise, Coteaux du Layon** and other **Loire dessert wines**.

Strawberries in red wine Drink more of the wine used in the recipe (**Beaujolais** is the usual option and it also goes with strawberries with pepper).

Strawberry ices and sorbets Strawberry-flavoured liqueurs.

Summer pudding

Australian sparkling Cabernet Sauvignon or a **sweet Recioto**.

Sushi

In practice, you're most likely to drink **green tea**, **Japanese beer**, **sake** or eat sushi with a bowl of *miso* soup. But **very crisp dry whites** such as **Muscadet** work well, as does (surprisingly) **non-vintage** or **blanc de blancs Champagne**. In fact, **Champagne** would be rather stylish.

Swedish

Iced vodka, **aquavit** or **pilsner** are the best options for pickled herrings or a smorgasbord. **Soft fruity reds** such as **Merlot** and **Zinfandel** go well with Swedish meatballs, particularly if accompanied by lingonberries; and also with venison, of which the Swedes are fond. (*See also* Gravadlax.)

Sweetbreads

A rare delicacy that needs a rarified wine to match. **Pinot Gris** from **Alsace** (or **California**, **New Zealand** or **Oregon**) would fit the bill. Or expensive **white burgundy**, **Condrieu** or **vintage Champagne**.

Sweetcorn

Corn has a terrific affinity with **Chardonnay** – particularly **rich oaky Chardonnays** from **Australia**, **California** and **New Zealand**. With a sweetcorn chowder you might want a slightly lighter example.

113

Swordfish

A meaty fish, often served seared and accompanied by a tangy salsa. Try a **zesty Sauvignon Blanc** from **Chile**, **South Africa** or **New Zealand**.

Syllabub

Despite the brandy and/or sherry, this doesn't taste wildly alcoholic so a **Australian botrytis** or **German Beerenauslese Riesling** should match up (except for Nigella Lawson's quince syllabub, which sounds as if it would be better with a **Tokaji**).

Tabbouleh

Often served as part of a selection of *mezze*, this minty Middle Eastern salad needs a **sharp lemony Greek white** or **Sauvignon Blanc**.

Tagines

See Moroccan.

Tandoori chicken

An inexpensive **crisp lemony white** such as **Vin de Pays des Côtes de Gascogne** or **Hungarian Sauvignon Blanc** with milder supermarket versions of this dish. Otherwise try an **Aussie Semillon/Chardonnay** or **Cabernet/Shiraz**. Or a bottle of **Kingfisher** or **Cobra lager**.

Tapas

Chilled fino or **manzanilla sherry** is traditional with these spicy Spanish snacks. Or go for a **crisp Spanish white** such as a **Rueda** or inexpensive **white Rioja**. Or **Spanish lager** such as **San Miguel**.

Tapenade

A **crisp dry Provençal** or **southern French white** or **rosé** will work with this black olive, caper and anchovy spread. Unless it accompanies meat, in which case go for a **spicy Rhône red** such as a **Vacqueyras**, **Lirac** or **Crozes-Hermitage**.

Taramasalata

Almost any **crisp lemony white** – **Greek** if you can get hold of one. **Dry Italian whites** such as **Pinot Grigio** would also fit the bill.

Tarragon

Most often associated with chicken or delicate creamy sauces. **Unoaked Chardonnay** or **Pinot Blanc** would do the job.

Tarts

See Quiches, Apple, Apricot, Lemon, Tomato, and so on.

Tarte Tatin

Ultra-fashionable upside-down tart that is normally made with apples, but occasionally with pears, pineapple or banana. There are also savoury versions, which are usually made with tomato or chicory.

What tatins have in common is their gooey, sticky, caramelised topping. Most **sweet Muscats** will cope (**Australian Liqueur Muscats** in the case of banana) and **Hungarian Tokaji** would be excellent. Savoury versions are trickier: try an **Australian Semillon** or **Spanish Albariño**, or a **soft fruity Sangiovese**.

Tempura (Japanese-style deep-fried seafood or vegetables)

Seems to work well with beer: a **Japanese lager** or a **wheat beer** such as **Hoegaarden** would be good choices; tempura also goes well with a **crisp dry white** such as **Muscadet**.

Terrines

The kind of starter you find in smart restaurants or serve up at a formal dinner party, terrines call for posher wines than pâté.

Light fish or vegetable terrines Pouilly-Fumé, **Sancerre**, **Chablis**. **White burgundy**, or **Champagne** if the terrine includes salmon or luxury ingredients such as lobster.

Roast vegetable or meat terrines A good **Beaujolais** such as a **Brouilly**, **light red burgundy** or **Californian Pinot Noir** (*see also* Pâtes).

Jellied fruit terrines **Moscato d'Asti** or any other kind of **fizz**.

Thai food

Hotter than Chinese, less spicy than Indian, the punchy flavours of Thai food need wines with plenty of personality. **Australian Semillon** and **Semillon/Chardonnays** hit the mark as do most **Sauvignon Blancs** and off-dry whites such as **Riesling**, **Gewürztraminer** and **dry Muscat**. Red wines aren't generally as successful, but super-fruity **Aussie reds** should get by so long as they're not too oaky. Beerwise, **pale ale** works better than lager.

Thai green (or red) chicken curry

Sauvignon Blanc, **Semillon** or a **pale ale**.

Thyme

See Herbs.

Tiramisu

Recioto di Soave or **Passito di Pantelleria** if the dish is home-made.
Moscato d'Asti or **Moscatel de Valencia** with supermarket versions.
Australian Liqueur Muscat if you've got a sweet tooth.

Toad in the hole

A **traditional English bitter** if it's on its own; **brown ale** or **porter** if it comes with an onion gravy. Or a **gutsy French red** such as **Fitou**.

Tofu

Tofu tends to pick up the flavour of whatever seasoning it's cooked with, so follow the advice for the other main ingredients in the dish (*see also* Chinese).

Tomatoes

Many tomato dishes come from the Mediterranean, so wines from those countries work best. **Dry French rosé**, **Spanish rosado** and **dry French** and **Italian whites** are good with light tomato dishes, **southern French**, **Italian** and **Spanish reds** with more robust ones. More contemporary ways of cooking tomatoes – sun-dried, oven-dried or roasted – open the door to new world wines such as **unoaked Chardonnay** and **Merlot**. (*See also* Bruschetta, Pizza, Pasta, Salsas, Tarte tatin.)

Tomato salad Inexpensive **dry French whites**, and **Italian whites** such as **Verdicchio** and **Orvieto**, **southern French rosés** and **Spanish rosados**. Or **Sauvignon Blanc**.

Tomato sauce Uncooked: **dry Italian whites** such as **Pinot Grigio**, **Vernaccia di San Gimignano** or **Sauvignon Blanc**. Cooked: **southern Italian reds** from **Puglia**, **Sicily** and **Sardinia**, or **Sangiovese**.

Tomato soup Heinz: **Australian Chardonnay**. Home-made: **Australian Verdelho** or **New Zealand Sauvignon Blanc**.

Tomato tarts *Pissaladiere* for example: **dry rosés** are good, otherwise treat as pizza and drink a **crisp dry Italian white** or **light Italian red**.

Stuffed tomatoes **Light southern French reds** such as **Côtes du Rhône-Villages** or **Côtes du Roussillon**.

Tongue

Tongue is such a classically English dish that beer seems more appropriate than wine, though a good **fruity red** such as **Beaujolais** or **Valpolicella** would go well with hot tongue. With cold tongue serve a **pale ale** or **light bitter**.

Tortilla

Chilled fino sherry if it's a *tapa* (*see* Tapas). A **light Chardonnay** or **Spanish Viura** if you're eating it on its own.

Treacle tart

Australian Late-Harvest or **botrytis Riesling** if it's got lemon in it. **Australian Liqueur Muscat** if it hasn't.

Trifle

Should be boozy enough already, if you've made it properly. If you don't think it is, and assuming that it's a sherry trifle, drink a glass of **sweet oloroso sherry**. With blander supermarket versions an inexpensive **Moscatel de Valencia** would be fine.

With less traditional trifles you can be more adventurous. Orange-flavoured trifles would go well with **Californian Orange Muscat**, **Tokaji** or **Passito di Pantelleria**, while with rhubarb trifle you could drink a **Beerenauslese** or **Australian botrytis Riesling**. And if you're making Delia Smith's butterscotch and banana trifle, serve a sticky **Australian Liqueur Muscat**.

Tripe

Needs something pretty powerful. A big **French** or **Spanish country red** such as **Madiran** or **Jumilla** with Continental tripe dishes such as *tripes a la mode de Caen*. A pint of **stout** (preferably **Mackeson**) with tripe and onions.

Trout

Trout isn't as obviously fishy as most fish so calls for **soft, not so sharply flavoured whites** such as **Chardonnay** and **Pinot Blanc**.

With almonds **Pinot Blanc**, a **light Vin de Pays d'Oc**, Chilean **Chardonnay** or **modern Sicilian white**.

With creamy sauce **German Kabinett Riesling**, or a **Riesling** from **Australia** or **Alsace**. Or **Chablis**.

Smoked trout or smoked trout pâté **Manzanilla sherry**, **Sancerre, Sauvignon de Touraine, Californian Sauvignon Blanc**, or **dry Alsace** or **Australian Riesling**. A **light malt whisky** if the smoke is strong.

Truffles

You'd might think it would be white wines with white truffles and red wines with black ones but it isn't quite that simple.

Because of their exotic scented mushroomy flavour, **reds** – particularly **mature reds** – go better than white wines. **Red burgundy** (the best you can afford) is the classic, but other **Pinot Noirs** are also good. With white truffles, **northern Italian reds** such as **Barbera, Barolo, Dolcetto, Valpolicella Ripasso** and **young Nebbiolo** go well, or try a **delicately scented white** such as **Arneis** or **Roussanne** – or even a top **Italian Chardonnay**. Dishes with truffle oil should be treated as white truffles.

Tuna

Raw tuna Sushi and tuna tartare for example: **Muscadet** or **dry Champagne**.

Tuna in a creamy sauce or pasta bake Inexpensive **Hungarian**, **Bulgarian** or **Italian Chardonnay** or **South African Chenin Blanc**.

Tuna salads Salad Niçoise or tuna and bean salad for example: **crisp dry whites** or **rosés** from **southern France** or **Italy**.

Seared or barbecued tuna **Pinot Noir**, **Merlot** or **light reds** from the **Loire** such as **Chinon**, **Saumur-Champigny** and **Bourgeuil**. If combined with southeast Asian flavours such as chilli and coriander drink **Sauvignon Blanc**, or **lager**.

Turbot

Eating turbot is good excuse for splashing out on a **top white burgundy**, **Pessac-Leognan** (as the best **white Graves** is known these days) or **vintage Champagne**.

Turkey

The fabled Christmas turkey with its stuffing and cranberry sauce needs a really **big fruity red** such as **Châteauneuf-du-Pape**, **St-Emilion** (**Pomerol** is even better), **Chilean Merlot**, **Californian Zinfandel**, or **Australian Shiraz**. Otherwise choose the same wines that you would pick for chicken (*see* Chicken).

Turkish

Very similar to Greek so follow the same advice (*see also* Aubergines).

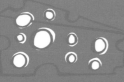

Vanilla

Simple vanilla-flavoured puddings go with most **dessert wines**, but, if they're served with a fruit coulis you might want something with a touch of sharpness, such as a **Late-Harvest Riesling**. (*See also* Panna cotta, Ice cream.)

You occasionally come across vanilla sauces with fish – a perfect excuse to crack open a good **white burgundy** or **blanc de blancs Champagne** or **sparkling wine**.

Veal

Veal isn't very PC these days. Most of the dishes that are still around are Italian and tend to go best with **Italian** wines.

Roast or grilled veal **Traditional medium-bodied reds** such as **Chianti Classico**, **Rioja Reserva**, and **soft fruity clarets** (**St-Emilion** for example), or **dry Italian whites** such as **Orvieto** or **Arneis**.

Veal in creamy or mushroom sauces *Blanquette de Veau* for example: **light Chardonnays**, **German** or **Austrian Riesling**, **Alsace Pinot Gris**, **Viognier**, **Vouvray** or **rosé Champagne**.

Veal escalopes In breadcrumbs or *al limone*: **dry Italian whites** such as **Pinot Grigio** or **Verdicchio**, or **Sauvignon Blanc**. Cooked with marsala: **fruity Italian reds** such as **Rosso di Montalcino**, **Rosso Conero** or **modern Sicilian reds**.

Braised or stewed veal Osso buco for example: **smooth dry Italian whites** such as **Soave**, **Bianco di Custoza**, **Gavi** or **Lugana**.

Vitello tonnato (cold veal with tuna mayonnaise) **Light Italian Chardonnay, Californian Sauvignon Blanc, Australian Sauvignon/Semillon**.

Vegetables

On the whole, vegetables served as a side dish or accompaniment to a meal don't have a powerful enough flavour to dominate the main course (the exceptions are strong-flavoured vegetable dishes, such as aubergines, braised red cabbage and ratatouille – *see* Aubergine, Cabbage, Peppers).

When it comes to main course vegetable dishes you'll find most of the options covered elsewhere in the A-Z: *see* Pasta, Risottos, Salads, Soups, Stir-fries, Terrines; or under individual vegetables and different national cuisines.

Vegetarian & organic food

Vegetarian wines – which are made without the use of animal products – are readily available these days (though some only say what they are on the back label). You may also feel you want to buy wines made from vines that are organically grown (that is, without the use of chemicals or pesticides). The range and quality of both vegetarian and organic wines have improved enormously, so it's possible to pick the same type of wine that you'd choose to go with a meat dish – a **Chianti** for example – with the vegetarian equivalent. Remember that what counts is the way you cook a dish rather than its basic ingredient. (*See also* Beans, Lentils, Nuts, Pâtés, Quorn, Tofu.)

Vegetable pies, pasties and crumbles With light creamy sauces: **pale ale**, **cider**, or **Chardonnay**. With tomatoes, peppers and garlic: a gutsy **southern French red** such as **Côtes du Roussillon**.

Veggie burgers and sausages An inexpensive **fruity vegetarian red** – the **south of France** is a reliable source. Or an **organic beer**.

Venison

Venison's flavour is similar to that of beef but it can be slightly richer and gamier, particularly when it's braised. **Languedoc reds** such as **Fitou** and **St-Chinian**, or a **Madiran** are reasonably priced options, but a huge haunch of venison is also a good opportunity to wheel out a serious **Rhône red** such as a **Hermitage**, or a **Ribera del Duero**, **Amarone**, **Californian Syrah** or **Australian Shiraz**. **Strong Belgian ales** would also be good. (*See also* Game pie.)

Venison medallions, noisettes and steaks **Fruity reds** such as **Australian** or **Chilean Cabernet Sauvignon**, **Aussie Shiraz** or **Californian Zinfandel** work well – particularly if the dish is accompanied by a sweet fruity cranberry or Cumberland sauce.

Smoked venison or venison pâté A **light red burgundy** or **Pinot Noir**.

Vichysoisse

This leek and potato soup, which is usually served cold, goes with a **crisp dry white** such as **Muscadet**, **Petit Chablis** or **South African Chenin Blanc**. Or try a **dry cider**.

Vietnamese

The flavours of Vietnamese food are slightly stronger than Chinese but milder than Thai. **Viognier** is a star choice but **Grüner Veltliner** from **Austria**, **Verdelho** from **Australia** and **dry Riesling** from just about anywhere work too. **Wheat beer** is also surprisingly delicious.

Vinaigrette

See Salad dressings.

Walnuts

Walnuts in salads make **Chardonnay** a better choice than Sauvignon Blanc. Walnut tarts – as with most nut tarts – go with **Australian Liqueur Muscat** or **sweet oloroso sherry**. Walnuts are often included in coffee cakes and gateaux, but are better partnered with **coffee** than wine.

Watercress

Almost all watercress recipes, including soups, salads and sauces, go with **smooth dry whites** such as **Chardonnay** or **Soave**.

Welsh rarebit

Good **British ale**, or a **light Chardonnay** if the rarebit is combined – as Gary Rhodes cooks it – with smoked haddock.

Whelks

See Shellfish.

Whitebait

Dry whites such as **Muscadet**, **Picpoul de Pinet** or **Sauvignon de Touraine**. A stronger **Sauvignon Blanc** if they're devilled.

Wild boar

A similar prescription to venison: **mature Syrah**, **Ribera del Duero** or **Italian reds** such as **Amarone**, **Aglianico del Vulture** or **Salice Salentino**. Or, if you fancy yourself as Obelix, a **strong Belgian beer**.

Wontons

See Chinese.

Worcestershire sauce

Very tough on wine. Don't overdo it. Devilled chicken or kidneys can get by with a **fruity red** such as an **Argentinian** or **Chilean Malbec**.

Y akitori

Sake, **dry fino sherry** or a **Japanese beer** are all a better bet than wine with this classic Japanese street food dish of skewered chicken.

Yoghurt

Yoghurt has a sharper edge than cream, though it has the same effect of modifying strong flavours. **Crisp dry whites** and **rosés** work best with savoury dishes such as kormas, yoghurt marinades, and cucumber salads such as raita and tzatziki. With yoghurt-based desserts it's also better to go for a wine with a hint of sharpness such as a **Late-Harvest** or **botrytis Riesling**, unless the dish includes honey or fruit, which would match a **richer dessert wine**. Iced yoghurts are not good with wine or spirits.

Yorkshire pudding

When served on its own, with gravy, drink **Yorkshire ale**; or maybe a **Newcastle Brown**. (*See also* Beef.)

Z abaglione

Has its alcohol (**Marsala**) already incorporated; if you want a glass as well, make sure it's a sweet one. **Vin Santo** or a **Passito di Pantelleria** are other possibilities.

Zampone

Authentic red Lambrusco (not the weedy, wishy-washy kind) is the wine to drink with this robust Italian dish of stuffed pig's trotters and lentils. If you're feeling particularly adventurous, try **sparkling Shiraz**.

Zucchini

See Courgettes.

Index

THE CAMEL

THE CAMEL

How Muslims Are Coming to Faith in Christ

by Kevin Greeson

The Camel
Copyright © 2007 WIGTake Resources, LLC.

WIGTake
What's It Gonna Take ? Resources

Published by WIGTake Resources, LLC, PO Box 1225,
Arkadelphia, AR 71923 e-mail: WIGTakeResources@pobox.com

Available for purchase from: Fresh Wind Distributing
PO Box 560967
The Colony, TX 75056
Website: www.FreshWindDistributing.com
1-(806)-853-8068 (Voice)
1-(866)-698-7564 (Toll Free Voice)
1-(806)-853-8076 (Fax)

Bible quotations in this publication are taken from the following sources:

The New King James Version (NKJV), Copyright © 1982 Thomas
Nelson, Inc. and The Holy Bible, New International Version (NIV),
Copyright © 1973, 1978, 1984 by International Bible Society. Used by
permission of Zondervan. All rights reserved.

English language quotations from the Qur'an are taken from:
The Holy Qur'an, translated by M.H. Shakir, published in 1982 by
Tahrike Tarsile Qur'an, Inc. and from Yusuf Ali and Mohammed
Pickthall's translations as found in Alim for Windows, 1999, ISL
Software Corporation.

Library of Congress Cataloging-in-Publication Data
Greeson, Kevin, 1961 -
The Camel / by Kevin Greeson

Summary: "216-page paperback on Christian ministry to Muslim"
– Provided by the publisher.
ISBN-13: 978-0-9747562-0-2

A Muslim Proverb ~

And we know that Allah has one hundred names. And that he has revealed 99 of his names to the sons of men that they may know and worship him. But one name, the one-hundredth name, he has told only to the camel. And, the camel, he is not talking.

The Camel's secret ~

God has highly exalted Him, and given Him the *Name which is above every name: That at the name of Jesus* every knee should bow, of those in heaven, and those on earth, and those under the earth, and that every tongue should confess that *Jesus Christ is Lord,* to the glory of God the Father.

Philippians 2:9-11 (NKJV)

Table of Contents

Foreword

Kevin Greeson

A Camel Testimony

I LOVE TO READ BOOKS. I like to read myself to sleep at night. Take a look at my bedside table and you will quickly see how true this is. There are always at least six or seven books, complete with bookmarks, stacked beside my lamp. Typically I like fiction with the occasional history book thrown in for good measure. Only rarely do I read anything related to work at the end of the day. One December night in 2004 I broke this rule and opened a book given to me by a fellow worker. The moment I started reading I knew that my ministry, and perhaps my way of life, was about to change forever.

In 1995 my family and I were assigned to work in Northern Africa and the Middle East. Our job description stated that our assigned country had a population of 50 percent Christian and 50 percent Muslim. That latter half was our target of interest. We felt that God had called us to work specifically with Muslims. We didn't really know a lot about the religion. We had heard of the pillars of Islam and a couple of other cultural beliefs but that was about it. Ultimately, we would spend the next nine years reading about Islam, talking with people, and attending any meeting or conference that was offered to us in an effort to engage Muslims more effectively.

I have a knack for meeting people. I can talk to anybody. Sometimes I talk when no one is listening. It doesn't bother me at all. This ability has helped me to build a strong platform that has produced many acquaintances and even several long term relationships. However, in my quest to see these relationships become something more fruitful I have always been stymied. I thought that I was doing all the right things. I loved the people, studied Islam, did the required company reading, went to the conferences, etc., etc., but at the end of the day I was still left with the question, "How do I best share the Gospel with Muslims?" But there was an even bigger question looming over me, "How do I get to a Church Planting Movement among our people?" If I couldn't share effectively at an individual level then a Church Planting Movement was just a pipe dream. Enter the *Camel*!

The *Camel* was introduced to me by a co-worker from my home church. He explained briefly that it was a bridge from the Qur'an to the Bible. Up till then I had never been a big fan of using the Qur'an in my witnessing, so I threw the book in my "to be read later" pile. A couple of weeks passed. One night, as I was preparing to go to bed, I noticed it sitting there and picked it up. From the opening pages I was hooked. As I began reading about the sheer numbers of Muslims who were coming to Christ I was in a state of disbelief. Here I was on the frontline for almost ten years and had never witnessed anything resembling this. As I continued to read I felt God speaking to me of the possibilities that existed through this methodology. I could envision Muslims giving their hearts to Jesus at the rate of one a day, perhaps ten, or even a hundred. This was just too much to hope for but I knew that God had spoken to me and that he had provided the very thing I had been lacking in my ministry. I read the book in two nights.

It isn't remarkable that I read another book. What is amazing is what happened when I went out and tried to do what the book said. In my very first encounter I shared a part of the Gospel

Kevin Greeson

with a complete stranger at an auto parts store. He then turned to his friend and shared what I had just told him. There I was, an obvious foreigner, not a great Arabic speaker, watching this Muslim telling his brother about Isa al-Masih (Jesus Christ). He was doing my job for me. The whole encounter lasted less than half an hour and no one was angry or offended in the process. I had never done nor seen that happen before. God had just confirmed what I was thinking. There may not be a magic bullet for Muslim evangelism, but the *Camel* is as close as it gets.

There may be some who have read the *Camel* or perhaps even tried it so I must clarify a couple of things. I believe that the Bible is the ultimate book that gives us both our mandate and our instruction. I also understand that the *Camel* is not an evangelism method in and of itself but rather a filter for finding the "person of peace" with whom we can share the Gospel. There are a couple of issues in the method that might even be considered controversial. Before you pass too quick a judgment, however, try this experiment. Imagine you have been working in the Muslim world for nine years. You are doing all kinds of good things like making friends, operating a platform, learning language, maintaining security, attending meetings, making out strategy plans and budgets and yet you still feel completely ineffective in breaking down the barriers of Islam. Now try to understand my excitement when I say that in just three months of using the *Camel* I have two groups of baptized Muslim background believers that I am meeting with for discipleship. God is greatly to be praised!

This is my experience. This is what the *Camel* method has done in my life. Is it fair to say that it has impacted my ministry? No. It has completely transformed it! I am more focused, I am bolder, and I am well equipped to answer any objections a Muslim may have toward Christianity. Will the *Camel* continue to be an effective tool for the future? This is anybody's guess. In the meantime I think it best that we let God work where and how He chooses and continue to praise Him for allowing us to be a part of it. If any of you reading this are struggling in your ministry to Muslims then I have a suggestion for you. Ride the *Camel*!

A Missionary in the Arab Muslim World

Kevin Greeson

A Firm Foundation

WHEN I WROTE *The Camel Training Manual* two years ago, my primary audience was missionaries and Muslim evangelists. No one was more surprised than I was when the book quickly went through multiple printings and found readers and practitioners all over the world.

This new book is aimed at that larger, broader audience of anyone who longs to see Muslims come to faith in Jesus Christ. Since I am no longer communicating primarily with missionaries, I can no longer assume some of the basic theological positions that my earlier book took for granted.

So let me take a few minutes to lay down some foundational principles that you will need to know in order to understand how best to use the Camel Method to reach Muslims for Jesus Christ.

1) Motivation. What is your motivation for reading a book about church planting among Muslims? Your motivation will color the way you approach this topic and likely determine whether or not God will use you to reach Muslims. In the book of Acts, we are introduced to a man named Simon Magus who sought the gift of the Holy Spirit, but for the wrong reasons. Peter condemned this ulterior motive saying:

> You have no part or share in this ministry, because your heart is not right before God. Repent of this wickedness

and pray to the Lord. Perhaps he will forgive you for having such a thought in your heart. For I see that you are full of bitterness and a captive to sin (Acts 8:21-23 NIV).

What is your motivation for learning about Muslim evangelism and church planting? Are you motivated by fear and anger? Do you see Muslims as an enemy that must be defeated? People who are winning Muslims to Christ have a different motivation. They recognize that our struggle is not against flesh and blood but against spiritual darkness. Spiritual darkness is lostness, and *lostness* is the real enemy. Islam, like Communism, Buddhism or any other *–ism*, is merely a human response to a condition of lostness. Apart from Christ, we are all lost in our sins and delusions (Romans 3:23).

If you have not yet experienced Christ's deep love for Muslims, then stop right now, and spend some time in prayer before you read any further. Find the heart of God for a world of lost Muslims, a heart that prompted him to make the ultimate sacrifice of His own Son for their salvation.

2) Origins of the Camel. As you will see in the following chapters, missionaries didn't invent the Camel Method. It is the method we learned from Muslim-background believers who are using it right now in what is the largest turning of Muslims to Christ in history. As missionaries, we have observed this method at work, examined it in light of the authority of God's Word, and found it to be a powerful tool in reaching Muslims everywhere with the Good News of Jesus Christ.

3) No other name. As followers of Jesus Christ, we have great confidence in saying that Christ alone is mankind's hope of salvation. For the New Testament is clear, "Salvation is found in no one else, for there is no other name under heaven given to men by which we must be saved" (Acts 4:12 NIV). We are also confident in proclaiming that the Christ who saves is the

Christ who has been revealed to us through the Bible alone. Any other teachings about Christ are dangerously deficient as guides to salvation.

4) Redemptive bridges. God has filled the world with redemptive bridges, analogies and metaphors that point both to our need for salvation and to the hope of salvation. If we use the bridges well, they can also point us to the Bible as God's revealed truth about our fallen condition and His plan of salvation.

Jesus modeled the use of bridges in His own ministry drawing illustrations of God's kingdom from agriculture, fishing and everyday life. Paul adopted the same method when he spoke to the Stoics and Epicureans at the famous Areopagus in Athens. There he paused to build a bridge for them from their "altar to an unknown God" to the Christ who had revealed Himself to a lost world. "Now what you worship as something unknown," Paul declared, "I am going to proclaim to you" (Acts 17:23b NIV). From Muslim-background believers who are winning their family, friends and neighbors to Christ, we have learned that the Qur'an contains many bridges that we, too, can use to introduce Muslims to Jesus Christ.

5) Lifting Jesus up. Our aim in the Camel Method is to exalt Christ. We deliberately do this without attacking or condemning the Muslim religion, lest our Muslim friends interpret our Good News about Jesus as an assault on their culture. Whenever we identify values, virtues or insights within Muslim culture we are not endorsing Islam, Mohammed or the Qur'an, but rather removing obstacles that might prevent them from seeing Jesus. Jesus promised, "And I, if I be lifted up, will draw all men unto me" (John 12:32 NKJV). This personal reference to His crucifixion is hailed throughout the Christian world, yet Muslims still fail to see the Christ who died for them. We want Muslims to see Christ, **so that they, too, will be drawn to Him.**

Like John the Baptist, we want to make the way clear,

> Prepare the way for the Lord, make straight paths for him. Every valley shall be filled in, every mountain and hill made low. The crooked roads shall become straight, the rough ways smooth. And all mankind will see God's salvation (Luke 3:4b-6 NIV).

Treating Muslims with gentleness and respect is not a sign of weakness or uncertainty. On the contrary, it is because of our great confidence in Christ that we can boldly approach Muslims with the Good News that God has graciously entrusted to us.

6)   Permission granted. Jesus taught His disciples that the Holy Spirit would "...convict the world of guilt in regard to sin and righteousness and judgment..." (John 16:8 NIV). As you will see in the pages that follow, the Holy Spirit is at work in the Muslim world, convicting individuals of sin and the need for salvation. But it takes more than conviction to produce salvation. Unless Christians are able and willing to share the Gospel in a way that overcomes the many barriers within the worldview of Muslims, the vast majority of these Muslims will never hear the Good News of Jesus Christ.

The Camel Method addresses this twin challenge by: 1) teaching Christians what to say to Muslims, and then 2) giving Muslims permission from their own most authoritative book, the Qur'an, to read the Bible and consider the claims of Christ.

Drawing from Qur'anic passages which speak favorably of Christ and affirm the reliability of the Bible, the Camel Method equips Christians to unlock the worldview chains that have long bound Muslims from the truth. As these Muslim seekers cross the Camel bridge and begin reading the Bible for themselves, the Bible's two-edged sword pierces their hearts and fulfills the yearnings that the Holy Spirit has been impressing upon them.

Kevin Greeson

Through God's Word, they find eternal salvation and freedom from their bondage to sin.

7) Biblical authority. While the Qur'an's teaching about Allah may echo many of the truths about God that were first revealed in the Bible, we must never confuse the Qur'an with the Word of God. Apart from the Bible, we have no revelation of the Father's *agape* love for us, Christ's saving death and resurrection for us, or the Holy Spirit's dynamic power within us. The Trinity, so central to the New Testament revelation, is not only absent from the Qur'an, it is rejected by the Qur'an. The biblical testimony of 2 Timothy 3:16 that "all Scripture is God-breathed, and useful for teaching, correcting, rebuking, and training in righteousness" does not extend beyond the Old and New Testament. The Apostle John's warning in Revelation applies equally to the whole of the Bible when he wrote:

> I warn everyone who hears the words of the prophecy of this book: If anyone adds anything to them, God will add to him the plagues described in this book. And if anyone takes words away from this book of prophecy, God will take away from him his share in the tree of life... (Revelation 22:18-19a NIV).

This may be obvious to many of our Christian readers but bears repeating before we proceed into a close encounter with Islam.

8) A Gospel that translates. Finally, it is important for readers to know that unlike Islam, which is bound forever to the Arab language and culture, we have a Gospel that translates. Every time the Gospel enters a new culture, it must be translated into the language and worldview of that culture. This is part of the genius and power of the Gospel: It translates eternal truth into local forms and expressions just as God in Christ translated Himself into a particular human form and Jewish expression.

It was his desire to communicate this eternal Gospel into the local culture that prompted the Apostle John to introduce his readers to Jesus as "the *Logos*" (the Word). *Logos* was a Greek philosophical term with wide circulation in the first century Greco-Roman world, but not a term that had ever been used as a bridge to the Gospel, until John filled it with new meaning. This *Logos*, John wrote, "...became flesh and dwelt among us, and we beheld his glory, the glory of the only begotten of the Father, full of grace and truth" (John 1:14 NKJV).

While it is biblical and appropriate to translate the Gospel into the language and culture of the Muslim community, we must never confuse the use of Arabic names for God (Allah) and Jesus Christ (Isa al-Masih) with an endorsement or acceptance of the Muslim religion. Bridges are built to take us from one place to another and should never become an end in themselves.

With this theological foundation now firmly under foot, we are ready to move forward. Let us begin at the beginning, in a small village, where a follower of Jesus Christ met a lost Muslim youth and shared with him a message that changed his world.

Kevin Greeson
November 2006

CAMEL BEGINNINGS

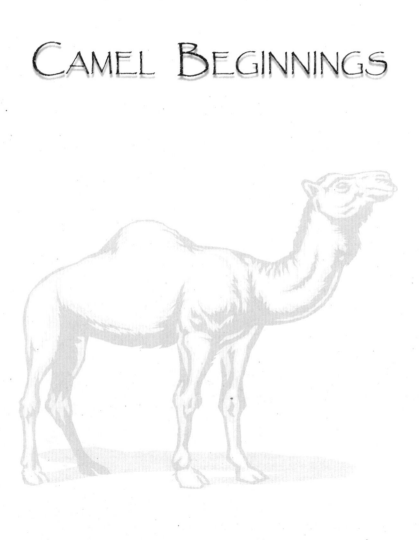

Chapter One

It Began in a Village

IN MAY 2002, A RESEARCH TEAM from the Southern Baptist International Mission Board traveled to a South Asian country to investigate reports of an unprecedented turning of Muslims to Christ. Local Christians from Muslim backgrounds were reporting nearly 90,000 fellow believers and thousands of new Muslim-background churches. After conducting extensive interviews, random samplings and on-site visits the team uncovered a vital church-planting movement of historic size and scope.

The movement had its origins in the late 1980s and had grown steadily through the decade of the 1990s. By 2002, it had spread to almost every corner of this South Asian country and was beginning to spill over into neighboring nations. Over the next few years, Christians from both Muslim and non-Muslim backgrounds have taken the lessons learned from this remarkable movement and begun impacting Muslim communities around the world.

How did this movement begin? This story of one of the largest Muslim church-planting movement in history began in a village, when a Christian missionary obeyed an impulse from God to share his faith with a Muslim boy.

A Sinner Boy

In South Asia, devout Muslim parents send their young boys to Islamic schools called *madrasas*, where they learn to read and memorize the Qur'an, in hopes that someday they might become an *imam*, an Islamic leader. For Abdul, life was no different, and at the age of nine his parents sent him to the local *madrasa* where he dedicated himself to his lessons and prayers. As he delved deeply into the Qur'an, Abdul began to have many disturbing questions about its meaning and validity. The first time he questioned the authority of the Qur'an the *imam* beat him and warned him never to question the meaning of the Qur'an again.

But Abdul soon forgot this warning as he found himself again asking questions. This time the *imam* banished Abdul from the *madrasa*, sending him home in disgrace. A note was placed on the bulletin board stating, "Abdul is a sinner boy and anyone who talks to him will also be shamed."

Abdul's father was humiliated and angry. He expelled the young boy from his family home. For the next three years, Abdul lived alone in a shack beside their house, forbidden to eat or socialize with his family. Abdul carried the brand "a sinner boy" in his heart, as his family and all who knew him treated him as though he were cursed.

A Muslim Meets an Angel

One afternoon as Abdul walked alone down a dusty village road, a white foreigner riding in the back of a rickshaw stopped and asked if he wanted a ride. This man was a missionary and the first white man Abdul had ever seen. Stunned by the invitation, Abdul wondered who this man was and why he had dared speak to him in public. As he rode beside the stranger in the rickshaw, Abdul recalled, "I quietly touched the white man's arm to see if he was a man or an angel."

When they arrived at the man's house, Abdul learned that the man was a Christian and the owner of several Bibles. Prior to this encounter Abdul had never even seen a Bible. The missionary's wife treated Abdul like a son, offering him fresh-baked cookies and his first cup of hot coffee. When Abdul left the missionary's house, he had a New Testament under his arm.

When he returned home, Abdul opened the Bible and began to read. Working his way through the Gospel of John, Abdul stopped when he read John 3:17 (NKJV), "For God sent not his Son into the world to condemn the world; but that the world through him might be saved."

Abdul was astounded. God did not condemn him. Since Abdul had been condemned by everyone for such a long time, he assumed that God must also have condemned him. But the Bible said God loved him! That same night, Abdul accepted God's love in the form of Jesus Christ as his personal Lord and Savior.

Abdul's cursed little room that his father had built became a glorious haven, for there he could study the Scriptures in total privacy. Desiring more understanding, Abdul asked the missionary to teach him. The missionary arranged for a local pastor to disciple Abdul as he began attending the pastor's church.

When he learned that his son was attending a Christian church, Abdul's father demanded that he stop. Abdul told his father that he would try to stop going. "When Sunday came," Abdul later recalled, "I tried not to go to the church, but my feet would not listen and they took me directly there."

Incensed at his son's disobedience, Abdul's father summoned his brothers and uncles to take action. When Abdul returned home, they seized him and beat him severely, demanding that Abdul renounce Jesus and burn his Bible. But Abdul knew that his life had been worthless before Jesus. He couldn't bear to give up the peace in his heart.

When he refused to renounce Jesus and burn the Bible, Abdul's father and uncles tied him to a stake in the family's courtyard until he would change his mind. He remained there throughout the night wondering what would become of him.

The next morning before the first call to prayer, Abdul's mother came to him and quickly untied him. "Your father is going to kill you," she said. "You must leave here." That was the last time Abdul ever saw his mother. She died before he ever returned to his village.

Abdul immediately went to the missionary's house. The missionary gave Abdul enough money to reach the capital city and instructed Abdul to meet him at his office compound there. He soon found his way to the office compound. There the missionary met him and helped Abdul establish himself in the city, introducing him to a local Baptist pastor who mentored him and prepared him for baptism.

At the baptismal service, the church leaders at first refused to baptize Abdul unless he changed his name to a Christian name. Abdul refused, telling the church leaders that his name was his testimony to other Muslims that they, too, could become followers of Christ. Abdul said, "Either you can baptize me, or I will baptize myself, but I will be baptized. And I will not change my name." Impressed by Abdul's courage and conviction, the pastor yielded and baptized him.

In the capital city, Abdul eventually earned an undergraduate degree and, subsequently, a master's degree in business and accounting. He also spent hours studying the Bible and the Qur'an. In the Bible he found spiritual nourishment. In the Qur'an, Abdul found bridges that he could use to draw other Muslims to faith in Christ.

The First Convert

Abdul was at a crossroads. He was no longer a boy. His heart grew restless as he felt God leading him to return to his home village. Returning to his boyhood village Abdul found that he was still barred from his family home, but a school classmate named Bilal welcomed Abdul into his home. Bilal was good-hearted and generous. "I have only one bed," he said, "but we will roll a blanket up and place it between us. Half will be your side and half will be mine." As the two men shared a room Abdul also shared the Gospel with Bilal.

When other villagers learned that Abdul had returned as a Christian, they conspired to kill him. One day as he was walking through an open field, a soccer team grabbed Abdul and began beating and kicking him. They might have murdered him had God not intervened through a local politician who was passing by and witnessed the beating. He asked the boys why they were beating this young man, and they replied, "We caught a Christian and we are going to kill him." The politician convinced the boys that they would only bring trouble on the entire community if they killed him, so they stopped their torment. As they left, though, each boy spat on Abdul's motionless body.

Hearing the news of Abdul's beating, Bilal rescued his injured friend and took him home. When Abdul recovered, Bilal asked Abdul to baptize him. Abdul replied, "How can I baptize you? Didn't you see what they did to me? Don't you know that they will do the same to you?" But now Bilal understood the nature of the Gospel. He said, "There is another who has suffered even more for you and for me. Come now and baptize me."

As Bilal stepped into the river and was baptized, Abdul said, "Yesterday I was one; today, we are two; tomorrow we could be two hundred."

Later that same year, Abdul learned that his father had become seriously ill and near death. Abdul went to his brothers and asked for permission to pray for his father. It had been nearly eight years since Abdul had seen his father. After Abdul had fled from his village, his father had gone to the courts and declared his son legally dead. And now Abdul went to his father and prayed for his recovery in Jesus' name.

The next day Abdul's brothers came and found him. "Father wants to see you," they said. Abdul's father had sent for his son because, to his amazement, he was feeling better. The old man had been praying to Allah for weeks and weeks for healing, but nothing happened. Yet when Abdul prayed for him in the name of Jesus, his condition significantly improved. He asked Abdul to pray for him again each day until he was totally healed! Now fully recovered, Abdul's father listened as Abdul told him about Jesus and the new life that Jesus had to offer him.

The old man who had so tormented Abdul bowed his head and prayed to receive Jesus as his Savior and Lord. Of the thousands of Muslims who would later come to faith, Abdul says he personally baptized only two: Bilal and his father.

As word of Abdul and Bilal's faith spread, Bilal's relatives sent word that they wanted him to visit them so that they could persuade him to return to Islam. Bilal left Abdul and journeyed to his relatives' village. Two weeks later Bilal returned. He told Abdul that his relatives were not successful in their cause, but instead had become followers of Jesus, too. Bilal reported, "I baptized seven families, 36 people, in my relatives' village."

Greatly encouraged by these baptisms, the two men began to travel together and share the miraculous love and grace offered to all Muslims by the Lord. They often used the Qur'an as a bridge to show Muslims that they were not forbidden from reading the Bible, but rather encouraged to read the "Scriptures that came before". It did not take long before they had won several hundred Muslims to faith in Jesus Christ. The Gospel spread quickly along family lines. Brothers would often travel together to the homes of their brothers-in-law to share with them the changed life they had found in Christ.

As the movement grew, Abdul found that he could use his education and business training to provide financial support for the evangelists and church planters in the growing movement. Abdul started a fish farm and then began a small leather bag factory. Employed as salesmen, more than 20 Muslim-background believers were sent out into distant villages to sell the leather bags on commission. These salesmen/church planters propelled the movement to remote districts where it continued to spread along family lines. The movement was becoming explosive.

While Abdul was the businessman supporting the movement, Bilal emerged as its discipler and leadership trainer. Never married, Bilal wedded himself to the movement. His modest bamboo house became a discipleship training center for an endless stream of new believers and emerging house church leaders. Over an eight-year period, Bilal trained more than 1,500 new Muslim-background believers and leaders.

Bilal's method of discipleship was as simple as it was effective. Anywhere from five to 15 new believers would travel to Bilal's humble house and stay for two weeks. Each morning, Bilal would have his students find a quiet place to read their Bibles, while he walked under the trees and read his own. After some time, he would call his students together, close his Bible, and tell them a Bible story that he had just read. "No one could tell a story as well as Bilal," some of them later recalled.

This was their morning devotional. After hearing the story, the students would discuss it. Then Bilal would reopen his Bible and read the story aloud. The remainder of the morning was spent looking for verses and passages in the Qur'an that they could use as bridges of understanding to help other Muslims come to read, understand and accept the Gospel.

After a late lunch, they would read more stories from the Bible and discuss them. Beyond this, they had no formal Bible study course or curriculum. When churches and new leaders had questions about what to do next, they would search the Scripture, often finding answers in the book of Acts, the book that most closely mirrored their own story of new faith, persecution and explosive church growth.

Late at night on February 14, 2003, Bilal answered a knock at his door to find a group of Muslim extremists who seized and stabbed him to death. Their goal was to deal a fatal blow to the leadership and discipleship of the movement, but they were too late. There were now more than 100,000 baptized Muslim-background believers, and Bilal's godly passion for the word of God and the souls of men had been forever infused into the movement. Even today, students of Bilal remember him fondly and imitate his style of pouring God's Word, and his own life, into the new believers and rising leaders.

Today, Abdul is one of many leaders in the movement. He continues to live with his wife and children in the village where he was born. He worships in the house from which he was once expelled, alongside his father, uncles and brothers who once beat him for the faith that they now share.[1]

---

[1] Listen to Abdul tell his own story with a video reenactment in *The Camel Workshop* (Richmond, VA: WIGTake Resources, 2007). Online from Fresh Wind Distributing at: www.FreshWindDistributing.com

Chapter Two

How I Got into This

I T WAS SEPTEMBER 1997. I was in Singapore attending a
training workshop for new missionary strategy coordinators. A
strategy coordinator is a missionary charged with developing
and implementing a strategy to plant multiplying churches among
an unreached people group. My people group was a large South
Asian Muslim people with a population of more than 100 million
lost souls.

Each night I returned to my hotel room filled with thoughts
about my people and ways to reach them. One night before
drifting off to sleep, I experienced a vision from God in which
I saw thousands of Muslims from my people plunging into the
flames of hell. The reality of the vision was so vivid that I began
to weep. My pillow was soon wet with tears of grief and sorrow,
so that I had to turn it over just to find a dry spot on which to lay
my head.[1]

Both the vision and the tears were unusual for me. It had been
years since I had wept over anything. Yet as this horrible scene
played out in my mind, I was gripped with fear, fear for my people.
In a few moments, though, the vision of hell was replaced by a
new vision. The Muslims that I had seen falling into the flames of
hell were being redirected and taken up into heaven. As I watched
this new vision unfold, I felt the presence of God wash over me,

and with this peaceful reassurance, I fell fast asleep.

The next morning, I opened my devotional guide and was surprised to see that it featured a profile and emphasis on my own Muslim people group. This meant that, the night before, while I was having my vision, there had been some 30,000 Christians in America praying specifically for my people. Because of our different time zones, these American prayer supporters would have been starting their morning devotionals at the very time that I was lying down to sleep.

This was a great beginning for a new strategy coordinator. As I completed my training, I was convinced that God was going to do something great!

I had already been trying to reach the Muslims in my country for some time before attending this strategy coordinator training. During my first two years of ministry, I had focused my efforts trying to mobilize the minority Christian population in our country to rise to the challenge of reaching the Muslim majority that lived all around them.

Unfortunately, these local Christians were fearful of Muslims and had little understanding of them. Most of them had come to Christ from Hindu, Buddhist or Animist backgrounds and could not relate to the Muslim worldview. They wanted to see Muslims converted but were afraid of Muslims and often confused cultural conversion with spiritual conversion.

In their traditional church practice, a convert was expected to adopt a new name from the Bible, such as John or Paul. He was also expected to worship in a manner that the local Christians had received from the missionaries who had introduced the Gospel to them over the past two centuries. As a result, the church worship styles ranged from 19th century English Baptist to contemporary American praise styles.

Nonetheless, these were sincere brothers and sisters in Christ, so I tried to work with and through the local churches whenever possible. That was my plan. Over the two years, our small team of church planters increasingly moved beyond the work of local churches using every kind of evangelistic outreach we could dream up.

We used the "JESUS" film, literature distribution, agricultural development ministry, disaster relief work, friendship evangelism and cross-cultural incarnational missionary witness. We made friends with Muslims, grew to love them, and extended real ministries to them.

At the end of two years, though, our small team of church planters could identify no new church starts or even baptisms. The only measurable success we could point to was 23 Muslim women who gathered in one of our micro-businesses to make baskets for export. After many fruitless attempts to evangelize these women, we began looking for a different approach.

One of the lessons from strategy coordinator training began to haunt me. Our training coordinator said, "If you keep doing what you've been doing, you'll keep getting what you've been getting." And its counterpart: "If you keep doing what you've been doing, but expect different results, you must be crazy."

Was I going crazy? Something had to change. I began to look around to see what other things God was doing that were producing different results. I remembered a young Muslim-background believer named Abdul that I had met at a conference in 1996. At the time, he was claiming 20,000 converts from Islam. I suppose I didn't realize just how outrageous that claim was until I had tried and failed for two years.

I sought out Abdul, and over the next months and years I got to know him well. I spent most of my time just being a brother to him, listening to him as he shared his life, his struggles and his ministry. At first I was skeptical. How was this brother seeing so much fruit when I was seeing so little? Other foreign workers in the country shared my skepticism. "It simply isn't possible," they said. So I decided to see for myself.

Many of Abdul's early reports came from his home district,

a place where foreign workers insisted there were no Muslim-background believers. In 1997, I went there myself and personally interviewed more than 150 Muslim-background believers in four different villages. One village alone had 54 families of believers.

Still struggling to believe, I quizzed these believers with Muslim names and Christian testimonies, probing to see if they were genuine. I asked them to sing songs for me that they used in their churches. They would smile and break into a Christian song that they had written themselves. I would ask them to tell me what Bible passage they had studied the previous Sunday. "We don't worship on Sunday," they said. "We meet on Friday." They then proceeded to tell me the Scripture passage they had studied.

From this initial investigation and many more that followed, I became convinced that God was doing something very special, something that I wanted to be a part of. If God was working through this brother, then I wanted to learn all I could. Perhaps God would use me, too.

We soon found several characteristics that set this growing movement apart from the ways we had been working.

Characteristics of the Movement

1. A Different Vocabulary

The first thing we noticed was that the Muslim-background believers used a different religious vocabulary. So long as it did not conflict with biblical authority, they retained familiar terms from their Islamic heritage. For example, they retained their Arabic names because they saw no reason to change them. They called their churches *Isa jamaats* (literally *Jesus groups*), and referred to their pastor as an *imam* (a term from the mosque literally meaning, *the one in front*).

As we discovered more of how they lived and spread their faith, we knew we would need to learn more about the Qur'an which defined so many things in their culture. The Qur'an's 114 chapters, or *surahs*, each have their own title. Muslims are more

Kevin Greeson

familiar with the surah's title than its number; so, surah 3 is called *al-Imran, surah* 46 is called "The Sandhills" and so forth. Each *surah* is filled with verses called *ayya* (singular) or *ayyat* (plural).

Following their Islamic culture, they called the Bible the *Kitab al-Moqaddis* (literally, the holy book), comprised of three parts: the *Taurat* (or Torah), the *Zabur* (Writings) and the *Injil* (New Testament or Gospels). They also retained the Qur'anic Arabic names for the characters in the Bible: *Nuh* for Noah, *Dawud* for David, *Musa* for Moses and most importantly *Allah* for God.[2]

2. Identity

When asked about their religion, most of these Muslim-background believers replied, "I am an Isahi Muslim." Since the word "Muslim" does not mean "follower of Mohammed", but rather "one who submits himself to God", they could say this in good conscience -- because they *had* submitted themselves to God by following Isa (Jesus); "Isahi" means "belonging to Jesus." The term "Isahi Muslim" fooled no one. Muslims knew that this meant "Christian". Yet, the use of "Isahi Muslim" did two things for them. First, it set them apart from "Western" Christians (considered corrupt by most Muslims) and secondly, they used this designation as an evangelistic opportunity to explain why they were followers of Isa.

3. How It Was Spreading

I wanted to learn *how* the Gospel was spreading, so I visited a remote village approximately 100 miles from Abdul's home town. In the village I found a small church with approximately 25 Muslim-background church members. As I interviewed the church members to discover how their church had begun, they told me that two years earlier, an Isahi from a church in Abdul's area had traveled to the village to meet with one of his relatives. At first, the relative had rejected the Gospel, but soon changed his mind and embraced Christianity. As the Isahi from Abdul's area baptized several of the new believers, the church was begun.

As I continued to interview church members, I soon realized that three of the church members were leading churches of their own in nearby villages. Each of these churches had been started through relatives or close friends. One particular jump of the Gospel struck me. The pastor of the church I was visiting told how the Gospel had jumped from his church to his sister's village some 40 miles away. He told me that his sister's village now had 100 Muslims who have become followers of Jesus.

This seemed to be the pattern of how the Gospel was moving throughout Abdul's country. A church member in one village would visit a "safe risk" relative, such as a brother-in-law or maternal uncle in another village. Eventually, his relatives and fellow villagers became followers of Jesus and formed a church. The only exception to this pattern of growth was when a church planter or evangelist intentionally traveled beyond areas of his relatives and preaches the Gospel in new frontier destinations.

From these patterns of growth we made two applications. First, we did all we could to encourage the Isahi to visit their distant relatives. Many of these Isahi would even take a church planter with them to their relatives' homes. Secondly, we did our best to map the spread of the Gospel along family lines. Once the area of coverage was determined, we began to send church planters to areas beyond the natural flow of family relationships to spread the Gospel into new areas.

4. Method of Evangelism

Church planter-evangelists in the movement used a variety of passages from the Qur'an as their primary way of moving a conversation with a Muslim to spiritual matters. They also used it to "test the waters" and find out who was responsive to their message.

Sharing the Gospel directly with a Muslim can be a problem,

Kevin Greeson

especially if you are a Muslim-background believer. Muslim-background believers have found it safer to first show Muslims specific verses in the Qur'an that speak positively of Jesus and the Bible. They avoid being side-tracked by Qur'anic verses that do not speak of Jesus or the Bible, keeping their focus on "bridge" verses. Depending on what sort of reaction they receive, they will discern whether to proceed or not.

After Muslims come to faith in Jesus Christ, they retain their Qur'an, not for spiritual development, but for use as an evangelistic tool. This method of evangelism is a major factor in the speed by which the Gospel is spreading. Muslim-background believers feel comfortable using the Qur'an as a bridge to the Gospel, because the Qur'an places them on common ground with the Muslims to whom they are witnessing.

As I listened to Muslim-background believers spend hours witnessing to Muslims using the Qur'an to point out analogies and raise questions as bridges to the Bible, I felt overwhelmed. I wasn't comfortable with this tool; I wasn't sure I even wanted to know enough about the Qur'an to use it in this manner. But I could not deny that this was a key tool they were using, and it was one method we had not tried.

5. Identity of Evangelists and Church Planters

Church planter-evangelists who started new work took on the role of micro-businessmen, selling wares or starting a new venture as an auto-rickshaw driver. This allowed them to earn most of their own salary and pay for their own transportation.

This was done for two reasons. First, funds for salaries were not available. Only a small amount of funds from foreign mission sources were occasionally used to help start new businesses and for church planters' transportation expenses into the new areas.

Secondly, the leaders and church planters in the movement did not *want* funds for salaries from foreign sources. In this South Asian country, non-government organizations (NGOs) had a reputation for "buying converts" through relief and development projects for poor Muslims. Muslims were also suspicious of NGOs as agents for advancing Western Christian culture. As businessmen, the Muslim-background believer church planters could enter new communities more easily because they were seen as normal people with whom others could identify.

6. Point of Conversion

Typically a Muslim did not receive Christ as Savior at the time of the first Gospel presentation. The average time between hearing an understandable Gospel presentation and actually coming to faith in Jesus Christ might range from three weeks to six months. The length of time usually depended on access the Muslim had to a Muslim-background believer who could help him work through his questions. We also noted that for most new believers, the actual point of conversion came when they were with a Muslim-background believer. Tracts, radio programs, Bible correspondence, and dreams played a role in drawing Muslim seekers to find Muslim-background believers from whom they could hear the Gospel.

We also found interesting the time of day that Muslim-background believers prayed to receive Jesus as their Lord and Savior. In a large meeting hall with 90 Muslim-background believers, I asked for a show of hands indicating the time of day each had prayed the prayer of accepting Jesus. I asked them to raise their hands if they prayed to receive Jesus in the morning, afternoon, evening, or "dead of night" (the hours between midnight and 4-5 a.m.). All but one indicated that he had prayed to receive Christ in the dead of night. I found this significant, because most of the foreign missionaries I knew were fast asleep in the dead of night. It was impossible to join in this Muslim harvest without local partners who were on call to witness around the clock.

7. Baptism

Baptism followed as soon after conversion as possible. Often

Kevin Greeson

new believers waited until a sizable group of them was formed before baptism. Most baptisms were conducted in secluded locations and performed at night in isolated ponds. Almost all converts were baptized by pastors, not by evangelists or church planters. Occasionally, for cultural reasons, women baptized women.

The "JESUS" film has impacted the world in more than one way. Baptisms in the movement were done according to the style performed in the "JESUS" film where the person being baptized bent his knees and dropped straight down into the water with the pastor's hand on top of his head. The person being baptized was totally submerged into the water. For this reason, it was not uncommon for baptisms to be delayed during cold months.

8. Contextualization through Indigenization

Most foreign missionaries spend years trying to make the Gospel fit contextually into the Muslim community. The movement I was now studying seemed to leapfrog over contextualization directly to indigenization as it naturally took on the cultural complexion of the Muslim community from which it sprang, because it was led by Muslim-background believers.

We had not realized how much local Christianity in the country was identified with Western culture. As we drew closer to the Muslims we were trying to reach and to our Muslim-background believer partners we began to see things through their eyes. In their eyes Western Christianity was associated with the same American culture they viewed on television, leading many of them to reject the Gospel as an extension of American culture.

Muslim-background believers overcame this obstacle by rejecting Western culture and, along with it, Western expressions of Christianity. Yet they were able to embrace the Gospel within their own cultural patterns. As a result the Gospel found an indigenous home and was able to spread rapidly through their community.

9. Worship Style

Typically, *Isa jamaats* worshiped on Fridays, meeting in homes, on verandas, in the villages or under a tree. Prayer, offerings, Bible message and singing made up the worship service. Some songs were written by new converts though most worship songs continued to come from traditional Christian music with some of the words changed to better fit the Muslim culture.

Unlike the traditional churches with their long wooden pews, these worshipers sat on the floor and held their open hands in front of them as they prayed.

In 1997, the Bible Society published a contextualized Bible[3], written in the common language of the Muslim population. Muslim-background believers began using it with great enthusiasm. For the movement, the contextualized Bible was like throwing a kerosene-soaked log into a fire.

10. Persecution and Boldness

Although virtually all of these new believers experienced persecution, it had not been as severe as anticipated. Intense persecution in the form of verbal abuse and rejection from the community typically lasted from six months to a year. As of this writing, only seven Muslim-background believers from the movement are known to have been killed as a direct result of local Muslims trying to stop the spread of the Gospel.

The relatively low number of martyrs and relatively mild persecution was probably due to the way these *Isahi* Muslims used the Qur'an as a bridge, conducted family-based evangelism and rejected association with Western culture.

When persecution did occur, it was met with a bold evangelistic response. One worker observed that, when a new Muslim convert proclaimed his faith in Christ, he might be severely beaten. As he recovered from his wounds, his family and neighbors would come to inquire. He would then take that opportunity to tell them about Jesus, and the movement would grow. Had the brother responded to persecution with a silent retreat, the movement would have ground to a halt.

One brother who had been beaten repeatedly declared, "They can cut my body into a thousand pieces and each piece will cry out, 'Jesus Christ is Lord!'"

Applying What We Learned

My co-workers and I then set about applying what we had learned. We knew that there were some things we could adopt and others that would be more difficult.

We immediately committed ourselves to be much bolder in our witness. Rather than cautiously hiding behind secular identities, we would use every opportunity to tell Muslims about Jesus, *especially when we were threatened.*

We didn't go so far as to call ourselves *Isahi* Muslims, but we did adopt the vocabulary that was more familiar to the Muslims we so wanted to reach. Rather than try to bridge new Muslim believers into the traditional Christian community, we encouraged them to start their own churches.

One of the bigger challenges was to sort through the many ways the *Isahi* evangelists were using the Qur'an. We knew we would never have their broad knowledge of the Muslim scripture, and we really did not want to know it that well, but we did need to come up with something manageable for non-Muslim-background evangelists like us.

It soon became clear to us that the shortest bridge available was found in the 13 verses of *surah al-Imran*, chapter 3 of the Qur'an, which spoke of *Isa al-Masih* (Jesus Christ). This passage declared that Jesus would be born of a virgin; that He would do miracles; that He would be a sign to the whole world; that Allah would cause Him to die and raise Him again to heaven.

To help us remember the key points in the chapter, we used the acronym C-A-M-E-L. These letters brought to mind the chapter's key teaching that Isa's mother, Mary, was **C**hosen to give birth to Isa; that **A**ngels announced the good news to her; that Isa would do **Miracles**, and that He knew the way to **Eternal Life**. In this way, the Camel Method was born.

We first tried our new approach with the 23 Muslim women basket weavers with whom we had been working. We asked them to call their husbands for a meeting. Each one brought her husband or father. At the meeting, we shared with them the verses in the Qur'an which spoke of Jesus.

Walking through the verses together, it was easy to show them that Jesus was much more than a prophet. They responded with both excitement and anger; excitement about the truth of Isa and anger at their *imams* who had been hiding this truth from them. All of them wanted to know more about the Jesus who was more than a prophet. We then showed them the "JESUS" film in their own heart language. What happened next was incredible.

The men insisted on meeting the next day. For four days in a row, they met and listened as we explained the Gospel to them. By the end of the week, the men were convinced that Jesus was the Son of God and the only way to heaven. We then helped organize them into six churches.

We continued to learn from the larger Muslim movement and put those lessons into practice witnessing to Muslims, winning them to Christ, and gathering them into churches. Over the next two and a half years, the harvest grew so rapidly we could hardly keep up, as our team saw 4,500 Muslims baptized and 314 new churches started. Nearly two years later, my church-planting teammates associated with this second movement reported more than 8,000 Muslims baptized and more than 500 new churches planted.[3]

In 2002, the Southern Baptist International Mission Board sent a research team to conduct an extensive assessment of the two movements. Although they were able to survey only portions of the movement, the team's report found that "...a church-planting movement of historic size, scope, and spiritual depth among Muslims (had) emerged...during the late 1990s and is continuing amidst significant and escalating persecution."⁴

Their assessment uncovered at least 90,000 baptized Muslim background believers. Over the next three years, the numbers of baptized Muslim-background believers and new churches continued to climb at a remarkable rate. Today both movements are thriving and spilling over into neighboring countries.

Why is this happening now? After all, hasn't God always loved Muslims and desired their salvation? Of course He has. God has not changed. We are the ones who are changing. After centuries of witness to Muslims using methods that seemed right to Christians, we are now taking a different approach. We are learning how Muslim-background believers witness to and win their own people. We see them answering questions that Muslims have and addressing concerns that are important to them. As we begin addressing those same concerns, we are finding Muslims equally willing to listen, and respond.

Our breakthroughs occurred as we began to apply the principles and insights that were already being used by our Muslim-background brothers. We are now convinced that these same principles are transferable to others. If God could use those of us who were not from a Muslim background to win Muslims to Christ in our country, perhaps he would use other Christians to bring His salvation to Muslims around the world.

And that is why I've written this book, to share with you the ways God is at work drawing lost Muslim men and women to Christ today in hopes that *you* will Him join in that wonderful harvest.

---

¹I call this a vision, because it came to me as a moving new insight from God. We can know it was from God because it was consistent with what He has revealed to us in the Bible.

²Christian readers who want a fuller understanding why we use of the name "Allah" for God should read the Appendix One "Ask the Camel" in the back of the book.

[3] See "Contextualized" or "Muslim-friendly Bible" in the Glossary.

[4] The International Mission Board has a detailed definition of church that is too lengthy to reproduce here but is consistent with the 2000 Baptist Faith and Message available online at www.sbc.net/bfm/default. asp. These churches were either fully consistent with this confession or were developing in that direction. The rounded numbers for baptisms and church starts are the team's best estimate in 2005.

[5] An executive summary of the report is on file with the Global Research Department of the Southern Baptist International Mission Board.

Kevin Greeson

Chapter Three

Is God up to Something?

A T A MEETING IN THE SPRING of 2006, mission leaders from Africa, the Middle East, South Asia, Central Asia and the Pacific Rim reported on where they saw God most actively at work. Though coming from different corners of the world, the same message resounded again and again: "We are seeing Muslims come to Christ as never before." To the surprise of all those present, the reports clearly revealed that Islam has become a great harvest field! Could the Muslim world be on the verge of a massive turning to Christ?[1]

Consider the evidence: "More Muslims have come to Christ in the past two decades than at any other time in history."[2] In North Africa, 50-60,000 Berber Muslims are now followers of Jesus Christ. A Turkic republic saw 4,000 Muslims come to know Jesus as Savior in one year. A mission group in India reported that they have seen an increase from three Muslim-background believers to 1,200 in only eight months. Another mission effort working in north India is reporting 9,500 baptisms among Muslims in only four years. Over the past decade and a half, 13,000 Muslim Kazakhs have come to faith in Christ.

Widespread reports of baptisms and new church starts are popping up all over the Muslim world. Nigeria reports several thousand baptized Muslim-background believers; Uzbekistan 80 new churches among former Muslims; Tajikistan reports 15,000 Muslim converts; Afghanistan 3,000 secret believers; Iran over 800 baptisms of Muslims in one city alone.[3]

Christian missionaries are not the only ones noticing Islam's faltering foothold. Sheikh Ahmad al-Qataani, president of *The Companions Lighthouse for the Science of Islamic Law* in Libya, an institution for training *imams* and Islamic preachers, was recently quoted on Al-Jazeera's television saying, "In every hour, 667 Muslims convert to Christianity. Everyday, 16,000 Muslims convert to Christianity. Every year, six million Muslims convert to Christianity."[4] Though Qataani's numbers may be exaggerated, his comments reveal a growing awareness among many Muslims that something is changing in what was once thought to be an invincible fortress of Islam.

When we view the state of the Islamic world from a global perspective, it bears similarities to the eve of the fall of Communism. Just as global Communism collapsed with a suddenness no one anticipated, God could be preparing Muslims for a great awakening to Christ.

Spotlight

In a theater, all eyes follow the spotlight. The one controlling the spotlight in a dark theater has control over what the audience sees. As the drama of history unfolds, the one controlling the spotlight has a beam of light fixed on the religion of Islam. Since 9/11 and the events that followed, Islam has been on everyone's mind as never before. The religion that presents itself as a religion of peace is facing harsh scrutiny. Where is this peace that Islam proclaims? Muslim leaders encouraging violence can no longer hide in the wings, they are at center stage.

The spotlight on Islam has also captured Christians' attention. Surf the Internet and you will discover numerous new Web sites inviting Muslims to consider Christianity. Across the Christian world, prayer for Muslims has escalated, especially during the month of Ramadan (the Muslim 30 days of fasting). After 9/11, the largest missionary sending agency in the world quickly altered its strategic focus from a non-Islamic emphasis to a three-year worldwide emphasis on the Muslim world.

Opening Borders

Many Islamic countries, long closed to missionaries, are now opening up for aggressive seed sowing and reaping activities. Borders to Afghanistan and Iraq have never been more open. Even countries that try to prevent missionaries from entering fail to prevent evangelistic Internet, radio and satellite television broadcasts.

Islam's Own Reformation

Prior to the Protestant Reformation in the year 1517, Roman Catholic priests maintained an advantage over the laity in that they were generally the only ones who could understand the Latin Bible. Abuses became widespread as priests misinterpreted the Scripture, taking advantage of parishioners who could not read Latin.[5] Once the Bible was translated into the language of the people, its truth exposed deceptive and self-serving practices. The gate-keeping role of Catholic priests was bypassed and massive reforms ensued. The foundation of Roman Catholic authority was altered forever.

In a similar way Islam today is going through its own reformation. In 1984, King Fahd of Saudi Arabia commissioned the translation of the Qur'an from Arabic into every language with a Muslim population. As long as the Qur'an remained in Arabic alone, *imam*s held enormous power and control over their followers. With Muslim lay people now reading the Qur'an in their own languages, misinterpretations by *imam*s are being exposed. They can now see that many common anti-Christian teachings about Jesus and the Bible do not have their origin in the Qur'an. This has led many Muslims to question their *imam*s' integrity and character.

It is not only the *imams* whose authority is being undermined. The Qur'an may prove to be its own worst enemy. As Muslims read the Qur'an in their own language they are seeing for themselves how surprisingly little it has to offer. Some Christian evangelists are even buying Qur'ans in the local languages and distributing them to Muslims! They want Muslims to read the Qur'an because they know that once they read it, their disappointment will compel them to continue their search for the Truth.

In May 1999, a national newspaper in Bangladesh quoted a member of parliament who stood before his peers and asked, "What is happening to our religion? Muslims are throwing their Qur'ans into dumpsters, and in one district, they are throwing their Qur'ans into the river."[6]

The newspaper story stemmed from an incident in a southern district of the country in which a local *imam* had boldly lifted up his Qur'an before the men of his mosque and said, "This book has done nothing to help us improve our lives." He then threw the Qur'an into the river. Rather than opposing him, the men of the mosque, numbering more than 3,000, joined their leader and threw their own Qur'ans into the river as well.

Abundant Tools

Missionaries and their local Christian partners are recognizing as never before that God has not only given Christians the mandate to go into the world and preach the Gospel, but He has also provided them abundant and effective tools to get the job done. In many Muslim countries, missionaries and Muslim-background believers are building bridges from the Qur'an to the Gospel as a powerful tool for winning Muslims to Christ. Muslim-friendly Bibles and tracts[7], the "JESUS" film, radio programs for Muslims, cassette distributions, Web sites and chat rooms for Muslim seekers are among the many tools being used today to reach Muslims for Christ. Ten to twenty years ago, many of these resources did not exist.

Kevin Greeson

Growing Missionary Force

Jesus said, "The harvest truly is great, but the laborers are few; therefore pray the Lord of the harvest to send out laborers into His harvest" (Luke 10:2 NKJV). Could it be that the increase of missionaries to Muslims is directly linked to the increase of prayer for Muslims? Our feet tend to follow our prayers.

Prayer for Muslims has been growing rapidly over the last decade. Since 1993 prayer guides such as the *30 Days of Prayer for Muslims* have become commonplace across the United States leading thousands of churches, ministries and prayer groups to pray for the salvation of Muslims around the world. Millions participate in the annual 30 days of prayer for Muslims which corresponds with Ramadan, the Muslim month of fasting.

The Center for the Study of Global Christianity at Gordon-Conwell Theological Seminary reports that the missionary force to Muslims nearly doubled between 1982 and 2001. In the mid-seventies, only two percent of mission organizations around the world had missionaries working among Muslims. Between 1982 and 2001, missionaries to Muslims increased from 15,000 to somewhere in excess of 27,000. *Time* magazine reporter David Van Bienna noted that, "Not for a century has the idea of evangelizing Islam awakened such fervor... Evangelicals have been rushing to what has become the latest hot mission field."[8]

Back to Jerusalem

"In China more than 30,000 believers are baptized everyday."[9] Missionaries describe the massive growth in China as "a church-planting movement on steroids". But believers in China do not see the winning of their nation as their ultimate goal. Those caught up in China's great awakening are looking beyond their borders.

Ask a house church leader in China what "B2J" means, and he will tell you, "B2J means 'Back to Jerusalem.' Two thousand years ago, the Gospel originated in Jerusalem. Finally, it reached us. Now it is time for us to take it back to Jerusalem."[10] Between

China and Jerusalem lies the Muslim world.

The massive house church network in China has a passion and burden for Muslims. Some of these networks have established underground training centers for pursuing B2J. In 2003, *The Camel Training Manual* was translated into Chinese and is being taught in many of these training centers. Their plan is to establish church-planting movements across the Muslim world. No missionaries are better suited or qualified to spread the Gospel into this most dangerous of mission fields. The leader of one Chinese house church network with 4 million members said, "The reason God has allowed us to face severe persecution in our country is only for practice...He is making us ready for the Muslim world."[11]

Dreams

Another indication that God's Spirit is mounting a massive movement among Muslims is the increasing number of Muslims having dreams in which Jesus appears to them. The second most prevalent reason named by Muslims for why they came to Christ was dreams. A survey of 600 Muslims who came to faith in Christ revealed that one quarter of them began their journey to faith in response to a dream. The most common way for Muslims to come to Christ, the survey found, was through direct personal witness.[12]

Even in places where missionaries are not present, God is at work through dreams and visions. The most common theme in these dreams is the appearance of Jesus wearing a bright white robe. Some Muslims have been instructed in their dreams to read about Jesus in the Qur'an. Two women in Pakistan documented their experience in which dreams directed them to follow Jesus. Esther Gulshan was instructed to read about Isa in her Qur'an. Upon reading the Qur'anic verses, she was compelled to find a Bible.[13]

In February 2003 in a South Asian country, a volunteer team filled a large handcrafted boat with 5,000 Bibles and set sail down the river. Their plan was to distribute God's Word to remote villages scattered along the riverfront. One day, an elderly woman stood at the top of the river's bank and yelled at the team as they were about to pass by. After docking the boat, a team member stepped ashore and approached the woman. It took a while to calm her down and understand what she was saying.

She explained that Allah had spoken to her in a dream the previous night. Allah told her that foreigners would be coming down the river that day and that they would give her Allah's book. When they placed a Bible in her hand, she raised it above her head and said, "I will take this book home and read it to my children and grandchildren, and then I can die in peace."

Farther down the river, a Muslim man approached the volunteer team. Like the elderly woman, he had also had a dream in which he was told to go to the river to receive Allah's book of Truth. With God's Word in hand, he disappeared into the crowd. Numerous churches have been planted along this river as a result of the volunteer team's Bible distribution trip.

Islam is coming out of the shadows and into the spotlight of the world's consciousness. Opening borders, abundant resources, a growing global missionary force, even the dreams of Muslims are being filled with invitations to Christ. Can there be any doubt that God *is* up to something? After years of waiting could this, at last, be the day of salvation for the Muslim world?

---

[1] As reported at the semiannual Regional Leaders Forum of the Southern Baptist International Mission Board, SBC. March 2006.

[2] David Garrison, *Church Planting Movements, How God is Redeeming a Lost World* (Midlothian: WIGTake Resources, 2004), p. 99.

[3] Unpublished reports and conversations with the author by missionaries and strategy coordinators working in the countries

referenced.

[4] Reported by Ali Sina, *Islam in Fast Demise*, March 31, 2004. (To see the entire transcript of the interview on Al-Jazeera television, go to http://www.faithfreedom.org/oped/sina31103.htm.)

[5] The most notorious of these excesses was the sale of indulgences, virtual passes into heaven, awarded in exchange for donations and favors to the church.

[6] This commentary and the story that follows were widely reported in a number of newspapers in Bangladesh.

[7] Muslim-friendly, or Muslim contextualized, Bibles and tracts use familiar Islamic names and terms such as *Kitab al-Moqaddis* (literally "Holy Book") for the Bible, Allah for God and Isa for Jesus. These names have their origin in Arabic and are typically different from the names used by the traditional Christian community.

[8] David Van Biema, "Missionaries Under Cover," Time, 30 June 2003, 52.

[9] Garrison, p. 49.

[10] Reported to the author in a conversation with the leader of a Chinese underground house church network in 2004.

[11] See Paul Hattaway, *The Heavenly Man* (London: Monarch Books, 2002), 351 pp.

[12] D. Woodberry/R. Shubin, March 31, 2004. "Why I Chose Jesus," see: http://missionfrontiers.org/2001/01/muslim.htm.

[13] Bilquis, Sheikh, *I Dared to Call Him Father* (Grand Rapids: Baker Book House Co, 2001) and Gulshan, Esther. *The Torn Veil* (Grand Rapids: Zondervan, 2001).

Kevin Greeson

CAMEL CONNECTIONS

Kevin Greeson

Chapter Four

Finding God's Strategy

WHEN I BEGAN WORKING with Muslims many years ago, I had a different mindset than I have today. At first, I thought that God needed my help. Going into Muslim villages to preach the Gospel, I pictured myself as planting a seed, my part of the job, so that the Holy Spirit could come behind me, to water it and grow it up. In those days, I saw few results. But then, I used *my* strategy, not God's strategy.

Later, I began to realize that God was already at work and that my assignment was to find out where He was at work and to join Him. God already had a strategy lined out for each community we entered. There was no need for a secondary strategy.

One week I went with two American volunteers to use the Camel Method in four rural villages to find where God was at work. In each village, we introduced ourselves to the *imam* and soon found ourselves surrounded by a crowd of 50-100 Muslim villagers. In three of the four villages, our team found where God was working. Within a few months, we were able to see a Muslim-background church established.

As we moved slowly away from one of the villages, I will never forget the sight of a middle-aged man who burst through the crowd riding wildly on a bicycle. He headed straight for us. When he reached us he caught his breath and said, "I did not get one of those papers you handed out." He was referring to the tracts that we handed out after the Camel presentation.

I told the crazy-looking man that we did not have any more. We talked for a moment, then it dawned on us that God was at work in this man. He did not want a tract. There were plenty of tracts in his fellow villagers' hands. He wanted more from us. God had been at work in him even before we arrived. The Spirit was telling him that something was wrong in his life, that he was being held prisoner to a lie. Recognizing the hunger for truth in this man, I made arrangements that day for him to come to the local church planter's house.

Soon, he and eleven others in his village were baptized. Today, he is the pastor of a little church that meets under a tree. No longer do we have the mindset that our job is to go and create spiritual activity among the lost (which we could not do in the first place). We now see that our job is to find the already-existing spiritual activity.

You may be asking yourself, "If God *is* at work among Muslims all over the world, how can I participate in this?"

Good news! You do not have to come up with your own strategy. God's Spirit is already at work unfolding a perfect master plan for the Muslims in your community. What you need to do is discover this divine conspiracy, identify where God is at work, and join Him.

It was never difficult for Jesus to see where the Father was at work; after all He and the Father were one (John 17:21-23). But Jesus knew that it would be more difficult for us. Our sinful nature would blur our vision and cause us to miss God's plan. So Jesus took on flesh, walked among us, and showed us the way.

At the age of 30, Jesus began His earthly ministry consciously modeling for us how to find the Father's strategy for winning the lost all around us. As our perfect example, Jesus wanted us to see how to identify where the Father was at work so that we, too, would know how to join Him in that work. Christ's great lesson for us is found in John 5:17-20 (NKJV).

> But Jesus answered them, "My Father has been working until now, and I have been working." Therefore the Jews sought all the more to kill Him, because He not only broke the Sabbath, but also said that God was His Father, making Himself equal with God. Then Jesus answered and said to them, "Most assuredly, I say to you, the Son can do nothing of Himself, but what He sees the Father do; for whatever He does, the Son also does in like manner. For the Father loves the Son, and shows Him all things that He Himself does; and He will show Him greater works than these, that you may marvel.

If you want to apply Christ's lesson, try personalizing these verses in your own life and ministry.

Jesus, Our Model

Let's take a look at some of the principles Jesus revealed in this model for discovering and pursuing God's master plan. Then, try to apply these principles in the local Muslim community where you live.

- Jesus showed us that the Father was still at work in the world.

- Jesus taught us that we should join the Father wherever He was working.

- Jesus showed us that apart from the Father *we* could do nothing.

- Jesus taught us to be attentive with our spiritual eyes and ears to learn where the Father is working.

- Jesus taught us, as soon as we see where the Father is at work, to stop what we are doing and join Him.

- The Father shows us where He is working, because He loves us and wants to work through us in amazing ways.

1. **Jesus showed us that the Father was still at work in the world.**

"My Father has been working until now..."

Sin came into the world separating man from God. Since that time, God has been working to reconcile man to Himself. Since man's fall in the garden, God has been seeking those who are lost. To see how God is already at work seeking lost Muslims in your community, use your imagination to consider the ways that God might be stirring their hearts. Here are some examples of what God might be doing:

- A Muslim man asks you for a Bible and says that he wants to read it.

- Last night a Muslim woman had a dream in which Jesus appeared to her and told her to search for Truth. Today, she is looking for someone to deliver this Truth to her.

- A Gospel tract was tossed on the ground by an angry Muslim. Another Muslim picked it up and began reading it. As he read it, his heart began to burn. Now he wants to discuss this burning feeling with someone like you.

God is at work all around us. He wants us to wake up, pay attention, see where He is at work and join Him.

2. **Jesus taught us that we should *join* the Father wherever He was working.**

"...and I have been working."

Jesus explained that He had come into the world to join the Father in the work of seeking and saving the lost: "...for the Son of Man is come to seek and to save that which was lost" (Luke 19:10 NKJV). Jesus always worked in perfect harmony with the Father.

Have you ever been in a church planning meeting in which plans were discussed, agreed upon and then written down? Finally, almost as an afterthought, someone says, "Let's commit these plans to the Lord and ask Him to bless them." Such a meeting illustrates how we often make *our* plans for evangelism and church planting, and then ask God to *join us.*

Jesus knew that God already had a perfect plan for the lost in our community. There was no need to develop a new plan. What we needed was to find where God was already at work. This is your task as well.

3. Jesus showed us that apart from the Father we could do *nothing*.

"Most assuredly, I say to you, the Son can do nothing of Himself..."

Jesus said He could do "nothing of Himself". Why would Jesus make such a statement? Jesus knew that, apart from God, there was nothing we could do to produce a church-planting movement. So, He modeled for us complete dependence upon the Father. If you develop your own strategy for a church-planting movement, you will fail. Instead, follow these two suggestions for finding God's plans and strategies:

- Make a plan to find where God is at work.

- Once you find where God is at work, make it your plan to join God where He is already working.

4. Jesus taught us to be attentive with our *spiritual eyes and ears* to know where the Father is working.

Use your spiritual eyes to see where God is at work. In Ephesians 1:18, Paul prayed that we would be able to see, not just with our physical eyes, but with our spiritual eyes. If we ask God, He will open our spiritual eyes to see the ways He is at work around us.

Second Kings 6:14-17 (NIV) tells the story of Elisha, his servant and a hostile Aramean army. The army arrived in Dothan at night in hopes of capturing Elisha. Early that morning, Elisha's servant awoke in a panic when he saw the Aramean army surrounding them. When he awakened Elisha, Elisha told him to not be afraid. "Those who are with us," he said, "are more than those who are with them." Then Elisha prayed, "O Lord, open his eyes so he may see," and God opened the eyes of the servant. Elisha wanted to align his servant's physical eyes with his spiritual eyes. When the servant opened his eyes he saw another army, full of horses and chariots of fire all around them. Then the Lord subdued the army of the Arameans.

Are you able to see what the Father is doing where you live and work? Jesus can help us in our efforts to recognize and see where God is at work. Let's consider the following examples from Jesus' ministry.

- **Zacchaeus** – In Luke 19:1-9, Jesus came into Jericho where He was surrounded by a large crowd. The tax collector Zacchaeus could not see Jesus, so he did *something unusual* and climbed a tree. Jesus, sensing God at work in this man, stopped what He was doing, left the crowd, and entered Zacchaeus' house as He joined the Father's redemptive work.

- **Bartimaeus** – In Mark 10:46-52, Jesus and a large crowd were departing Jericho when a blind beggar cried out to Him. Sensing the Father's leadership, the Bible says, "Jesus stopped...." Though others tried to dissuade Him, Jesus exhibited a life fully attuned to the Father. So, that day, salvation and healing came to Bartimaeus.

- **The Samaritan woman** – In John 4:1-42, Jesus and his disciples took a shortcut through Samaria on their way to Galilee. Beside a well, Jesus talked with a woman who came to believe that He was the Messiah. Jesus delayed His trip to Galilee and stayed in Samaria, where the Father was working.

You should also use your spiritual ears to find where God is at work. "My sheep listen to my voice," Jesus said, "I know them, and they follow me" (John 10:27 NIV). "He who belongs to God hears God's words," He says, "The reason you do not hear is that you do not belong to God" (John 8:47). We must hear God's words and listen for His voice to speak to us. From these two verses we can see that true followers of Jesus hear God when He speaks.

Listen with your spiritual ears and perhaps you will hear where God is at work. Have you ever heard a Muslim say:

- "I am ashamed of the way we Muslims have been acting." (See John 16:8-11.)

- "I had a dream in which a prophet spoke to me." (See Acts 10:30-33.)

- "I want to know what the truth is." (See John 16:13, 17:17.)

- "I want to understand what the Bible is saying." (See Matthew 13:10-11.)

- "I think that Allah is speaking to me." (See John 10:26-27.)

- "I want to know more about Isa." (See John 6:44.)

- "What will happen to me when I die?" (See Hebrews 2:15.)

If you hear a Muslim make comments like these, your spiritual ears should tell you that God is at work inside that person. The Bible tells us that only God can do these things.

5. Jesus taught us, as soon as we see where the Father is at

work, to stop whatever we are doing and join Him.

"...for whatever He does, the Son also does in like manner."

When God shows you where He is at work, He also invites you to join Him. The invitation is not for later, it is for now. If you recognize where God is at work but first have to check your calendar to see if you are free, you just might miss God's invitation. Train yourself to respond quickly to God's invitations. When you join Him, you will see the hand of God at work and will be amazed at what He will do.

- In Luke 8:41-56, we read that the daughter of Jairus was dying. Jairus asked Jesus to come and heal his daughter. Surely, Jairus had one thing on his mind, "Jesus, be quick! Heal my daughter!" On the way, though, there was an interruption (or was it a divine invitation?) when a woman who had been suffering from a flow of blood for years touched Jesus' clothing and was healed. Even though Jairus' daughter was at the point of death, Jesus stopped to spend time with the woman because He sensed this was where the Father was working.

- Abdul relates the story of how God "interrupted" his own life one day as he was riding a bus on his way home from a long and hard journey. Sensing God's leadership, he began sharing the Gospel with a young Muslim man sitting next to him. Excited by what he was hearing, the young man invited Abdul to come to his home with him and share the Gospel with the Muslims of his village. Abdul was tired and anxious to go to his own home, and the young man's village was out of his way. Nevertheless, sensing that God was at work, Abdul accepted the invitation. As night fell on the village and lanterns were lit, Abdul continued to share with the people. At one point, a man interrupted Abdul and asked, "I have killed a man, can Isa forgive me?" This caused a chain reaction. Another man interrupted and asked, "I am a thief, can Isa forgive me?" An outbreak of confessions erupted. In the end, eleven men came forward, confessing their sins, and asking Isa to forgive them. Salvation visited the village that night.

God is still at work among the lost all around us. He wants us to be a part of His saving activity, but it requires us to open our spiritual eyes and ears. When you see and hear God at work, stop what you are doing and join Him.

6. The Father *shows us* where He is working, because He loves us and wants to work through us in amazing ways.

"For the Father loves the Son and shows Him all that He Himself; and He will show Him greater works than these."

Amos 3:7 says, "Surely the Sovereign Lord does nothing without revealing his plan to his servants the prophets" (NIV).

God does not need us to implement His plan of salvation, but because of His love for us, He invites us to join Him. He knows that when we find where He is at work, we will find God Himself. Our encounters with God will change us forever and will enhance our worship of Him.

If you ask me to introduce my children to you, I can tell you exactly who they are because I see them each and every day. But if you ask me questions about a remote figure such as the President of the United States, I have to rely on what others say about him because I do not know him personally.

If your children or grandchildren ask you who God is, will you have to tell them what you have read or what others have told you about God, or will you be able to tell them who God is from your own personal encounters and experiences with Him?

God is inviting you right now to join Him in His new work of turning Muslims in your area to faith in Christ. By joining God in the work He is doing, you will have your own personal encounters with Him. These encounters will truly amaze you. Then, when someone asks you who God is, you will be able to share *your own* story of being on mission with God.

Kevin Greeson

Chapter Five

The Person of Peace

IN LUKE 10:1-20 JESUS provides us with His master plan
for missions. It is the story of Jesus sending out the seventy
disciples into the harvest field. The story begins with Christ
declaring the ripeness of the waiting harvest and ends with the
disciples reporting the amazing harvest they have reaped. Between
these two bookends, Jesus teaches us an invaluable lesson that is
known and practiced by every successful evangelist. The lesson
is that the Holy Spirit has already gone before us and is arranging
divine encounters for us within the new communities we are
about to engage.

It was in 1995 that I first heard a sermon that opened my eyes
to what Jesus was teaching His disciples in Luke 10: "How to
Find a *Man of Peace*". It would be five years before I decided
to actually try to find a *man of peace* by following as closely as
possible the instructions Christ gave His disciples in Luke 10.

Today, the quest for divine appointments that will reveal
a person of peace has become commonplace in missionary
strategies. In reference to Luke 10, we began to call this sort
of adventure "L10 Evangelism". On my first L10 journey, two
American volunteers accompanied me. We decided that we
would take nothing with us except one change of clothes, a Bible,
a "JESUS" video, and a small amount of money. We charted out

a city that would be our destination. No Muslim-background believer churches had been planted in that city or its vicinity.

As we were dropped off on the side of the road to begin our journey, immediately a crowd gathered, and we spent time sharing the Gospel with them. Throughout the day, we continued to share the Gospel with Muslims all along our route instead of going straight to our city of destination.

Finally, at the end of the day, we arrived at the city and felt discouraged because, despite our persistence, no one had responded to our evangelizing efforts. We had assumed that we would find a *man of peace* who would provide us with food and shelter. We shared with a few more people and handed out some tracts. Then, at the conclusion of our discouraging day, we found a government office with a small guest room attached to the back of the building and retired for the night.

Just as we were going to bed, there came a knock at the door. We opened it to find two Muslim men who told us that they had heard from people in the city that three foreigners had come to town speaking about Isa. They had been told that one of us could speak their language and was using Muslim-friendly words. They then told us their story.

A few years earlier, four foreigners had come to the city and visited the home of one of the men. "My daughter had a crippled leg," he said. "The men prayed for her healing in the name of Isa. Within a few weeks, my daughter was healed." As a result of this, the two men had become convinced of the power of Isa.

"We believe that Isa has power and that He loves us," said the one man, "but we need to know more about Him. Can you help us?"

"We have been waiting years to hear more about Isa," the other man exclaimed.

We asked the men why the visiting foreigners had not told them more about Isa. "They could not speak our language," they said. We then asked, "Why didn't you just go to the Christian community a few miles away?" The men admitted that they had been raised to distrust Christians. They also said that they had difficulty understanding these Christians even though they seemed to speak the same language. We could see how our use of Muslim-friendly terms had distinguished us from the traditional Christian community.

Totally exhausted from our long day's travel, I asked the men to come back the next day. I did not pick up on the fact that God was showing me that He was at work in these two men. Fortunately, one of the volunteers with me poked me in the side and said, "Let's not put this off; let's talk to them now." I was reminded why Jesus sent His disciples out in pairs. While my spiritual radar was not working due to fatigue, my partner's spiritual radar picked up God's activity. He knew that when God gives an invitation to join Him, the invitation is for that moment, not for later at a more convenient time. With this in mind, we spent the next two hours explaining how God offers salvation through Isa. We concluded with prayer.

Before the men of peace left, we asked if they could arrange a meeting in which we could share Isa's story with some Muslim women as well. We hoped that if these Muslim women became believers in Christ, then their entire families would follow. Gaining access to Muslim women to share the Gospel had always been difficult, especially for foreign men.

Early the next morning, the two men arranged the meeting we had requested. What seemed to be impossible for us was easy for them. They led us to a home in the village. As we entered the house, we were amazed to see 25 Muslim women sitting on the floor waiting for us. For three uninterrupted hours, we shared the Gospel with them.

When it came time to tell the story about the birth of Isa, we told the two men that we wanted to show a film (the "JESUS" film). The two men of peace quickly went into the city and returned with a rented television and video player. After the women saw the "JESUS" film, the two men fed everyone lunch. The only expense we incurred that day was the cost of a rickshaw ride to and from the meeting place. These men of peace were used of the Lord to meet our needs and facilitate our witness. Once we had fully explained the Gospel to them, we left. We immediately notified a local church planter of this event and he began to follow up with these soon-to-be new believers.

Six months later, we asked another national church planter to travel to the city and visit the two men. To his amazement, he discovered that 125 Muslims had been baptized and five new churches had been formed. Two years later the number of baptisms had risen to 300 and there were 15 churches.

Finding a Person of Peace

We have learned that finding God's person of peace is a vital first step to a multiplying movement of new believers to Christ.[1] Jesus is our model for finding where God is already at work raising up persons of peace. He took the time to teach His disciples how to do this. Jesus used His encounters with Zacchaeus and the woman at the well as examples to teach the disciples how to find those who were responding to the Spirit of God.

Luke chapter 10 tells the story of the disciples' on-the-job training, where they were sent out into the surrounding villages with the assignment of finding men of peace.

Read Luke 10:1-20 (NKJV)

> [1]After these things the Lord appointed seventy others also, and sent them two by two before His face into every city and place where He Himself was about to go. [2]Then He said to them, "The harvest truly is great, but the laborers are few; therefore pray the Lord of the harvest to send out laborers into His harvest. [3]Go your way; behold, I send you out as lambs among wolves. [4]Carry neither money bag, knapsack, nor sandals; and greet no one along the

road. [5]But whatever house you enter, first say, "Peace to this house.' [6]And if a son of peace is there, your peace will rest on it; if not, it will return to you. [7]And remain in the same house, eating and drinking such things as they give, for the laborer is worthy of his wages. Do not go from house to house. [8]Whatever city you enter, and they receive you, eat such things as are set before you. [9]And heal the sick there, and say to them, "The kingdom of God has come near to you.' [10]But whatever city you enter, and they do not receive you, go out into its streets and say, [11]"The very dust of your city which clings to us we wipe off against you. Nevertheless know this, that the kingdom of God has come near you.' [12]But I say to you that it will be more tolerable in that Day for Sodom than for that city. [13]"Woe to you, Chorazin! Woe to you, Bethsaida! For if the mighty works which were done in you had been done in Tyre and Sidon, they would have repented long ago, sitting in sackcloth and ashes. [14]But it will be more tolerable for Tyre and Sidon at the judgment than for you. [15]And you, Capernaum, who are exalted to heaven, will be brought down to Hades. [16]He who hears you hears Me, he who rejects you rejects Me, and he who rejects Me rejects Him who sent Me." [17] Then the seventy returned with joy, saying, "Lord, even the demons are subject to us in Your name." [18]And He said to them, "I saw Satan fall like lightning from heaven. [19]Behold, I give you the authority to trample on serpents and scorpions, and over all the power of the enemy, and nothing shall by any means hurt you. [20]Nevertheless do not rejoice in this, that the spirits are subject to you, but rather rejoice because your names are written in heaven.

Jesus' Instructions for Finding the Person of Peace

Let's examine closely Luke 10:1-20 and make notes on each aspect of the assignment Jesus gave them. Add your own thoughts you go.

10:1 Go Two by Two *"...the Lord... sent them two by two..."*

Besides this verse, there are other passages in the Bible that encourage us to travel with a partner. Deuteronomy 17:6 says that the testimony of two is required to establish the truth. Could it be that Jesus knew that when we see God's amazing work our testimony about it may seem unbelievable? Yet if we have a witness, then even our amazing stories will be confirmed.

In the same way, Muslims often find the good news of the Gospel hard to believe. For people raised in a religion that teaches that a person must earn his way to heaven, the Gospel seems too good to be true. They ask, "Can it be that God wants to give man a free gift even though he does not deserve it?" This "unbelievable" Gospel is more believable for Muslims when it comes from two persons.

Ecclesiastes 4:9-12 tells us that if one falls, the other can pick him up. Evangelism among Muslims is risky and dangerous, not because Muslims are dangerous people but because Satan will try to stop you from capturing his territory. Going out in pairs is safer. You can pray for one another, help one another, and hold one another accountable, just as the volunteer from America held me accountable to share the Gospel with the two Muslim men who visited our room late that night. When we hold one another accountable, we tend to be more motivated and follow through with our work.

Persecution also tends to be more bearable when two endure it together. It makes a world of difference to not be alone and to know that someone else identifies with our pain. Moreover, when we know that someone else is suffering along with us, we have compassion for them, and this causes us to feel less of our own pain and suffering.

Jesus' instructions do not appear by accident. Jesus was modeling an effective strategy for us. In Matthew 10 we read that Jesus sent out the Twelve, and in Luke 10 that He sent out seventy. Jesus mobilized and deployed evangelists into the harvest field in

Kevin Greeson

search of persons of peace. We should do the same.

10:2 Believe in the Harvest *"The harvest truly is great, but the laborers are few; therefore pray the Lord of the harvest to send out laborers into His harvest."*

Many Christians cannot see the harvest of Muslims that are coming into the Kingdom of God. Instead, they believe that the harvest is yet to come. Their earnest prayers are full of requests for God to open up the heavens and pour out his Spirit. Yet, right under their noses, a great harvest of Muslims is already ripening. Jesus did not speak of a future harvest, He spoke of a present harvest. He did not ask us to pray for the harvest to come, He instructed us to pray for workers to go out into the existing harvest.

When I first went to the Muslim country where I served, I thought my job was to plant seeds, the Holy Spirit's job to water those seeds, and someone else in the future would reap the harvest. Slowly, I learned that the Holy Spirit was already at work cultivating a great harvest in the hearts and minds of Muslims. My job was to join in that harvest.

In 1988, tomato pickers in California went on strike to win better wages. Over the following months, countless tomatoes ripened and fell rotting on the ground. The lack of harvesters left the tomato farms with a powerful stench.

Jesus reminds us that the Father has been at work from the beginning until today (John 5:17). Muslim communities already have a harvest ripening in their midst. Where Muslims are not yet coming to faith, it is not that God is not working. It may be that a harvest is just around the corner. As we adopt the ways taught to us by Lord of the Harvest, we maximize our chances of joining in that harvest. What a tragedy it is when "ripened" Muslims are experiencing God's call and yet do not hear the Gospel, because the harvesters have abandoned the fields.

Your job is *not* to pray for the harvest, your job is to go out, find *ripened* Muslims, then win and disciple them. If you want to pray, pray for harvesters, not that God would do more work in preparing the harvest. Church-planting movement practitioners must mobilize as many "L10" trained church planters as possible into the Muslim fields that are already white unto harvest.

10:3 Watch Out! *"...behold, I send you out as lambs among wolves."*

No disciple sent into the harvest field to find the person of peace should go without first counting the cost. Do not expect the world to act favorably towards you. Knowing ahead of time that you could end up with a black eye takes much of the sting out of the pain. A boxer knows ahead of time that he will pay a price. The punches are painful, but the boxer's mind has prepared his body to endure the pain. Unexpected pain tends to hurt more than expected pain. Jesus gave sufficient warning of what could happen.

10:4 Go Needy *"Carry neither money bag, knapsack, nor sandals;"*

The man of peace is looking for you just as much as you are looking for him. One of the keys for an evangelist or church planter to meet up with a person of peace is to travel as a person in need of basic food and shelter. Men of peace stand ready to take care of them. This is the God-given duty of the person of peace. Let him perform the assignment God has given to him as evangelists and church planters perform their assignment of searching for the person of peace. His acts of generosity will be a confirmation that he is the man of peace.

Does this mean L10 evangelists do not need financial support? No. If they have families at home, these will still need their daily bread provided, and it is the church's job to provide it. The point Jesus is making is this: *If we go into the harvest field self-sufficient, lacking nothing, we may miss the kindness, openness and generosity of a man of peace who is looking for us.*

While support for L10 evangelists and non-local harvesters does not necessarily affect the emerging church-planting movement, giving funds to the person of peace *will negatively affect* the movement! The person of peace is a local resident who should not need financial support. It is these local, resident persons of peace who will start the first churches and multiply the movement.

Therefore, follow Jesus' model by training your co-workers to go into the harvest fields, find the person of peace, and disciple him so that he can pursue a church-planting movement in his own community. The L10 evangelist's job is not to launch the movement himself, but rather to find the person of peace who may become the first fruit and the leader of a church-planting movement among his own people.

Not every person of peace that you find will prove to be the sort of contagious evangelist who will start a movement, but among the many persons of peace who are awaiting your visit expect to find some who will reap a great harvest.

Can you imagine having seventy fully committed workers going out into your Muslim people group looking for men of peace? We must do whatever we can to mobilize workers into the harvest fields and find these movement catalysts.

10:5-6 Make Your Presence Known *"...whatever house you enter, first say, 'Peace to this house.' And if a son of peace is there, your peace will rest on it; if not, it will return to you."*

Jesus directs us to proclaim our peace to "whatever house we may enter". The point is to remember that the man of peace is looking for you just as much as you are looking for him. If you are too secretive or clandestine in your approach, you may miss him. It is vital to the church-planting movement that the evangelist and the person of peace find each other.

We are to share the peace of Christ with those we encounter

and then be spiritually alert to see if the peace rests upon them or returns to us empty.

Too often, missionaries working among Muslims are afraid to boldly enter the homes of Muslims and share the Good News of Jesus Christ. They cautiously guard their Gospel witness as if it were a precious secret. A secretive witness may assure years of presence within a Muslim community, but it will frustrate the search for a man of peace.

10:7 Stay *"And remain in the same house, eating and drinking such things as they give..."*

This is an important missionary principle. When you find the man of peace, adapt yourself to his culture; do not insist that he adapt to yours. If we are going to see Muslims come to faith in Christ, we must resist the temptation to attack the outward forms of their culture and religion. Jesus went into Zacchaeus' house, sat down and ate with him. The text says, "Remain in the same house." In church-planting movements, the lines are blurred between evangelism and discipleship. By spending time with the person of peace, you can accomplish both.

Because the man of peace is not yet a follower of Christ, the evangelist is still the primary channel for God's saving activity. As the person of peace becomes a follower of Christ, the evangelist must disciple into him the vision, skills and responsibility for launching a church-planting movement in his own community and beyond.

A typical person of peace is anxious to see this vision unfold. One such man that I met in Pakistan did not wait for me to give him a vision for a movement. He told me he already had a plan. Then, without my prompting, he told me that he was going to gather ten of his family and friends into a room and share the Gospel just as I had shared with him; then he would charge these ten to go out and tell another ten!

Sowing the Gospel without looking for persons of peace may

reveal our lack of faith that God has already prepared persons of peace to receive our message. God wants to raise up *local* believers from within the community whose testimony will command much greater hearing than will our random seed sowing.

Persons of peace are members of the community; we (the evangelists) are outsiders or strangers. Community people accept the testimony of those they know more so than from strangers.

People like Zacchaeus or the Samaritan woman at the well have powerful testimonies of the change God can make in a person. We must remember that a changed life speaks louder and connects with lost people more than an impersonal Gospel distributed through radio broadcasts, tracts, media products, etc.

Most Muslim-background believers give testimonies that they were drawn to the Gospel through a radio broadcast, a tract, or even a dream, but the moment of actually giving their hearts fully to Christ came when a follower of Jesus was present. When the Gospel message comes through a familiar face, a response is much more likely.

10:8-9 Heal and Proclaim *"...eat such things as are set before you. And heal the sick there, and say to them, 'The kingdom of God has come near to you.'"*

Whether you like the person of peace's food or not, eat it! Sometimes this is hard to do in cultures where they eat strange things. Nonetheless, allow the person of peace to do his job and take care of you. You may be tempted to critique those customs and practices that you find unpleasant, but your job is more limited in scope and more important.

Do not hesitate to pray for healing for the man of peace, and do not be surprised when God answers your prayers! But do not limit your prayer to his physical well being. One of our Indian partners has taught us to pray a BLESS-ing on any potential man of peace.[2]

The B-L-E-S-S prayer reminds us to pray for five aspects

of a person's life: **B**ody (physical needs), **L**abor (where they work), **E**motional well-being, **S**ocial relationships, and **S**piritual condition. As we offer these prayers, we are modeling the reality of the Kingdom of God in our own lives and the potential it holds for the man of peace, should he accept it.

Never offer this prayer apart from a bold proclamation of the Gospel, offering every prayer in the mighty name of Isa al-Masih. Ministry, even the ministry of prayer, is incomplete unless it obeys Christ's mandate in verse 9 to "...say to them, 'The kingdom of God has come near to you,'" so we always include a Gospel presentation using such tools as Bible storying, showing the "JESUS" film, using the Evangecube, walking down the Roman Road, or reviewing the Four Spiritual Laws. The important thing is not to miss these proclamation opportunities.

10:10-16 Know When to Leave *"[when] they do not receive you..."*

God is at work everywhere, but not everyone is responding to the work of God in and around them. If you are not welcomed or received, walk away. Staying in an area that clearly has rejected God's message and messenger makes a statement to God. Staying is a declaration that we can do a better job than the Holy Spirit. Be reminded of Jesus' words, "...the Son can do nothing of Himself, but what He sees the Father do; for whatever He does, the Son also does in like manner" (John 5:19 NKJV). Do not linger in a community that is unresponsive. Not only is it unproductive, wasting your time laboring in an unresponsive community can even be dangerous.

Do not take rejection personally. When they reject you, it is not you they are rejecting, it is Jesus they are rejecting. Maintain the theme, "I will work only where I see the Father working."

10:17-20 Expect Results *"Then the seventy returned with joy..."*

There is more to L10 evangelism than finding the person of peace. When you find where God is at work, you find God. Our team has ventured on many L10 trips. Each time, we found several persons of peace and each time we found at least one of them who initiated a movement in his community.

One of the greatest joys as a follower of Christ is to find a person of peace who starts a church-planting movement in his community. Jesus expressed this joy himself in Luke 10:21:

> In that hour Jesus rejoiced in the Spirit, and said, I thank thee, O Father, Lord of heaven and earth, that You have hidden these things from the wise and prudent, and revealed them to babes. Even so, Father, for so it seemed good in Your sight" (Luke 10:21 NKJV).

Summary

Here are the key principles from Luke 10 for seeking and finding the person of peace.

- Go in faith with a partner searching for where God is working, and look for the person of peace.

- Travel light. Do not be self-sufficient, but rather go as a person in need.

- Depend on God's guidance. He is at work before you and will show you the way.

- Offer your peace. If it is accepted, stay there. If not, move on. Sometimes you will not find the person of peace until you walk away, and you discover that he is following you.

- Expect to encounter Muslims who have been prepared by God, possibly through a dream or other means, to hear your witness.

- When you believe you have found the person of peace, go to his home, trusting that he will provide what you need.

- Whether you are accepted or rejected, always remember that God is with you and the Kingdom of God is near. Pray for their needs.

- Recognize that your mission is to lead the person of peace to receive Christ and equip him to share the Gospel with his family and friends.

---

[1]While Luke 10 speaks of finding a "man" of peace, other Bible examples reveal that gender is not the issue. In John 4, Jesus works through the Samaritan woman of peace; in Acts 16:9 Paul's Macedonian call leads to a woman of peace, Lydia, who awaits him and his message of salvation.

[2] The BLESS prayer was first communicated to IMB missionaries by Dr. Raju Abraham working with the UP (Uttar Pradesh) Mission in India.

Kevin Greeson

Chapter Six

When Dreamers Dream

I T SHOULD COME AS NO surprise that God is disturbing the sleep of men and women across the Muslim world. In Joel 2:28 (NKJV) God promised:

> ... I will pour out My Spirit upon all flesh; your sons and your daughters shall prophesy, your old men shall dream dreams, your young men shall see visions.

The prophet Joel presents this prophecy as a prelude to a great outpouring of the Spirit of God upon all flesh. Certainly this promise was fulfilled at Pentecost, but what about those who are still awaiting that outpouring? Dreams can never take the place of biblical revelation, but they do point to the mighty power of the Holy Spirit drawing men and women to have a curiosity about and even hunger for the Gospel message.

This is happening to thousands of Muslims around the world. Tragically, many of these spiritually hungry Muslim dreamers will never meet someone who can explain to them the meaning of their dreams or the Good News of salvation in Jesus Christ. Without these Gospel messengers, the dreamers will remain lost in their sins and trespasses. "How then shall they call on Him in whom they have not believed? And how shall they believe in Him of whom they have not heard?" (Rom. 10:14 NKJV).

If we want to see where God is at work in the Muslim world, we will do well to talk to the dreamers. Many of them are being prepared by God to serve as persons of peace. Let's listen now to what they have to say.

The Man in the White Robe

One of the most common themes in the dreams that Muslims are experiencing is "a man in a white robe" whom they come to see as Isa. Other dream encounters involve different scenarios such as a command to read the Bible or talk to a Christian to find the Truth. What these dreams all share in common is that they point to Jesus.

The Bible reminds us that God has long been speaking to non-believers through dreams.[a] So we should not be surprised to find the same thing occurring across the Muslim world today.

Most of the dream encounters I have come across have occurred among Muslims who have not had access to the Gospel. With so many "Isa dream" reports, one can safely assume that we are only seeing the tip of the iceberg. A search of the Internet reveals scores of sites dedicated to "Isa dreams". Whether this is a new phenomenon or God has been doing this to Muslims previously in history, we cannot know. What is clear, though, is that this phenomenon is widespread and common.

We are not hearing reports of dreams of this nature so much among non-Muslim people groups. We dare not ignore this phenomenon. It is evident that God is at work among Muslims today preparing a massive harvest. Perhaps these dreams have been there for generations. Perhaps it is only today that missionaries are learning of them as they penetrate more deeply into Muslim communities than ever before. Regardless, it is good to know that God is at work even where we are not.

After the Christmas tsunami of 2004 hit the Maldives, I traveled there to see what could be done to help. The Maldives claim to be 99.9 percent Muslim. In the capital city of Male, I

Kevin Greeson

stepped into a taxi after using the Camel Method in the largest mosque in the Maldives. I asked the taxi driver to take me to my hotel. As we were driving, I asked him if he knew of any Muslims in his community who were having dreams in which a prophet appeared.

The taxi driver looked at me with wide eyes and said, "Yes, so many of our people are having this dream." I asked him to pull over to the side of the road and describe for me the prophet that they are seeing. He said this prophet had a white face and white hair, and wore a glowing white robe. I asked if this prophet had any power. His reply astounded me. "Yes," he said, "he has power to get us to heaven."

I asked the taxi driver if his people knew the name of this prophet, and he said they did not. At this point, I told him that I knew the name of this prophet and proceeded to share the Gospel with him. This taxi driver is now reading the Bible with his daughter.

After this encounter I was reminded of Jesus' appearance on the Mount of Transfiguration found in Matthew 17:2 and also Jesus' appearance in Revelation 1:12-14a (NKJV):

> ...and He was transfigured before them. His face shone like the sun, and His clothes became as white as the light.

> Then I turned to see the voice that spoke with me. And having turned I saw seven golden lampstands, and in the midst of the seven lampstands One like the Son of Man, *clothed with a garment down to the feet* and girded about the chest with a golden band. *His head and hair were white like wool, as white as snow*...(italics added)

Three weeks later in India another taxi driver told me that he never had a dream where a prophet spoke to him, but his mother recently called the family together to reveal her dream. She told them that a prophet in a bright white robe had appeared to her and said, "You Muslims are traveling on the wrong road. Follow me on the correct road of righteousness and light." Once again, I told the taxi driver that I knew the name of this prophet and promptly shared the Gospel story with him.

In a city in the heart of Pakistan a Muslim-background church planter introduced me to his new Isahi friend. The friend had been drawn to Isa through a dream where he saw a powerful being that was directing him to walk toward the light. Later he realized that the powerful being was Isa. Immediately after hearing this story I turned to the Muslim-background believer church planter and asked, "How many Muslims in this city are having this kind of dream?" The answer came, "I know of more than 60 Muslims who have had this kind of dream."

The following stories from Muslim-background believers (MBBs) have been collected by missionaries working across South Asia. We will discuss the meaning of these stories at the end of the chapter.

Habib

In 1984, Habib went to visit his sister. That night as he slept, he saw in his dream a tall man with a long beard and white clothes. He asked Habib, "Why are you not following the straight path? You are following the winding path." Habib asked, "What is the straight road?" The answer came, "I will explain to you," then he disappeared.

Habib promptly woke up. The next morning he went to a Muslim-background believer and asked him to interpret his dream. The friend explained that Isa is the straight path to Allah. Habib thought to himself, "How can I follow Isa, I am a Muslim?" Five days later, the same dream occurred. This time Habib heeded the call and became a follower of Isa.

Raymond & Jan

In the spring of 2002, Muslim terrorists launched a series

of attacks against Christians across Pakistan. In the days that followed many Americans evacuated the country. Among these was a young American couple named Raymond and Jan who had been living in the interior of the country when the attacks occurred.

Raymond and Jan's hasty departure meant they were unable to say goodbye to their many Pakistani Muslim friends. Two years later the couple, expecting their first child, prepared to return to Pakistan for a brief visit. They felt strongly that God wanted them to return to their Muslim friends in the mountains and give them a word of testimony and copies of the New Testament. Friends and family in America immediately voiced their concern, but the couple pressed ahead.

Upon reaching Pakistan, harsh travel conditions within the country nearly stopped them. At one point an avalanche blocked the mountain road to their destination, but they continued.

Eventually they reached their destination, the remote city in which they had lived and worked. They visited the house of one of Jan's female friends. When Jan handed her a New Testament, her friend began to cry. She told Jan of a dream she had had a few months earlier in which she saw a mountain. She heard Allah say that the mountain was Isa. There was written on the mountain something that she could not read, so she asked Allah what was written there. Allah said that Raymond and Jan would come and explain the writing to her. Immediately, the couple began to share the Gospel.

Shahid

In 2001, a South Asian Muslim named Shahid felt a desire to know more about Isa. He knew of a Muslim-background believer living not far from his village. One day he sought out the believer and asked him for information about Isa. The believer invited Shahid to a training program taking place the next day.

That night Shahid developed a high fever. When he finally

went to sleep, he had a dream. In the dream, a man in a white robe told him that he needed to attend the training program. Shahid told the man that he could not because he was running a high fever. At that, the man in the white robe touched him and made him well.

When Shahid woke up in the morning, the fever was gone. Shahid attended the training meeting and became a follower of Isa. He concluded his story stating that he has not had a fever since that time.

Pakistan Earthquake

On October 8, 2005, during Ramadan, the Muslim month of fasting, a devastating earthquake struck northern Pakistan killing approximately 80,000 people. I visited the country with three American volunteers. One night I shared the Gospel with a staunch Muslim in the privacy of a hotel room. After five hours, it became evident that we were not getting anywhere.

We took a break and stood on a balcony overlooking a refugee camp and began to talk about the earthquake. Many tragic stories accompanied the earthquake. I casually asked the Muslim man, "What is the most amazing story you have heard related to the earthquake?"

He told a widely known story of a woman who was pulled out from under the collapsed roof of her house. She had been pinned under the rubble for 17 days. When they pulled her out, they immediately offered her food and water. The woman refused to eat or drink, insisting that she would continue to observe the fast of Ramadan. The rescuers continued to urge her to eat and drink. Finally, she told them that she did not need anything because each night a man in a white robe had come to her and given her nourishment.

Immediately, we went back inside the hotel room and I read Revelation 1:12-15 (NKJV) to our Muslim friend. Upon hearing the description of Jesus "clothed with a garment down to the feet

Kevin Greeson

….His head and hair were white like wool, as white as snow...." the man changed his attitude. I placed the Bible on the coffee table in front of him. For the next three hours, he kept one eye on the Bible. At the end of our conversation he asked if he could take the Bible home with him.

Peshawar

We had been told that you cannot do any bold evangelism in Peshawar, Pakistan. Peshawar is a frontier city near the Afghan border. We went to Peshawar after hearing a Christian living there tell us of five Muslim doctors who had been having dreams about Isa. The doctors told our Christian friend that, as a result of their dreams, they wanted to become followers of Isa. We were disappointed that we were unable to find the five doctors, but we did find a particular Sufi mosque that I had heard about.

The mosque was home to a Muslim Sufi sect whose members stretched from Pakistan across northern India and finally into Bangladesh. This Sufi sect claimed to have about six million followers. I knew that a handful of these Sufis in Bangladesh had become followers of Isa.

As we entered the Sufi mosque, a young man visiting the mosque took it upon himself to be our translator. During our three hour visit in the mosque, the young man shared with us the reason why he was there. He said, "Last night I had a dream where I saw this mosque (he had visited this mosque only once before). It was such a powerful dream that I felt compelled to come." We told him that it was no accident that we were here at the same time he was.

He proceeded to translate for us as we shared the Camel passages and the plan of salvation. A total of 25 Muslims including the *imam* listened as we shared the Gospel. They asked us to stay and eat with them. After the meal, we left.

Two months later, the *imam*'s son telephoned a Sufi friend who lived in Bangladesh. He did not know that his friend had already become an Isahi. The *imam*'s son told him that two foreigners had come to his mosque and had shared with him something amazing. He said that he would be coming to Bangladesh in a few months and would tell him all about it. We are praying that God will bless this meeting.

Maleek

Maleek was a factory worker in Pakistan. One day a Christian co-worker shared his faith with Maleek. Maleek was not interested. But that very night Maleek had a dream in which he saw God on His judgment throne. Stretched out to His left were millions of Muslims. On His right were a similar number of Christians. God was pronouncing judgment as He separated the religious adherents. Maleek could see that God was punishing some while accepting others, but he could not determine who was receiving punishment and who had been blessed. The next day Maleek told his Christian co-worker about the dream. The Christian told Maleek of the final judgment passage in Matthew 25. He explained that, according to Scripture, those on the right hand of God will be accepted and those on the left will not. Maleek was amazed by this revelation, but he was still not ready to believe.

When the Muslim month of Ramadan arrived, Maleek spent 10 days in fervent worship and prayer in the mosque. One night he prayed with all his might, asking God over and over again, "Where is the truth? What should I believe?" Maleek was stunned to hear a voice saying clearly to him that his prophet is a liar and a fraud. This disturbed Maleek greatly. He was even more amazed when another young man who was there with him told him that he had just seen a vision of a man dressed in white with a white beard and who shone brightly. This other young man said that he thought the man in the vision must be a Muslim saint, but Maleek wondered silently if this man in white was the one who had spoken these words to him. Maleek did not reveal to anyone the words that he had heard. He still did not accept the Gospel.

Kevin Greeson

Maleek's third encounter proved too much, even for his skeptical nature. One day as he was praying, Maleek felt a power seize him and physically shake his body. He heard a voice say, "Why have you not listened to me? I have shown you already what Truth is. Now obey it." At this, Maleek accepted Jesus as his Lord and Savior.

Hossain

Hossain, a Muslim-background believer from Bangladesh, tells his story of a dream he had in which he saw Isa standing in the middle of a large crowd. Everyone in the crowd surged forward to see. Isa's face which was hidden beneath the hood of His robe. Longing to see Isa's face, Hossain pushed his way through the crowd, but just before reaching Isa, he woke up.

For the next four years, Hossain felt a deep longing to see Isa's face. Finally, while on a trip to the capital city, Hossain wandered into the foyer of a Catholic church where an artist's painting of Isa hung on the wall. For the first time in four years, Hossain felt a deep satisfaction and peace. He immediately found a group of Christians who told him more about Jesus. Soon afterwards, he became a follower of Christ.

Raja

Taken to the madrasa at age five by his parents, Raja became an *imam* as a teenager. Consumed with pride, Raja felt that he knew everything. One day a Bengali Christian woman visited his *madrasa* and spoke briefly to the students. Raja was instantly filled with anger at the woman and shouted at her until she left the *madrasa*.

That night, Raja had a disturbing dream. In the dream, he was at home with his family when suddenly the house was surrounded by an angry mob. The mob was angry with Raja for driving the Christian woman from the *madrasa*. Raja awoke, deeply disturbed by his dream.

Raja said, "Still to this day, the hatred that I showed the

Christian woman haunts me." Recurring memories of this incident led Raja to look more closely at the Christian woman's beliefs. She had told the students that Isa was born of a virgin and is the only one who can guarantee salvation.

Several years later, Raja decided to become a village doctor. He received training from an experienced doctor who had once been a Muslim but had become a follower of Isa. This doctor helped Raja study the passages in the Qur'an that speak of Isa. Raja learned and accepted that Isa was righteous and honorable and is the way to heaven. Raja was subsequently baptized and went on to lead more than 300 Muslims to place their faith in Christ.

As a doctor, Raja gives medicine to his patients but never fails to pray for healing in the name of Isa. Raja said, "I have dedicated my life to sharing Isa with the world." He wrote a book for Muslims so that they can understand that Isa is the only way to heaven.

Raja's boldness is contagious as he stands up for the Lord. One evening in December 2002, he attended the mosque where he once was an *imam*. It was a special night in the Muslim calendar, the night that Muslims believe Allah sends out his heavenly angels to listen to people's petitions. Three hundred Muslim men were in the mosque that night as Raja stood before them and taught them through the Qur'an that Isa is more than a prophet. Then he shared from the Bible that Isa is the Savior. As Raja concluded his message, he said to them, "This is the night to find salvation in Isa. If you want to be baptized, come with me right now to the pond and be baptized." Eight Muslims walked out of the mosque with Raja that night as they experienced for themselves the salvation that Raja had found and were baptized.

Ali

Ali admitted that everyone in his village who knew him considered him an unruly boy. Not knowing what else to do with his rowdy son, Ali's father sent him to the *madrasa* where Ali did well, delving into his studies of the Qur'an and the Hadith and learning the importance of being holy.

For 12 years Ali served as the *imam* of his village mosque, striving to be faithful to Islam. In the back of his mind, though, there was a nagging thought: "How can a man become truly holy?" Frustrated, Ali began looking for good men who would instruct him in holiness.

Eventually, he met a Muslim friend who had become a follower of Christ. After hearing the message that Isa was the one and only Savior, Ali went home and pondered this truth. That night, Ali dreamed that a man in a white robe showed him a village pond and said, "Go into the water for a bath." In his dream, Ali obeyed the man and went down into the water. Coming out of the water, Ali noticed an open cut over his heart. Suddenly, the man in the white robe touched him and the cut closed.

Ali awoke in a cold sweat and rushed to the home of his believer friend. He was desperate to be baptized, knowing without a doubt that Jesus was the one true way to God. Today, Ali is the pastor of a small Muslim-background church. He chooses to follow Isa and no other.

Capturing a Harvest of Dreams

These are but a few of the countless dreams that God is pouring out across the Muslim world. What are we to make of these dreams? Do they replace or supplement Scripture? By no means! They do point to a reality, though, that we must not miss. God's Holy Spirit is at work across the Muslim world. But God's plan of salvation is not to evangelize the world through dreams. He commands *us* to take the Gospel to a world that is lost apart from salvation in Jesus Christ.

These dreams are God's invitation to Muslims to come to the light of the Gospel. They should also be a reassurance to us that we are about a mission that is divinely ordained and empowered by the Holy Spirit of God. We do not go into our mission alone or under our own power. God is already at work among Muslims and invites us to share in the joy of reaping where we have not sown.

If you obey God's commission to enter the Muslim world, you should look for and listen for Muslims who are having dreams. The Apostle Peter instructed us to "Always be prepared to give a reason for the hope that is within you" (1 Peter 3:15 NIV). If you are ready, you may be the one to answer a Muslim dreamer's questions about the man in the white robe or an unknown being of light who is haunting his dreams.

You might ask a Muslim whom you meet, "Do you know of any Muslims in your community who are being visited in their dreams by a prophet in a white robe?"

This question puts no one on the spot, nor is it threatening. They may actually be flattered that you would ask. Dreams play a much more prominent role in the life of Muslims than they do in Western society. So do not be surprised if they mention that a prophet in a white illuminated robe is visiting them. Listen carefully as your Muslim friend describes this prophet. Offer to show him the description of this same prophet in the New Testament.

Read to them the account of Jesus on the Mount of Transfiguration in Matthew 17:2 (NKJV):

> ...and He was transfigured before them. His face shone like the sun, and His clothes became as white as the light.

Then show them how John described Christ's appearance in Revelation 1:12-14a (NKJV):

> Then I turned to see the voice that spoke with me. And having turned I saw seven golden lampstands...One like the Son of Man, *clothed with a garment down to the feet*

Kevin Greeson

and girded about the chest with a golden band. *His head and hair were white like wool, as white as snow....*(italics added)

If they recognize the prophet from their dream in these passages, you can point them to the *Injil* as a source for learning much more about Isa. Offer them a copy of the New Testament and exchange contact information so you can follow up with them after they have read more.

Start a Muslim Dream Team

If you are in a prayer ministry for Muslims, you can be a part of what God is doing among Muslims through dreams. Enlist and challenge members of your prayer team or prayer network to pray specifically for Muslims throughout the Islamic world that they would respond openly to their Isa dreams. Designate these prayer warriors as your *Muslim Dream Team.*

If you are living in the western hemisphere, your morning prayers will coincide with the time when most Muslims in the eastern hemisphere are lying down to sleep. Pray that the man in the white robe will appear and speak to them.

Now you need to prepare yourself to answer the questions that a Muslim dreamer will have. It's time to learn to ride the Camel!

---

[1] See for example: Gen. 20:3 – to Abimelech, 31:24 – to Laban the Syrian, 40:9 – to Pharaoh's butler, 40:16 – to Pharaoh's baker, 41:7 – to Pharaoh himself, Dan. 2:1 – to King Nebuchadnezzar. And in the New Testament: Matt. 2:12 – to the Magi; and 27:11 – to Pilate's wife.

Riding The Camel

Kevin Greeson

Chapter Seven

Walking the Camel

O N A RECENT TRIP to Pakistan, I prayed for God to open my eyes to find a Muslim person of peace, but not just any person of peace; I wanted to find one who would be a catalyst for igniting a church-planting movement. Working against me were two factors: I only had two days in my schedule to give to this project, and I did not speak the local language.

I hired a taxi driver named Mahmood who spoke English in addition to the local language. He was extremely helpful in driving me around the city. When I would see individuals that appeared to understand English, Mahmood would stop the car and I would get out and talk to them. At one point, Mahmood expressed interest in my message. Not wanting to anger him, I told Mahmood that I was doing a survey to find out what Muslims in Pakistan thought about Isa.

The first day, I set a goal of talking with 10 individuals, but at the end of the day no one had seemed interested in hearing about Isa. The next morning, Mahmood picked me up at my hotel. Immediately, he told me that last night he had talked with his wife about Isa and both of them wanted to know more.

My spiritual radar time is sometimes dull in picking up signals of where God is working. I told Mahmood that we would talk again later, but right now I needed him to take me to a mosque. Mahmood drove me to a mosque that I would not have chosen. I was nervous until I realized that Mahmood was not going to drop me off alone. He parked the car and escorted me into the mosque. I was his guest.

We walked deep into the inner part of the mosque looking for the *imam*. We passed several Muslims who stared at me as if I did not belong there. Finally, Mahmood took me into a back room where seven older Muslim men with long beards sat. Mahmood took charge of the meeting. He boldly said, "This foreigner has some questions for you, will you talk with him?" They were all taken aback at first, but finally agreed to do so.

I ventured into the Camel presentation but was not able to get very far. They were more interested in other matters. After fifteen minutes, Mahmood turned to me and asked, "Are you satisfied?"

Fumbling, I said, "I guess so." At that, I thanked the men and said goodbye.

When we got back into Mahmood's taxi, he turned to me and said, "I don't like those men." I asked him why. He said, "They are liars. They say one thing and do another." I listened as he spoke harshly about all the Islamic leaders he had encountered.

Finally, my spiritual radar detected that God was at work in my taxi driver. Mahmood was not only interested in hearing more about Isa, he was totally frustrated with Islam and its leaders. I asked Mahmood if we could sit and talk. He took me to a local restaurant where I shared the Camel presentation along with the *Korbani* Plan of Salvation. All throughout the presentation, Mahmood would say, "Why hasn't anyone ever told our people these things? Why have our religious leaders hidden this truth from us?" After two hours of sharing with Mahmood, he said that what he heard from me must be the truth.

Kevin Greeson

Then something amazing happened. Mahmood looked beyond himself and became deeply burdened for all the Muslims the truth about Isa and the way of salvation. He said, "Kevin, you can't do this anymore." He was referring to my running around the city talking to people on the street about Isa. I asked him why. He said, "This is too dangerous for you, I have a better plan." I asked him to give me his plan.

His plan was to gather 10 of his family members and friends into a private room. He told me, "What you just told me, you will tell these 10 people." Without any prompting from me, he said, "And then I will tell the 10 to go and tell another 10. This way we can cover Pakistan with this message." I was amazed at his plan and that God had answered my prayer.

As I look back on this encounter, I realize that I disobeyed God in Pakistan. Years earlier, I had told Him that when I found where He was at work, I would drop everything and join Him. Yet my plane was leaving in just two hours after sharing the Camel presentation with Mahmood. This was my moment of truth to demonstrate to God that He was the master and I was the servant. I failed this test as I got on the plane headed home.

Before leaving Mahmood though, I made arrangements for him to have the 10 gathered in a private room when I came back in four months. He agreed and drove me to the airport. I called Mahmood two months later and asked if he was ready for me. He told me that I was too late. He had already shared about Isa with 10 of his fellow taxi drivers. I asked him what their reactions were. He said that three wanted to kill him, three thought he was crazy and four were interested to know more.

My experience with Mahmood illustrates how God has already selected special persons of peace and will direct us to find them. A simple tool like the Camel Method can help us discover where God is at work. Here are some steps to prepare you for a successful Camel ride.

Preparation for a Successful Camel Ride

#1 Pray!

Camel riding is a spiritual endeavor, more about being on mission with God than mastering a technique. So, pray that you will have the compassionate heart of God as you go into the Muslim community. Pray that God will already be nurturing persons of peace, and that you will be spiritually alert to find them. Pray that Satan will be bound from this effort. Pray in faith expecting results, confident that God is already at work and that persons of peace are just waiting on your arrival.

#2 Have a Humble Heart

Muslims, by and large, are a proud people. The last thing they want is for a Christian to approach them with a superior attitude trying to teach them something about Allah and the Qur'an. You *will* teach them something, but you will receive a better hearing if you approach them with a humble attitude as a genuine learner.

This should be an encouragement to anyone doing Muslim evangelism for the first time. It is okay not to be a knower. For the first time in your life, a good measure of ignorance just might make you more effective at something.

#3 Where to Use the Camel

If the Apostle Paul was a missionary to Muslims today, what would his strategy look like? Where would he use the Camel Method? Paul's custom when entering a new area was to go to the synagogue and then begin revealing Christ to them through their own Hebrew Scriptures.

> Now when they had passed through Amphipolis and Apollonia, they came to Thessalonica, where there was a synagogue of the Jews. Then Paul, as his custom was, went in to them, and for three Sabbaths reasoned with them from the Scriptures.... (Acts 17:1-2 NKJV).

Kevin Greeson

Of course, Muslims are not Jews, and the Qur'an is not the Old Testament, but the value of exalting Christ through the scriptures sacred to those we are trying to reach has a similarly powerful effect today.

The Camel Method can be used in a mosque, in a coffee house, in a village, or in a private setting. It can be used with a single Muslim or with large groups. Sharing it in a large group will increase the likelihood of finding a person of peace.

It is not uncommon for Muslims to invite you to sit with them, especially if you want to discuss with them something about Islam. By accepting their invitation, you can count on being on safe ground. Muslims often love to entertain guests. It is a huge embarrassment for a Muslim if his guests are harmed.

#4 Expect Good Will

To encourage a climate of good will, you might want to keep in mind a passage from the Qur'an that anticipates good relations between Muslims and Christians. It is found in *surah* 5, The Table Spread, verses 82 and 83:

> ...And thou wilt find the nearest of them in affection to those who believe (i.e. Muslims) to be those who say: 'Lo! We are Christians.' That is because there are among them priests and monks, and because they are not proud.

#5 Do Not Be Deceptive

Your friendliness and desire to discuss the Qur'an may lead your Muslim hearers to ask, "Are you a Muslim?" It is important for you to understand that this is not a simple question, because the word "Muslim" has two meanings. On the surface, it simply means "one who has submitted to God's will". At this superficial level, no Christian would want to respond with "No! I have not submitted to God's will." But the other meaning of the term must not be forgotten. Being a Muslim is being part of a religion and cultural heritage, a religion that exalts Mohammed and the

Qur'an, while rejecting the Trinity, the Incarnation and the very heart of the Christian faith. You do not want a hint of deception on this point. Pretending to be a Muslim or playing a semantic game will earn you no points in your efforts to win your new friend to faith, but neither will an abrupt denial.

In South Asia, Muslim-background believers typically respond to the question, "Are you a Muslim?" by saying, "I am an Isahi Muslim." This reply literally means, "I am one who has submitted to God's will by belonging to Jesus." The meaning may not be immediately obvious to the Muslim who hears it, but neither does it close the door to relationship and further communication. If the Muslim proves to be a seeker and wants to know more, the term "Isahi Muslim" invites a Gospel presentation.

For a Christian-background believer to say, "I am an Isahi Muslim" may be more problematic, leading to charges of deception. Many of us who are not from a Muslim background simply reply, "I am an Isahi who loves Muslims." This accomplishes what you desire: You have shown him respect both by affirming him and by using *his* term for a Christian, while making it clear that *you* are a follower of Isa.

Finally, some Christians give the answer, "I am a Christian, but I am reading the Qur'an." This gives a clear answer to your identity as a Christian. The second part of your statement, though, typically catches their attention and keeps the conversation moving forward toward the Qur'anic text. It also prevents a lengthy discussion on the things Muslims may dislike about Christians.

#6 Qur'an or No Qur'an

Though the Camel Method requires the use of a Qur'an, it is always best to use your Muslim friend's Qur'an. A non-Muslim walking into a conversation with a Qur'an in hand would probably only offend Muslims. You may have a copy of the Qur'an in your bag, but it is best to rely on your Muslim friend's copy when discussing the Qur'an's passages used in the Camel Method. Since most Muslims do not carry a Qur'an around with them, you will have to be patient as they either go and get their Qur'an or take you to their home or mosque.

It is not unusual at this point for the Muslim you are talking with to pass you off to another Muslim whom they consider to have a better knowledge of the Qur'an and of the Arabic language. To avoid being handed over to someone else, gently tell him that you would prefer to talk with him first. Tell him that if you come across a question that he cannot answer, then you will go to someone who is more knowledgeable.

What do you do if your Muslim acquaintance has no access to a copy of the Qur'an? Here are some things you can do, even if there is no Qur'an handy.

You will still be able to recall the C-A-M-E-L outline that we will introduce shortly, and share with him the three key points about Isa that you have gleaned from *surah al-Imran* 3:42-55: that Isa is holy, is powerful and can lead us to heaven. Then encourage him to go home or to his mosque and read it for himself. By all means, leave your contact information and ask if you can meet again later.

Stick to your goal of finding a person of peace. If your Muslim friend is unable to produce a Qur'an, you might still introduce yourself as an Isahi who would like to pray for people in this area. Ask him, "How may I pray for you? Do you or anyone in your family need prayer for healing? Are there needs in your community that I can pray for? May I pray for God's blessings upon you and your family (knowing that God's greatest blessing is found in Jesus Christ)?" Be sure to close your prayer, "…in the powerful name of *Isa al-Masih*." Assure your new friend that you will be praying for him, and exchange contact information. It is important to check back with him at a later time to see if there is any spiritual activity taking place.

Finally, remembering that God has been pouring out dreams

across the Muslim world, you might ask if he has had any interesting dreams lately, and see where it leads. You just might find a dreamer who is looking for a guide to reveal the identity of the prophet in white.

#7 Use Leading Questions

In your encounters with Muslims, you will be much more effective if you ask leading questions and draw the truth out of them rather than preaching the truth to them. Leading questions are questions for which you already know the answer. Jesus used leading questions as a powerful yet non-threatening way to draw out the truth from others. Jesus asked Peter, "...who do you say that I am" (Matthew 16:15 NKJV)? Jesus knew the answer to His question, but wanted to draw the answer out of Peter, so that Peter could hear himself say, "You are the Christ, the Son of the living God" (Matthew 16:15 NKJV).

You, too, should use leading questions as you walk a Muslim through the Camel Method. Sometimes, you may need to help him verbalize the correct answer. At other points you may build on his answer to lead him into a deeper truth.

As long as you stay within the Qur'an and ask your questions respectfully, Muslims cannot blame or attack you for proselytizing about Isa. However, once you have drawn out the person of peace, you will be able to leave the Qur'an behind and teach him exclusively from the Bible.

#8 Bridge to the Bible

Remember, there is not enough light in the Qur'an to bring Muslims to salvation, but there are enough flickers of truth to draw out God's person of peace from among them. As soon as possible, you want to bridge them out of the Qur'an and into the Bible where they can see the truth for themselves. A person of peace will recognize the truth in God's Word; your job is to get him there.

Kevin Greeson

#9 Lift Up Jesus

Jesus said, "...if I be lifted up, I will draw all men unto me" (John 12:32 NKJV). Walking through *surah al-Imran* 3:42-55 provides us with an excellent opportunity to lift up Jesus in the eyes of Muslims, elevating Him from the status of a prophet to much, much more. After reading *surah al-Imran* 3:42-55 and listening to you explain it, no Muslim will be able to honestly say that Isa was merely a prophet. From the text of his own Qur'an, he will see that Isa is far more than a prophet.

Offering spiritual food will draw out a seeker who is spiritually hungry. *Surah al-Imran* 3:42-55 attests to divine attributes of Isa that no Muslim can deny. From this passage in the Qur'an he will see that Isa is holy, and all powerful, and can show us the way to heaven. Thoroughly discussing this passage will most likely trigger something in the heart of a Muslim who is already under the conviction of the Holy Spirit.

#10 Turn on Your Radar

Finally, turn on your spiritual radar. Remember, God is already at work in this community. Your job is to find out where! Ask God to give you discernment, patience and faith to follow wherever He leads. Do not be surprised when He shows you the person or persons of peace who have been waiting for your message of Good News.

The number one cause for missing persons of peace is a busy schedule. Take your time and be patient. Some will appear as persons of peace, but after spending some time with them, it will be clear that this person is not responding to God's promptings. The only way to know is to spend time. Finding a person of peace is *so* important. The next person of peace you find just might be the one to ignite a church-planting movement. Now let's ride the Camel!

CAMEL 101

The central text you will use in the Camel Method is found in *al-Imran* 3:42-55. You can remember its content with the acronym: "C-A-M-EL".

C – Chosen (Maryam was chosen by Allah for a special purpose.)

A – Announced by Angels (Angels announced the birth of the Messiah to Maryam.)

M – Miracles (Jesus' power is revealed in His miracles.)

E L – Eternal Life (Jesus knows the way and *is* the way to heaven.)

Surah al-Imran 3:42-55

As you read through this passage keep in mind these three main points: 1) Isa is holy, 2) Isa has power over death, and 3) Isa knows and is the way to heaven.

If you have difficulty understanding the following translation of the Qur'an, you can review several others at www.quranbrowser.com.

C
42 And when the angels said: O Maryam! surely Allah has **chosen** you and purified you and chosen you above the women of the world.
43 O Maryam! keep to obedience to your Lord and humble yourself, and bow down with those who bow.

A
44 This is of the **announcements** relating to the unseen which We reveal to you; and you were not with them when they cast their pens (to decide) which of them should have Maryam in his charge, and you were not with them when they contended one with another.

Kevin Greeson

45 When the **angels** said: O Maryam, surely Allah
gives you good news with a Word from Him (of one)
whose name is the Messiah, Isa son of Maryam,
worthy of regard in this world and the hereafter and
of those who are made near (to Allah)
46 And he shall speak to the people when in the
cradle and when of old age, and (he shall be) one of
the good ones.
47 She said: My Lord! when shall there be a son
(born) to me, and man has not touched me? He said:
Even so, Allah creates what He pleases; when He
has decreed a matter, He only says to it, Be, and it is.
48 And He will teach him the Book and the wisdom
and the Taurat and the *Injil*.

M

49 And (make him) an apostle to the children of
Israel: That I have come to you with a sign from
your Lord, that I determine for you out of dust
like the form of a bird, then I breathe into it and it
becomes a bird with Allah's permission and **I heal
the blind and the leprous, and bring the dead to
life** with Allah's permission and I inform you of
what you should eat and what you should store in
your houses; most surely there is a sign in this for
you, if you are believers.
50 And a verifier of that which is before me of the
Taurat and that I may allow you part of that which
has been forbidden you, and I have come to you with
a sign from your Lord therefore be careful of (your
duty to) Allah and obey me.
51 Surely Allah is my Lord and your Lord, therefore
serve Him; this is the right path.
52 But when Isa perceived unbelief on their part, he
said "Who will be my helpers in Allah's way?" The
disciples said: We are helpers (in the way) of Allah:
We believe in Allah and bear witness that we are
submitting ones [literally in Arabic, "muslims"].
53 Our Lord! we believe in what Thou hast revealed
and we follow the apostle, so write us down with

EL

those who bear witness.
54 And they planned and Allah (also) planned, and

Allah is the best of planners.
55 And when Allah said: O Isa, *I am going to terminate the period of your stay (on earth) and cause you to ascend unto Me* and purify you of those who disbelieve and make those who follow you above those who disbelieve to the day of resurrection; then to Me shall be your return, so I will decide between you concerning that in which you differed. [italics added for emphasis]

Walking the CAMEL

We will start our Camel ride slowly with *Camel 101 - for beginners.* This basic level emphasizes the three points: 1) Isa is holy, 2) Isa is powerful and 3) Isa knows the way to heaven.

Opening Lines

The universal greeting for Muslims around the world is, *"Salaam aleikum"* (*Peace be upon you*) which the hearer will echo with *"wa-aleikum As-salaam"* (*And upon you, peace*). This is a beautiful greeting that Christians can embrace, since Jesus said: When you enter a house, first say, 'Peace to this house.' If a man of peace is there, your peace will rest on him" (Luke 10:5-6 NKJV).

Follow this greeting with a friendly introduction of yourself. Then use one of the statements below to move the conversation in the right direction.

> I have been reading the Qur'an and have discovered an amazing truth that gives hope of eternal life in heaven. Would you open your Qur'an to *surah al-Imran* 3:42-55 so we can talk about it?

Or you can say:

> I have been reading the Qur'an and found that it says some very interesting things about Isa. Could you read *surah al-Imran* 3:42-55 from your Qur'an so that we can talk about it?

After Reading *Surah al-Imran* 3:42-55

After your friend reads this passage carefully bring out the three key points:

I. Isa Is Holy

3:45-47 Point out that Isa, like Allah, is holy. Then ask, "Does this *ayyah* say that Isa came directly from Allah, and that He did not have a father?"

He will most likely agree that Isa came directly from heaven. Then you can ask: "Did Isa have an earthly father?" If he remains true to the Qur'an, he must agree that Isa did not have an earthly father. Now ask some leading questions.

First, "Are there any other prophets who did not have a father?"

He may reply that Adam did not have a father. If so, help him recall the story of Adam in the garden and how Adam walked with Allah because when Adam was first created, he had no sin. Because Adam was holy, he could be in the presence of holy Allah. After Adam disobeyed Allah, he could no longer be in Allah's presence. Allah is 100 percent holy and nothing unholy can be in His presence. This means that if anyone wants to go to heaven to be with Allah, he must also be holy.

Now you can point out that Isa also came from Allah. Ask your friend, "Was Isa holy? Did Isa ever commit a sin?" He will certainly reply, "No, Isa was *very* holy." Press a little further by asking, "Did Isa ever kill anyone? Did He ever have sexual relations with a woman? Did He ever try to make Himself rich?" These leading questions will gently draw a contrast in the mind of your Muslim friend between Isa and another prophet whom he knows all too well.

Conclude this point by saying, "Isa lived his entire life without committing any sin. *Isa is holy.*"

II. Isa Has Power over Death

3:49 After reading the list of Isa's miracles in this *ayyah*, emphasize Isa's miracle of raising the dead. You might ask your friend, "Would you agree that one of people's greatest fears is death?" Point out that death causes all of us to worry. Physical death is the most feared enemy of man.

Then ask, "Do you know of any other prophet who was given the power over death?" He will respond with, "No."[1] You can now agree that Isa was very powerful.

You may wish to relate the story of Isa raising his friend Lazarus from the tomb (John 11: 38-44). *Isa has power over death.*

III. Isa Knows the Way to Heaven

3:55 Finally, use this *ayyah* to help Muslims understand that Isa knows the way to heaven because He Himself has traveled the straight path from Allah to earth and returned to Allah in heaven. To get to heaven is a great desire for most Muslims, and yet they do not know of anyone who for sure has gone to heaven, except Isa. Most Muslims believe, as the Qur'an says, that Isa is with Allah in heaven right now. Use the following illustration to show them that *Isa knows the way to heaven.*

Ask him, "If you wanted me to come to your house and you knew that I needed directions, who would be best suited to show me the way?"

Say to him, "Naturally, you are the one most capable of leading me to your house. You know the way and who better to show me the way than you?" You can then proceed to say, "I am a sinful person. Though I have done many good things in my life, still I am still a sinner and share Adam's curse. I know that by my own power I can never become holy and get to be with Allah in heaven. *Out of all the prophets, which one do you think is most capable of helping me get to heaven?"*

If he answers, "Isa is the one most capable to help me get to heaven," then you may have found your person of peace. Walk him through the *Korbani* Plan of Salvation (see chapter 8).

If he answers, "Mohammed is the one most able to help me get to heaven," then you may need to take him to one verse that is outside *surah al-Imran*. Ask him to read *surah* 46, The Sandhills, verse 9 in which Allah instructs Mohammed to say:

> I am nothing new among the Prophets; what will happen to me and to my followers, I do not know; I am only a plain warner.[2]

This *ayyah* states that Mohammed did not know where he or his followers would go after death. Do not be combative at this point. Instead, gently say, "If you had to choose between someone who says he does not know what will happen to him after he dies and one who is already in heaven, which one would you rather have to lead you?"

If your Muslim friend wants to discuss the topic of Isa further, he just might be a person of peace. If he is willing, you should cancel everything on your schedule and spend time with him.

> And if a man of peace is there, your peace will rest on it [the house]; if not, it will return to you. And remain in the same house, eating and drinking such things as they give, for the laborer is worthy of his wages. Do not go from house to house (Luke 10:6-7 NKJV).

Practice and Pray Before You Go

Now that you have seen how easy it is to ride the Camel, go back and read through this chapter again, familiarizing yourself with its content. After you finish, find a partner and practice role-playing the Camel. One of you play the part of a Muslim while the other rehearses the key points of the Camel. Switch roles and try it again. As you become more comfortable with the material, set a time to meet with your partner, pray for a person of peace, then go and share with Muslims in your community.

---

[1]Since it does not appear in the Qur'an, most Muslims do not know the story of Elijah reviving the widow's dead son. They will most likely reply that they do not know of any other prophet with this power over death.

[2]In some translations of the Qur'an, this verse may not be found in 46:9. It may appear one or two verses on either side of verse 9.

[3]*The Camel Workbook and DVD* is a newly developed resource to help you practice through the Camel Method. It is available from Fresh Wind Distributing at www.FreshWindDistributing.com.

Chapter Eight

Camel Destinations

IF A MUSLIM LISTENS to you through the entire Camel presentation, keep in mind that he has still not heard the Gospel. Your Camel presentation allowed him to see Isa in a way he has never seen Him before and gain an eye-opening glimpse into who He really is. The presentation lifted Jesus out of prophet status and raised Him nearer to Savior status. A foundation for hearing the plan of salvation is now in place.

In your Camel journey thus far you have begun a relationship with a Muslim or a group of Muslims, but your journey is far from complete. There are three very important destinations ahead of you. In this chapter you will learn how to reach these three destinations: 1) Presenting the plan of salvation to a Muslim, 2) Bridging a Muslim into the Bible and 3) Launching a new Muslim-background believer into a church-planting movement.

Your First Destination: Sharing God's Plan of Salvation
Before setting out for your first destination, it is time to look within yourself and determine how serious you are about going the distance. This is not a television drama which requires nothing more from you than to sit and watch. This is the real world with real lost people, and it will take a strong and active commitment from you to see it through.

Once you find a Muslim person of peace, recognize the struggle he will be going through and decide if you have the time and energy to walk beside him. In the mind of a Muslim who is considering Christ, a war is raging. He needs you to be sensitive and understand his inner struggle. If you cannot walk beside him all the way, you must make arrangements for someone else to continue the journey with him.

The Cost

The decision to become a follower of Isa is more costly for Muslims than for us. We must understand that a Muslim has stronger ties to his family, to his community and to his heritage than most Westerners can appreciate. Whether or not to accept Jesus as Savior is not the only challenge facing a Muslim. He must also weigh the cost to his family. Becoming a follower of Jesus could affect his marital status, his home, his family, his job, where he shops, where his kids go to school, etc.

Perhaps an even greater crisis for a Muslim convert is the threat to his heritage. A Muslim contemplating a decision to follow Isa will most likely ask himself, "Who am I among my forefathers to make a decision to change religions? By doing so, I am accusing my father, his father and all my ancestors of believing and propagating a lie."

Your Muslim friend has a lot to think about. For this reason, be patient with those who listen to your Camel presentation. They have a difficult journey ahead.

The Nicodemus Factor

Remember Nicodemus, the Jewish ruler who came to Jesus by night? Jesus did not turn him away. Instead, He met Nicodemus where He was and answered his questions, even though they were offered in secret.

Always respect a Muslim's need for confidentiality in meeting with you or another Christian. Be creative in establishing a safe

Kevin Greeson

place for a Muslim seeker to meet with you. Your job is to make yourself available to his needs and help him with creative ways to meet in privacy.

If you understand what is going on inside a Muslim seeker and the level of commitment needed, then you are ready to continue your Camel journey.

The *Korbani* Plan of Salvation

In order to share the plan of salvation with a Muslim in a manner that he will more readily understand, consider using the *Korbani* Plan of Salvation. The *Korbani* Plan uses natural bridges within the culture of every Muslim to introduce the New Testament message of salvation. Some Camel practitioners go straight into the *Korbani* Plan of Salvation from the initial Camel presentation. Yet for most, a waiting period follows the Camel Method to see if a person of peace will reveal himself. When a person of peace surfaces, you can easily transition from the Camel Method to the *Korbani* Plan of Salvation.

The word *korbani* (kor BAHN ee) comes from the word *korban* which has both Hebrew and Arabic roots. As a verb it means *to draw near*, but as a noun it means *a sacrifice*. For Jew and Arab alike, the connection was clear: the way for people to draw near to God was through a sacrifice.

Each year, Muslims observe a sacrifice called *Korbani-Eid* (also known as *Eid-al-Adha* or *Bakr-Eid*). *Eid* (eed) means feast or holy day. This special event is as important for Muslims as Christmas is for Christians.

The inspiration for using the Muslim *korban* as a bridge to the Gospel comes from the New Testament pattern of building redemptive bridges from Old Testament religious practices to New Testament truths.

In Acts 17:2, we see how Paul went to the synagogue and reasoned with the Jews from the Old Testament Scriptures. The author of the book of Hebrews followed a similar pattern of building bridges between the Old Testament sacrificial system and the final sacrifice offered by Jesus Christ when he wrote,

> The law is only a shadow of the good things that are coming—not the realities themselves. For this reason it can never, by the same sacrifices repeated endlessly year after year, make perfect those who draw near to worship. If it could, would they not have stopped being offered?
>
> For the worshipers would have been cleansed once for all, and would no longer have felt guilty for their sins. But those sacrifices are an annual reminder of sins, because it is impossible for the blood of bulls and goats to take away sins. Therefore, when Christ came into the world, he said: "Sacrifice and offering you did not desire, but a body you prepared for me; with burnt offerings and sin offerings you were not pleased." Then I said, "Here I am—it is written about me in the scroll—I have come to do your will, O God."
>
> First he said, "Sacrifices and offerings, burnt offerings and sin offerings you did not desire, nor were you pleased with them" (although the law required them to be made). Then he said, "Here I am, I have come to do your will." He sets aside the first to establish the second. And by that will, we have been made holy through the sacrifice of the body of Jesus Christ once for all (Hebrews 10:1-10 NIV).

In the same spirit, we can approach Muslims with a redemptive bridge between their sacrificial system and the final great sacrifice presented by God in Christ Jesus.

Throughout the Muslim world today the *korbani* practice is basically observed in the following way:

Kevin Greeson

- The father, or recognized head of the family, buys a sheep, goat or cow which is healthy and without any defects. They use the word *pure* to describe the condition of the animal.

- The animal is brought home and tied up in the yard, where it is well fed.

- On the morning of *Korbani-Eid*, family members dress in their finest clothes. Male members gather around the animal. They place their hands on the animal as a local hired expert prepares to slit the animal's throat with a knife.

- In the father's possession is a piece of paper with the names of relatives or individuals close to the family. Before the animal is killed, the father reads out loud the names on the paper. The *korban* is intended to atone for the names on the paper as well as those placing their hands on the animal.

- After the father says a prayer, the animal's throat is cut and he dies. The *korban* is now complete. Meat is divided up among family, friends and poor people in the community.

- Some Muslims will untie the animal before the throat is cut. This symbolizes the willingness of the animal to be used as a sacrifice.

This is the backdrop to the *Korbani* Plan of Salvation. This ritual will serve as our bridge for relating God's plan of salvation to them.

Introducing Allah's Perfect Plan

Transition into the *Korbani* Plan of Salvation by referring to the act of *korban* and to *al-Imran* 3:54-55.

> And they planned and Allah (also) planned, and Allah is the best of planners. And when Allah said: "O Isa, I am going to terminate the period of your stay (on earth)

and cause you to ascend unto Me and purify you of those who disbelieve and make those who follow you above those who disbelieve to the day of resurrection; then to Me shall be your return, so I will decide between you concerning that in which you differed" (*surah al-Imran* 3:54-55).

Ask, "How do Muslims practice the act of *korban*?" Allow him time to tell you how they practice *korban*. Then say, "In *surah al-Imran ayyah* 54, we see that they (the Jews) had a plan to kill Isa and that Allah had a plan to cause Isa to die. *Ayyah* 55 clarifies Allah's plan to cause Isa to die. Of course, Allah is the best of planners. How was causing Isa to die a part of Allah's plan?"[1]

At this point, ask your Muslim friend if you can share what you have come to understand about why it was in Allah's plan to cause Isa to die.

You will use four points to guide them.

The four points to the *Korbani* Plan of Salvation:

Point 1: The First Great *Korban*
Point 2: The Second Great *Korban*
Point 3: Allah's *Korban* for Us
Point 4: Receive Allah's *Korban* for You

Point #1: The First Great *Korban*

After Adam sinned and was removed from Allah's presence, the tradition of *korban* was begun. The first *korban* occurred when Allah killed an animal to provide clothing for Adam and his wife to cover their shame and nakedness. This meant that an animal had to die in order to cover their sinfulness. This act of *korban* was an example or a picture for us. Through *korban*, God is teaching us that anyone who commits a sin against God has committed a serious offense. Sin produces guilt, shame, death and a break in relationship with Allah. The guilty person can no longer remain in the presence of holy Allah and must be punished.

The first *korban* clearly shows that instead of the guilty person receiving the punishment, an innocent animal sacrifice was substituted. In Allah's mercy, he transferred the guilty person's punishment to one who was innocent. In this way, Allah demonstrated both His mercy and His justice.

Point #2: The Second Great *Korban*

Now relate the familiar story of the second *korban*. One day, Allah directed Ibrahim to take his blessed son[2] to the mountain. He was instructed to use his own son for the *korban*. Ibrahim obeyed Allah's instructions.

Once they were on the mountain of sacrifice, Ibrahim's son asked his father, "Where is the animal to be sacrificed?" Ibrahim answered, "Allah himself will provide the animal for the sacrifice." (see Genesis 22:7-8) At the last moment, just before Ibrahim would have killed his son, Allah stopped him and provided a ram for the sacrifice.

This story helps us better understand the significance of Allah's *korbani* system. Allah tested Ibrahim's love for Him, and Ibrahim passed the test by showing Allah how much he loved Him. A father who is willing to sacrifice his own son is revealing enormous faith and love, and yet, a love of equal value is a son who is willing to be sacrificed.

Point #3: Allah's *Korban* for Us

Since Allah is 100 percent holy nothing unholy can come into His presence. In order to restore mankind's relationship with Allah, all of our sins must be completely removed. The *korbani* system is a picture revealed by God to teach us the penalty for our sins and how they might be transferred to one who is innocent. Only when our sins are transferred to another are they removed from us, and we once again become like Adam in the garden, holy and in relationship with God. With our penalty satisfied and our sins transferred to another, we are free to join Allah in heaven after we die. The full truth of this wonderful gift from Allah is fully revealed in the *earlier Scriptures* (i.e. the Bible).

Surah al-Imran 3:54-55 tells us that Allah was the best of planners and that He Himself would cause Isa to die. The *Injil* tells us the rest of the story. It reveals that Allah's *korban* of Isa would cover the sins of all people. To accomplish this, Allah would provide the most holy, innocent and righteous sacrifice possible. In *al-Imran* 3:45-49, we see that in the entire world, Isa, the child of the virgin, who came from heaven and returned to heaven, is the only one who fits this description.

Allah chose Isa for the *korban*. This was Allah's plan from the beginning. The prophet *Yahya* (John the Baptist) said when he first saw Isa, "Behold! The *Lamb* of God who takes away the sin of the world" (John 1:29 NKJV)! Allah transferred our sins to Isa who then paid for our sins with the sacrifice of His own life for us.

The disciples of Isa knew this plan. The *Injil* states what they understood, "For as by one man's [Adam's] disobedience many were made sinners, so also by one Man's [Isa's] obedience many will be made righteous" (Romans 5:19 NKJV). After Isa was killed and ascended to heaven, the disciples of Isa stopped the practice of *korban*. Still to this day, the followers of Isa do not practice *korban* because they fully understand Allah's plan that the *korban* of Isa al-Masih was the last, greatest and final *korban*.

Allah's reason for doing *korban* for mankind is simple: He loves us. What Allah did not allow Ibrahim to do to his son, Allah did to Isa, His Son by the Holy Spirit. Isa, who had no earthly father and knew only Allah as His Father, became Allah's *korban* for you and for me. Offering His own Son as a sacrifice reveals Allah's great love for us. *Allahu Akbar* (God is great)!

An animal that is to be sacrificed for *korban* is unaware of what is about to happen to it. But what if the innocent sacrifice knows what is about to happen to it and yet goes through with the sacrifice? The *Injil* says, "Greater love has no one than this, than to lay down his life for his friends" (John 15:13 NKJV).

Isa knew that He was to be used for Allah's *korban* and yet He willingly submitted Himself to it. The *Injil* records Isa's words, "No one takes it from Me, but I lay it down of Myself. I have power to lay it down, and I have power to take it again. This command I have received from My Father" (John 10:18 NKJV).

Recall that when a Muslim practices *korban* he keeps a list of relatives' and friends' names in his pocket. When Allah performed His *korban*, He had the name of every person, past, present and future on His list. *Your name was on His list.* Allah sacrificed Isa, His *korban*, for you.

Point #4: Receive Allah's *Korban* for You

You can do nothing to cleanse yourself from your sin, but Allah can and already has done that for you. All those who receive Allah's gift and believe in Him will gain entrance into heaven when they die.

Receive Allah's gift, His perfect and final *korban* for you. Give thanks to Isa for allowing Himself to be used for Allah's *korban*. Isa willingly took your punishment on Himself.

Would you commit to pray to Allah? You can pray a prayer from your heart like this:

> O Allah, I confess to You that I am a sinner and that I deserve to be forever separated from You when I die. I thank You for demonstrating Your love and mercy by doing *korban* for me. I thank Isa for taking my sin upon Himself along with my punishment. I believe that it is through Isa that I am able to be forgiven of my sins and come to live with You in heaven when I die.

Now that you've read the *Korbani* Plan of Salvation, go

back through it again and familiarize yourself with its four key points. Then find a partner and practice going through the plan, sharing with your partner as you would with a Muslim friend or acquaintance.

Your Second Destination: God's Word

As we have already noted, it is rare for a Muslim to make a decision for Christ the first time he hears the Gospel. In South Asia, it typically takes anywhere from three weeks to six months for a Muslim to come to faith after first hearing God's plan of salvation. So what can you do in the meantime that will increase your Muslim friend's prospects for accepting the Gospel?

If you can leave your Muslim friend reading the Bible or New Testament, you have reached another significant destination. The Word of God is powerful:

> For as the rain comes down, and the snow from heaven,
> And do not return there,
> But water the earth,
> And make it bring forth and bud,
> That it may give seed to the sower
> And bread to the eater,
> So shall My word be that goes forth from My mouth;
> It shall not return to Me void,
> But it shall accomplish what I please,
> And it shall prosper *in the thing* for which I sent it.
> (Isaiah 55:10-11 NKJV)

If your Muslim friend receives a copy of God's Word and begins to read it, you have a reason to celebrate. God's Word will continue to accomplish the purposes for which He sent it, even in your absence.

A good way to bridge into this destination is to return to the Camel passage, *surah al-Imran* 3:50. Point to the verse where the Qur'an says that the duty of Muslims to Allah is *to obey Isa.*

[Isa says:] And I come confirming that which was before me of the Torah and to make lawful some of that which was forbidden to you. I come unto you with a sign from your Lord, *so keep your duty to Allah and obey me* (*Surah al-Imran* 3:50) [italics added].

Of course it is impossible to obey someone if you are not familiar with his commands. In order to know Isa's commands, we have to read the *Injil*. Ask your friend, "Since the Qur'an commands you to obey Isa, how can you do it if you do not know what He said?"

In order for a Muslim to know what Isa commanded, he must read the *Injil*. Open the New Testament to the Sermon on the Mount in Matthew 5-7. From these chapters, you can show your Muslim friend what the Qur'an was talking about. Tell him that *ayyah* 50 is correct when it says that Isa brought about change to some of the Old Testament laws.

You might show him, for example, an old law that he will recognize: "An eye for an eye and a tooth for a tooth." Then you can point out how Isa instituted a new law when He said: "If someone hits you on your right cheek, turn to him your other cheek" (Matthew 5:38-39 NKJV). Another old law he may recognize is: "Love your neighbor and hate your enemy." Isa's new law says you should "...love your enemies, bless those who curse you, do good to those who hate you, and pray for those who spitefully use you and persecute you" (Matthew 5:43-44 NKJV).

If we are to do our duty to Allah by obeying the commands of Isa, then we must read the *Injil* in order to know these commands.

Anticipate and Prepare

Just as we were able to anticipate the responses a Muslim would give to your Camel presentation, we can likewise prepare for the objections he may have to receiving the Word of God.

For example, you might expect him to say to you, "We do not accept your Bible. You Christians have changed and corrupted it." If you ask him, "*Who* changed it and *when* was it changed?" his answer will be, "I don't know." Try all you want to convince him that the Bible has not been changed or corrupted; in the end it will be your word against his.

You can avoid the stalemate by once again calling upon that unexpected ally, the Qur'an. The Qur'an has many *ayyat* that confirm the Bible and its trustworthiness. As Christians, we do not need the Qur'an to confirm the Bible, but for a Muslim who submits to the Qur'an's authority it will have a powerful effect for him to see that the Qur'an actually encourages him to read and believe the Bible. Camel practitioners who have used the Qur'an in this manner have had great success.

Here are some ways to bridge Muslims to the Bible and some Qur'anic verses that will be your allies. Start by asking your friend, "If a Muslim ever has doubts or questions about Allah's revelation to mankind, where does the Qur'an tell him to go to get the answer?"

The answer you can guide him to is *the same place that Allah told Mohammed to go*. Then show him *surah* Jonah 10:94. Here Allah tells Mohammed that if he has any doubts about what has been told to him, he should consult those who read the "Scripture that was before you" (i.e. the Bible):

> And if you (Mohammed) are in doubt concerning that which we reveal unto you, then question those who read the Scripture (that was) before you. Verily the Truth from the Lord hath come unto you. So be not of the waverers (*Surah* Jonah 10:94).

Then you can point out to your friend that the Qur'an promises guidance, light and blessings to those who read the *Taurat* and the *Injil* (i.e. the Old and New Testaments). Ask him to read *surah* The Dinner Table 5:46 and 66:

Kevin Greeson

And We sent after them in their footsteps Isa, son of
Maryam, verifying what was before him of the Taurat
and We gave him the *Injil* in which was *guidance and
light*, and verifying what was before it of Taurat and a
guidance and an admonition for those who guard (against
evil) (*Surah* The Dinner Table 5:46).

If only they would uphold the Torah and the Gospel, and
what is sent down to them herein from their Lord, they
would be showered with *blessings* from above them and
from beneath their feet (*Surah* The Dinner Table 5:66a,
Rashad Khalifa, transl.) [italics added for emphasis].

After reading this passage, ask your friend, "What will happen
to those who observe the *Taurat* (Torah) and the *Injil* (Gospel)"?
The answer is, "…they will be showered with blessings."

At some point your Muslim friend will probably object to
reading the Bible by saying that it has been changed or corrupted.
The Qur'an does not say this though. In fact, the Qur'an affirms
the reliability of the "Before Scriptures" (i.e. the Bible). Ask your
friend to read *surah Cattle* 6:115:

Perfected is the Word of the Lord in truth and justice.
There is nothing that can change His words. He is the
Hearer, the Knower (*Surah Cattle* 6:115).

Now you can ask him: "When you say that Allah's words have
been changed, what are you saying about Allah? Is He too weak
to protect His words?" If this does not bring your Muslim friend
to accept a Bible, just wait. Be patient and allow the Holy Spirit
time to do His work of conviction.

Handing a Bible to a Muslim
Do you remember the first time you touched a Qur'an, how

Camel Destinations   123 it felt awkward in your hand? Perhaps someone challenged you to read it, and it made you feel uncomfortable. This is the same feeling a Muslim will have when he touches a Bible.

You will find it easier for a Muslim to receive the Bible if you give him a version that does not look *foreign* to him. So be prepared to give him a contextualized version of the Bible for Muslim readers. He will find the cover design appealing and inviting. It should be in his heart language with familiar Arabic names for the key terms and persons in the Bible. Several Bible publishers now offer a version of the Bible that is attractive for Muslims.[3]

Your Final Destination: A Church-Planting Movement

There are 1.3 billion lost Muslims in the world, so being satisfied with leading a single Muslim to salvation is dangerous, dangerous for the rest of the Muslim world. Each Muslim convert has the potential to lead hundreds of fellow Muslims to faith in Jesus Christ resulting in dozens of new churches.

No doubt, leading a Muslim to accept Jesus as Lord and Savior is one of the greatest joys a Christian can experience. But if you rest in that joy, you will fall short of the most important destination. We must find, disciple, and guide Muslim persons of peace to become catalysts for multiplying new churches within their own communities.

In the Muslim church-planting movements we witnessed in South Asia, each believer who became a follower of Isa had the potential of leading his entire circle of influence, up to 200 fellow Muslims, to faith in Christ. We are beginning now to see a common pattern among the thousands of new believers. One out of one hundred may prove to be a catalyst who will lead 200 other Muslims to saving faith in Christ over the next two to three years.

We cannot grasp all the ways God is at work, but it appears that He already has a chosen few waiting in lost communities for

His touch of salvation and His command to go! God has saved these persons to lead movements that will sweep through their communities. When we find such persons, we must pour into them discipleship that will launch them into their God-given vocation of leading a church-planting movement.

Imagine the joy of reaching this final destination. Imagine leading a new Muslim-background believer to facilitate a massive church-planting movement among the Muslims in his community. This joy must have been part of what the disciples expressed when they returned from their L10 adventure (Luke 10:17). They knew that they had tapped into something that was bigger than anything they could have dreamed. They had a hand in the destruction of Satan's kingdom. The next Muslim you lead to Christ just might be the one to launch a church-planting movement (CPM).

What is a church-planting movement? Church-planting movements are *rapidly multiplying indigenous churches planting churches that sweep across a people group or population segment.*[4]

There are some distinct characteristics to these movements; they are:

- Rapidly Reproducing

- Multiplying

- Indigenous

- Churches Planting Churches

Let's look closer at each of these elements.

Rapidly Reproducing

Rather than waiting years to mature before sharing their faith, in church-planting movements new believers feel an urgency to spread the message of the Gospel with their lost family and friends.

When they learn how to form house churches that can be easily reproduced, it is only natural that these new churches, or *Isa jamaats*, spread rapidly through their communities. Only rapidly reproducing churches hold forth the possibility of reaching a world of 1.3 billion lost Muslims.

Multiplying

Church-planting movements multiply churches and new life in Christ, much like the new cells that exponentially multiply within a newborn infant. One church starts two churches, those two churches start four, the four start eight, and so on. As this process unfolds, the movement goes beyond the control of those who helped start it; the movement becomes explosive!

Indigenous

In church-planting movements, the churches *fit* into the culture and are easily reproduced by the new believers. They do not look like foreign churches. If we want to see a church-planting movement, then we should encourage and help to start the kinds of churches that fit into the Islamic culture and can quickly become indigenously reproduced. These churches may not look like our Western-style churches, but they will multiply new believers in Christ and new discipleship communities of faith.

Churches Planting Churches

As the movement builds momentum, new churches will no longer be planted by outsiders, but by the local churches themselves. If new churches are *not* being started by churches, then there is something wrong. New believers who truly believe that Isa is Good News will share their faith. Indigenous house churches have an almost infinite capacity for reproduction within a community.

Understanding church-planting movements can help inform and guide our strategies toward that goal. If we attempt shortcuts, such as assimilating new believers into our Western churches rather than helping them start their own indigenous churches, we may derail the movement. Each step we take toward a church-planting movement offers hope of salvation to the world's 1.3 billion lost Muslims.

So, never be satisfied with a single new Muslim-background believer. Any Muslim drawing near to belief in Jesus Christ as the one and only Savior must be viewed as the first member of a new Muslim-background church. Then, do not satisfy yourself with one new Muslim-background church. The new *Isa jamaats* must be filled with a passion to reproduce and multiply into a movement.

A survey of church-planting movements around the world has revealed that there was typically an outsider behind the scenes who had a passion for the lost and for church planting. The outsider had a vision beyond winning a single lost person to faith in Christ, a vision for seeing an entire people come to Christ.

Where do you stand? What destination are you willing to settle for? The fate of millions of lost Muslim souls may depend on your answer.

Using the Camel Method you have shared the plan of salvation with a Muslim or group of Muslims and inspired them to read the Bible for the first time. Perhaps, by God's grace, you will see Muslims come to faith in Christ and start their own *Isa jamaat*. Perhaps God already has chosen one of them to be a CPM catalyst consumed with a passion to see *Jesus groups* multiply exponentially throughout the Muslim community.

---

[1]The use of the phrase, "Allah's plan to cause Isa to die" may seem awkward for Christians. The purpose of using the phrase in this presentation is to remain aligned with *al-Imran* 3:54-55. One could argue that this phrase is accurate based on such verses as Isaiah 53:10 which says, "Yet it pleased the Lord to bruise Him; He has put Him to grief. When You make His soul an offering for sin" (NKJV). You will see as the *Korbani* Plan of Salvation unfolds, that Jesus willingly offered Himself to be sacrificed.

[2]This is not the time to argue about which son was taken by Ibrahim to the mountain for the sacrifice. The story of Ibrahim attempting to sacrifice his son is found in the Qur'an, *surah as-Saffat Ruku* 37:100-111. Note that this passage in the Qur'an does not mention which son was taken for the sacrifice. There are other passages in the Qur'an that strongly suggest that it was Isaac, even though conventional Muslim teaching is that the son was Ishmael.

[3]You can purchase a contextualized Arabic language Bible called the *Kitab al-Sharif* from Good News for the Crescent World at: http://www.gnfcw.com/. To obtain a contextualized Bible from the Bible Society, make personal contact with foreign languages division of the American Bible Societies at 1-800-32-BIBLE or World Bible Translation Center at 1-888-542-4253. Explain that you are looking for a contextualized or *Musulmani* version of the Bible or New Testament in the language of the Muslims in your community (Arabic, Turkish, Farsi, Urdu).

[4]For a fuller treatment of church-planting movements see David Garrison, *Church Planting Movements, how God is redeeming a lost world* (Midlothian: WIGTake Resources, 2004) available from Fresh Wind Distributing at www.FreshWindDistributing.com.

Kevin Greeson

Chapter Nine

Crossing Bridges and Barriers

O NCE YOU BECOME comfortable with the basic Camel Method and the *Korbani* Plan of Salvation, you might try moving on to a more advanced level. The advanced Camel Method allows you to go deeper with your Muslim friends. Recognizing that most Muslims do not come to faith right away, it anticipates the questions they will raise and shows you how to respond. As the advanced Camel digs deeper into the Qur'an it offers you a number of additional bridges to the faith and overcomes barriers your Muslim friend is likely to face.

When you use the advanced Camel Method with groups of Muslims, they will probably not give you time to present everything in this chapter. So pick and choose which portions you want to emphasize. Once again, we want to avoid arguments and keep our focus on the main goal of lifting up Isa by pointing to His holiness, power and ability to lead us to heaven.

We will start with more bridges found in the primary Camel text *surah al-Imran* 3:42-55, and then tackle some of the most common barriers that Muslims must overcome as they consider the Gospel. We will continue to use leading questions as bridges to help our Muslim friends cross over into the truth of the Gospel. Whenever a bridge appears, we will identify it with the word (*Bridge*) so you will be sure not to miss it! As you become more familiar with the advanced Camel Method, you will be amazed at how often these bridge questions come to mind as you share your faith with a Muslim friend.

I. Isa Is Holy

C

42 And when the angels said: O Maryam! Surely Allah has chosen you and purified you and **chosen** you above the women of the world.
43 O Maryam! keep to obedience to your Lord and humble yourself, and bow down with those who bow.
44 This is of the **announcements** relating to the unseen which We reveal to you; and you were not with them when they cast their pens (to decide)

A

which of them should have Maryam in his charge, and you were not with them when they contended one with another.
45 When the **angels** said: O Maryam, surely Allah gives you good news with a Word from Him (of one) whose name is the "Messiah," Isa son of Maryam, worthy of regard in this world and the hereafter and of those who are made near (to Allah).
46 And he shall speak to the people when in the cradle and when of old age, and (he shall be) one of the good ones.
47 She said: My Lord! when shall there be a son (born) to I me, and man has not touched me? He said: Even so, Allah creates what He pleases; when He has decreed a matter, He only says to it, Be, and it is.

Bridges to the Gospel

3:42-43 No need to linger on verses 42-44; they are only an introduction to verse 45.

3:44 Muslims generally explain this story as a reference to the Jewish leaders who gathered some bachelors in the synagogue and cast lots to determine which one would take Maryam as his wife. According to their tradition, the lots fell on Joseph.

3:45 (*Bridge*) Allah gave Maryam "his Word whose name is

the Messiah." This offers a valuable bridge. Besides Messiah (in Arabic, *masih*), Muslims have two other prominent names for Isa. He is referred to as *Kalimatullah* (kah lee mah TUU lah) which means the Word of Allah (*kalim* + Allah). He is also called *Ruhullah* (ruh HUU lah) or the Spirit of Allah (ruh + Allah). (*Bridge*) You can ask your Muslim friend "Do you recognize the names, *Isa-Kalimatullah* and *Isa-Ruhullah*?"

Point out that the Word and the Spirit of Allah are part of Allah Himself. Just as you cannot remove a person's breath or spirit without destroying that person, so too, Allah's breath and spirit are part of Him. (*Bridge*) You might ask him, "Do you know of any other prophet who was called the Word of Allah?"

Should he be unfamiliar with Isa's identity as the *Ruhullah* or Spirit of Allah, you can point him to *surah* 4 The Women *ayyah* 171:

> ...Speak the truth; the Messiah, Isa son of Maryam is only an apostle of Allah and His Word which he communicated to Maryam and *a spirit from him.*

Do not be alarmed that this passage was intended to diminish the divinity of Christ, by saying He was only an apostle; the Qur'an is not the Bible. What is useful as a bridge is the way Christ's divinity still shines through, as Isa is called a Spirit from Allah, a testimony to His divinity that is not shared by any other prophet in the Qur'an.

The Qur'an reiterates this point in *surah* 21 The Prophets verse 91:

> And remember her (Maryam) who guarded her chastity, so we *breathed* into her of our word and we made her and her son a sign for all peoples.

(*Bridge*) Ask your Muslim friend and he will admit that no other prophet is given the title *Ruhullah* or Spirit of Allah.

Your goal here is not to prove Christ's divinity through the Qur'an. The Qur'an is incapable of doing that; instead, you want to show that Isa's close association with Allah reveals Isa's unequalled holiness.

The Qur'an teaches, and most Muslims readily accept, that Isa *Kalimatullah* or Isa *Ruhullah* was sent directly from heaven by Allah as the child of the virgin Maryam.

Verse 45 concludes with the claim that Isa would be honored by all people in this world and forever in heaven (in the hereafter), and is one who is near to Allah. It is easy for Isa to be near Allah since He is Allah's *Kalimatullah* and *Ruhullah* (*word* and *breath*).

(**Bridge**) You can say, "The Qur'an is right when it says Isa is worthy of regard in this world and in the hereafter. I cannot think of any major religion (Christianity, Islam, Hinduism, Buddhism) that fails to give honor and respect to Isa. Isa is a sign and Messiah for the entire world."

3:46 Allah said that Isa would be among the righteous (literally, one of the good ones). *(Bridge)* Ask your friend, "Did Isa ever sin?" Most Muslims will agree that Isa never sinned.

(**Bridge**) Now ask these leading questions, allowing time between each question for your hearer to respond: "Did Isa ever marry or have sexual relations with a woman? Did He ever kill anyone? Did He ever accumulate wealth?"

In most Muslim cultures, these three qualities of chastity, non-violence and poverty are considered holy traits. Most Muslims will also realize that these three traits are in direct contrast to their prophet Mohammed.

3:47 Maryam was shocked by the news that Allah had given. How could she have a baby? No man had ever touched her. But Allah explained to her that He could do anything He wanted. All He has to do is say "Be!" and it is so.

Do not let yourself be distracted by this false Islamic teaching that Isa was created by Allah. The point you want to make is that

Allah *can do anything.* Your Muslim friend should agree with you on that point. If Allah is able to cause a virgin to conceive, then what is to prevent Allah from also taking on flesh and dwelling among us?

(**Bridge**) The Qur'an teaches that Maryam would give birth to Isa the Messiah even though she was a virgin. Ask, "Do you know any other prophet who did not have a father?" He may respond that Adam (whom Muslims list among the prophets) also did not have a father. *Surah al-Imran* 3:59 says that Isa is like Adam, and this is true, because both men did not have an earthly father.

Adam and Isa share something else in common. Before Adam disobeyed God in the garden, he was sinless and walked in fellowship with Allah. Adam could live and walk with Allah because he did not have any sin. Though he began his life in righteous and holy fellowship with Allah in the garden, once Adam sinned, he and all of his descendants became unholy and could no longer live in fellowship Allah. The curse of sin and death took hold of Adam and all of his descendents.

If your Muslim friend does not remember what the Qur'an says about this, you can direct him to *surah Ta Ha* 20:121:

> Then they (Adam and his wife) both ate of it, so their evil inclinations became manifest to them, and they both began to cover themselves with leaves of the garden, and Adam disobeyed his Lord, so his life became evil.

(**Bridge**) Ask, "How many sins did it take for Adam to be removed from Allah's presence and from the garden?" This question is important because Islam is a works-based religion. To Muslims, good deeds cancel out bad deeds. If a person does enough good deeds, he can eventually earn his way to heaven. Remind your Muslim friend that it took only one sin for Adam to be removed from Allah's presence. The descendants of Adam are just like Adam. An apple tree only produces apples, it will never produce oranges. In the same way, Adam's descendants always turn out exactly like him, sinful.

(*Bridge*) How can sinful people like us ever hope to be with a holy God like Allah? With the virgin birth of Isa, Allah was beginning again with a new Adam. Like the first Adam, Isa had no earthly father. The Qur'an even makes the point (in 3:42) that Isa's mother, Maryam, was purified before giving birth to Isa, so that she would be a holy vessel for the birth of the Messiah. But unlike Adam, *Isa never sinned.* He remained holy, just as Allah is holy.

Clearly this is the reason that Allah did not allow Isa to have an earthly father. Allah's plan was for Isa to be a holy Messiah. Isa did not inherit Adam's curse of sinfulness, and unlike Adam, Isa lived a sinless life of holy perfection.

(*Bridge*): "Since we are all sons of Adam and sinners like him, who is powerful enough to save us from our sinful condition?" Ask your friend to read *surah al-Imran* 3:48-49.

II. Isa Has Power over Death

M

48 And He will teach him the Book and the wisdom and the Taurat and the Injil.

49 And (make him) an apostle to the children of Israel: That I have come to you with a sign from your Lord, that I determine for you out of dust like the form of a bird, then I breathe into it and it becomes a bird with Allah's permission and I **heal** the blind and the leprous, and **bring the dead to life** with Allah's permission and I inform you of what you should eat and what you should store in your houses; most surely there is a sign in this for you, if you are believers.

Bridges to the Gospel

3:48 This *ayyah* tells us that Allah taught Isa from the *Taurat*, the *Zabur* and the *Injil*, the books that make up our Bible today. If Allah thought it was important enough to teach Isa, don't you

Kevin Greeson

think it might be important for us to know as well?

(*Bridge*) You might ask your friend if he has a copy of these "earlier Scriptures", and offer to discuss them with him further. With all your friend has now heard about Isa, he will want to hear from you that the *Injil* is where he can learn more stories of the miraculous power of Isa. ·

3:49 Allah demonstrated His power through Isa. The Qur'an says that Isa made a live bird from a lump of clay, the lepers and the lame were healed, the blind received their sight, and even the dead were raised to life again.

The Gospel of Thomas

This first miracle of Isa mentioned in verse 49 is one that Mohammed learned from a book called The Gospel of Thomas. If you take the time to explain to your Muslim friend why we do not accept this book, you just might miss a useful bridge to the truth. Verse 49 says Isa breathed life into dust and it became a bird; do not let this slip by without making a quick observation.

(*Bridge)* You might say, "Isn't it interesting that this story says Isa created life out of the dust by breathing life into it? How did Allah create man?" Your Muslim friend may recall that Allah formed man from the dust of the earth and then breathed His life into man. "According to the Qur'an," you can say, "Isa was able to do the same thing by breathing life into birds made of dust. Isa had the power to create life." Then follow with, "Do you know of any other prophets who had this power to create life?"

(*Bridge*) Ask, "What is man's greatest enemy?" The answer is death! Take the opportunity to drive home the fact that Isa has power over our greatest enemy. No man has ever overcome the power of death – but Isa did! Say, "Once again, this passage in the Qur'an gives us great hope. Isa had the power to raise the dead back to life. Isa has power over death! This is amazing. The world has been waiting for one who can demonstrate power over our greatest enemy--death!"

(*Bridge*): "Do you know of any other prophet who was given

the power that Isa had?"

III. Isa Knows the Way to Heaven

50 And a verifier of that which is before me of the Taurat and that I may allow you part of that which has been forbidden to you, and I have come to you with a sign from your Lord therefore be careful of (your duty to) Allah and obey me.
51 Surely Allah is my Lord and your Lord, therefore serve Him; this is the right path.
52 But when Isa perceived unbelief on their part, he said "Who will be my helpers in Allah's way?" The disciples said: We are helpers (in the way) of Allah: We believe in Allah and bear witness that we are submitting ones (literally in Arabic, "muslims").
53 Our Lord! we believe in what Thou hast revealed and we follow the apostle, so write us down with those who bear witness.
54 And they planned and Allah (also) planned, and Allah is the best of planners.

EL

55 And when Allah said: O Isa, I am going **to terminate the period of your stay (on earth)** and **cause you to ascend unto Me** and purify you of those who disbelieve and make those who follow you above those who disbelieve to the day of resurrection; **then to Me shall be your return**, so I will decide between you concerning that in which you differed.

Bridges to the Gospel

3:50 *Ayyah* 50 offers many helpful bridges. Isa said that His life verified or fulfilled what the prophets had spoken of concerning Him in the "the earlier Scriptures" (i.e. the books of the Bible written before the Qur'an). (*Bridge*) Ask, "What did Isa verify and what things that were forbidden did Isa made allowable?" The point here is not to make a list of things that Isa make allowable, but to gently lead your friend to see that he must read the *Injil*,

Kevin Greeson

the New Testament, in order to know these things. Once your Muslim friend finishes with his attempt to answer your question, tell what you have found in the Before Books.

Say, "When I read the Before Books, the *Taurat* and *Zabur*, I found over 300 prophecies about Isa spoken by the prophets. For example, I found one *ayyah* that was written over 700 years before the birth of Isa which says:

> Therefore the Lord himself will give you a sign: The virgin will be with child and will give birth to a son, and will call him Immanuel (Isaiah 7:14 NKJV).

Explain to him that in the Hebrew language, the name Immanuel means God with us. In this way, you are continuing to sow in him the truth that Isa and Allah are one.

(**Bridge**) Finally, this *ayyah* closes with the Qur'an warning us to be careful to obey the commands of Isa. Yet in order for us to obey Isa's commands, we must know what His commands are. We must read the *Injil* to learn those commands.

3:51 Other English translations refer to the straight path instead of a right path. You can tell your friend, "There is only one straight path to Allah. Isa knew that straight path because He traveled it." Isa came straight from Allah in heaven and returned straight to Allah.

3:52-53 In *ayyah* 52, Isa seeks someone to assist Him in turning unbelievers to faith. A small group of men called the disciples came forward and said that they would help Isa. According to the Qur'an, these disciples of Isa were *muslims* (submitted to God's will) because they would turn the unbelieving to faith in God. In addition, these disciples said that they believed in Allah's message and the messenger (Isa) that He sent down (note that most, but not all, translations say "that He sent down"). Down from where? Obviously, Isa was sent down from heaven.

The followers of Isa are called *muslims*. Use this opportunity to build a bridge. (**Bridge**) Say, "Isn't it interesting that according to the Qur'an those who submitted to Allah's will as disciples of Isa were called muslims?"

3:54 Most Muslims see in this verse a reference to the Jews as those who planned to kill Isa. Point out that Allah also had a plan and that He is the best of planners. Allah's ways are not our ways. His plans are far superior to any plan we could devise. Before the creation of this world, Allah had a plan. Nothing happens by chance.

3:55 (*Bridge*) What was Allah's plan? Verse 55 reveals Allah's plan and presents one of the most important and challenging passages for Muslims in the entire Qur'an. According to *ayyah* 55, it was Allah's plan *to cause Isa to die*. Many Muslims will try to gloss over this point, even denying that Jesus died on the cross. But the Arabic word used in the Qur'an here is unmistakeable, *mutawaffika* – "to cause to die". It was Allah's plan to cause Isa to die. Be sure to have your Muslim friend read *ayyah* 55 twice, first in Arabic then in the local language.

Phonetically in Arabic, *ayyah* 55 reads:

> Iz qa_lalla_hu ya_ 'isa_ inni **mutawaffika** wa ra_fi'uka ilayya wa mutahhiruka minal lazina kafaru_ wa ja_'ilul lazinattaba'u_ka fauqal lazina kafaru_ ila_ yaumil qiya_ mah(ti), summa ilayya marji'ukum fa ahkumu bainakum fima_ kuntum fihi takhtalifu[1]

When you hear your friend pronounce the word *mutawaffika* ask him to stop and discuss this word. (*Bridge*) Ask him, "What does the Arabic word, *mutawaffika* mean?" He may answer that he does not know. If not, you can explain it to him. If he does know Arabic, he should answer, "The word means 'to die', 'to cause to die,' or 'to kill.'" Allah goes on to say I will "...cause you to ascend unto me". (*Bridge*) Capture this truth by asking, "Does *ayyah* 55 say that Allah would cause Isa to die and then raise Him to Himself?" We will look more closely at the significance of this word further as we explore Barrier #2 below.

Let's turn our attention now to the barriers that will exist in the mind of your Muslim friend. If he does not raise these objections right away, he will be thinking them. So let's go ahead and prepare for them.

Barrier #1: You Cannot Trust the Bible

It is common for Muslims today to say that the Bible has been corrupted and cannot be trusted. This argument is largely an invention of *mullahs* and *imams* who use it to retain their control over the Muslims who follow them. They know that if Muslims ever accept the truth of the Bible, it will shatter their control. By contrast, the Qur'an often speaks positively of the Bible and denies that it can ever be corrupted.

You can demonstrate the trustworthiness of the Bible by using the example of Mohammed himself as a bridge. You might ask, "When Mohammed was alive in this world did he ever say that the Bible had been changed or corrupted?"

The answer is, "No," but some Muslims may refer you to *Surah al-Imran* 3:78.

> And verily, among them is a party who distort the Book with their tongues: (As they read) you would think it is part of the Book, but it is no part of the Book; and they say, 'That is from God,' but it is not from God: It is they who tell a lie against God, and (well) they know it! (Hilahi-Khan trans.)

This *ayyah* mentions a group, most likely referring to a local Jewish party, who twisted the meaning of the Scriptures. Be sure to point out that the *ayyah* does not say that this group was able to change the *written* Scriptures, only their spoken interpretations of the Book were distorted.

In *surah* Jonah 10:94 Allah Himself commends to Mohammed the counsel of those who "read the previous scripture (i.e. the

Bible)" if he has any doubts:

> If you have any doubt regarding what is revealed to you from your Lord, then ask those who read the previous scripture. Indeed, the truth has come to you from your Lord. Do not be with the doubters.

Muslims should also know that the Qur'an states that the Bible cannot be changed. *Surah An-'aam* (in English "Cattle") 6:115 declares:

> Perfected is the Word of the Lord in truth and justice. There is nothing that can change His words. He is the Hearer, the Knower.

You can build an overcoming bridge with your Muslim friend by pointing out, "Despite what others may have told you, you and I can agree with the Qur'an's statement that the Word of the Lord is perfect and nothing can change His Words." After all, who is strong enough to overcome Allah and change His Words?

Finally, in *Surah* 4 *Nisaaa* (in English "Women") *ayyah* 136, Allah admonishes all Muslims not to wander from "the Scriptures which He revealed aforetime (i.e. the Bible)" saying:

> O you who believe! Believe in Allah and His messenger and the Scripture which He has revealed unto His messenger, and the Scripture which He revealed aforetime. Whosoever disbelieves in Allah and His angels and His Scriptures and His messengers and the Last day, he verily has wandered far astray.

This passage goes so far as to say that anyone who disbelieves the Scriptures (i.e. the Bible) has surely wandered far astray.

Barrier #2: Jesus Did Not Really Die

Muslims commonly believe that Jesus did not die on the cross. They have been taught that somehow God blinded those who tried to crucify Jesus and put someone else in his place who looked like Jesus. It is critical that we do our best to answer this objection because the fact that Jesus died is at the very core of the Gospel. It is important to note that the Qur'an does not state that Isa did not die! Here is the actual passage in the Qur'an that Muslims use to prove Jesus did not die.

> And because of their [the people of the Scripture – Jews] saying: "We slew the Messiah Jesus, the son of Maryam, Allah's messenger" – They slew him not nor crucified, but it appeared so unto them; Lo! Those who disagree concerning it are in doubt thereof; they have no knowledge thereof except pursuit of a conjecture; they slew him not for certain (*surah Women* 4:157).

Point out that this passage does not say that Isa did not die. It only says that the Jews did not kill Him. The *Injil* agrees! The Jews did not crucify Jesus. They did not have the authority to crucify Him. They were under Roman occupation and Roman authority. They could have killed Him, but not legally. They had to turn Jesus over to the Romans and hope that the Romans would crucify Jesus for them. And the Romans, not the Jews, did crucify Him. The next verse in the Qur'an (*surah* Women 4:158) states that Allah took Jesus up to Himself. The *Injil* agrees, but goes on to explain that Jesus was resurrected after He died.

You can also return to *Surah al-Imran* 3:55 which uses the Arabic word *mutawaffika* "to cause to die" in relation to Jesus. If your friend has the Arabic Qur'an, ask him to read verse 55. Phonetically, it should sound something like this: "Iz qa_lalla_hu ya_ Isa_ inni mutawaffika...." The key word is *mutawaffika*[2]; which means *Allah caused Isa to die*.

To have Muslims confess that Isa died is significant. Two more *ayyat* from the Qur'an that also testify to Isa's death are:

> And Muhammad is but a messenger. Verily all Messengers have passed away before him (*surah al-Imran* 3:144a, Maulvi Sher Ali's translation).

> So peace is on me the day I (Isa) was born, the day that I die, and the day that I shall be raised up to life (again) (*surah* Maryam 19:33, Abdullah Yusuf Ali translation).

Finally, you can point out that the primary Qur'anic text that Muslims use to question the death of Isa is *surah* Women 4:157 which also says, "those who disagree [concerning Isa's death] are in doubt thereof". At best 4:157 is unclear as to whether Isa died, while other passages (*surah al-Imran* 3:55, 3:144a, *surah* Maryam 19:33) all seem to indicate that He did.

Remind your friend what Allah said to Mohammed in *surah* Jonah 10:94: "If you are in doubt concerning that which We reveal unto you question those who read the Scripture that was before."

If a Muslim doubts or does not understand that Isa died, he should "question those who read the Scripture that was before." Those of us who read the Scripture that was before can tell them: Isa died!

Barrier #3: Isa Was Not the Son of God

When Christians say that Jesus is the Son of God, Muslims have been conditioned to misunderstand this title. They have been taught that the title Son of God means Allah had physical relations with Maryam. To them, this is an evil insult against Allah. If this issue is raised, you can assure them that Christians are in agreement with them that Allah never had physical relations with Mary.

At this point, the Qur'an will only be of limited help. The Qur'an clearly says that God has no son and that Jesus is nothing

The Camel

more than a prophet. *Surah* Cattle 6:101, *surah* Children of Israel 17:111 and *surah* The Pilgrimage 23:91 are examples of many verses in the Qur'an that say the same thing. But we have already said that a Muslim will not come to saving faith in Jesus through the Qur'an. So if a Muslim insists on clinging to the Qur'an, he will never be saved, because he will never understand that Jesus is the Son of God who died for his sins.

However, you can remind him of what the Qur'an did say about Isa, calling Him the Messiah, the Word of Allah and the Spirit of Allah:

> We breathed into her (Mary) of our Spirit and made her and her son a token (sign) for all peoples" (*surah* The Prophets 21:91).

> O Mary! Lo! Allah gives you glad tidings of a word from Him whose name is the Messiah, Jesus" (*surah al-Imran* 3:45).

Show him that these two verses in the Qur'an (*surah* 21:91 and 3:45) actually affirm what the *Injil* says about Jesus.

Next, pose this question: The first day a Muslim boy goes to school what two questions is he asked? The answer is: "What is your name and what is your father's name?" Now ask, "If Isa went to school the first day, how would He answer these two questions?" He would surely answer the first question by saying, "My name is Isa." But how would He answer the second questions? Of course, the only answer He can give is that God is His Father. Your Muslim friend may have difficulty admitting this point, but he will certainly be thinking it.

Then explain to him what the *Injil* (New Testament) teaches about Jesus:

> The angel said to her (Mary), "the Holy Spirit shall come

Crossing Bridges and Barriers

upon you, and the power of the Highest shall overshadow you, therefore, also that Holy One who is to be born of you will be called the Son of God" (Luke 1:35 NKJV).

In the beginning was the Word and the Word was with God and the Word was God ... and the Word became flesh (human) and dwelt among us. (John 1:1, 14 NKJV).

The reality of God taking on flesh was difficult for the first century disciples of Christ to grasp as well, so be patient with your Muslim friend. Only as he spends time in the Bible and allows the Holy Spirit to "lead him into all truth (John 16:13)" will he surrender to this unparalleled revelation that "the Word became flesh and dwelt among us, and we beheld His glory, the glory of the only begotten Son of the Father, full of grace and truth" (John 1:14).

Barrier #4: What Do You Say about Mohammed?

This is *the big question*. Muslims take great offense at those who would profane their prophet. The best bridge to overcome the barrier of Mohammed is to simply say: "I agree with what the Qur'an says about Mohammed."

The Qur'an does not say that Mohammed was the greatest prophet. It does say that he was the "seal of the prophets" in *surah al-Ahzab* 33:40; seal only means the last, not the greatest. (Please note: We are not saying that Mohammed is a true prophet or the seal of the prophets; we are only making you aware of what you might face from the Qur'an.)

Then ask your friend to read *surah al-Ahqaf* (the Sandhills *surah*) 46:9 in which Allah instructs Mohammed to say:

I am no new thing among the messengers, nor know I what will be done with me or with you ... I am but a plain warner.

Kevin Greeson

Likewise in *surah al-Imran* 3:144, Allah says of Mohammed:

> Mohammed is but a messenger, messengers (the like of whom) have passed away before him.

We see in these passages that neither Mohammed nor his followers claimed that he was the greatest prophet.

Then you can ask your friend: "What is life's greatest question?" The greatest question of life is, "What will happen to me when I die?" We see from *surah al-Ahqaf* 46:9 that Mohammed did not claim to have a certain answer to that question, for himself or for his followers. Then you can take your Muslim friend to the *Injil*. Show him passages such as John 6:47 and especially John 14:1-6.

> Do not let your hearts be troubled. Trust in God; trust also in me. In my Father's house are many rooms; if it were not so, I would have told you. I am going there to prepare a place for you. And if I go and prepare a place for you, I will come back and take you to be with me that you also may be where I am....I am the way and the truth and the life. No one comes to the Father except through me (John 14:1-4, 6 NIV).

Clearly Jesus does have the answer to life's greatest question.

At this point, you have completed the advanced Camel Method. You have not engaged in an argument, but you have turned on the Gospel light and you have done it in a way that is uniquely adapted to the worldview of the Muslims with whom you are sharing.

Now it is time to prayerfully turn on your spiritual radar and see where God is at work. Look for a person of peace; it may be the Muslim with whom you have been talking, but chances are it is someone behind you or just around the corner who has been listening in on your conversation. Let everyone know how they can reach you if anyone wants to discuss this matter further.

Begin even now to schedule a return visit. If anyone expresses an interest in your message, share with him the *Korbani* Plan of Salvation.

---

[1]By looking at four different English translations of 3:54, we can get a better understanding of this *ayya*:

Pickthall – "And they (the disbelievers) schemed, and Allah schemed (against them): and Allah is the best of schemers."

Hilali-Khan – "And they (disbelievers) plotted [to kill 'Iesa (Jesus) <><>], and Allah planned too. And Allah is the Best of the planners."

Sher Ali – "And Jesus's enemies planned and ALLAH also planned, and ALLAH is the Best of Planners."

Palmer – "But they (the Jews) were crafty, and God was crafty, for God is the best of crafty ones! "

[2]This word *mutawaffika* is debated among Islamic scholars. Every time I discuss the word *mutawaffika* with Muslims they either confess that it means, "to kill" or "to cause to die" or they go and excuse themselves to go and research the word. It is difficult for a Muslim to accept that Allah's plan in 3:54 was to kill or sacrifice Isa. Examine the diversity of nine English translations of the Qur'an. In each case I have put the translation of the word *mutawaffika* in italics.

Pickthall – "(And remember) when Allah said: O Jesus! Lo! I am *gathering thee* and causing thee to ascend unto Me,"
Yusuf Ali – "Behold! God said: "O Jesus! I will *take thee* and raise thee to Myself "

Shakir – "And when Allah said: O Isa, I am going *to terminate the period of your stay (on earth)* and cause you to ascend unto Me."

Sher Ali – "Remember the time when ALLAH said' 'O Jesus, I will *cause thee to die a natural death* and will raise thee to Myself...."

Khalifa – "Thus, GOD said, "O Jesus, I am *terminating your life*, raising you to Me...."

Arberry – "When God said, 'Jesus, I will *take thee* to Me and will raise thee to Me."

Palmer – "When God said, 'O Jesus! I will *make Thee die* and take Thee up again to me."

Rodwell – "Remember when God said, "O Jesus! verily I will *cause thee to die*, and will take thee up to myself."

Sale – "When God said, o Jesus, verily I will *cause thee to die*, and I will take thee up unto me."

Because Christians never say that God killed Jesus, *ayyah* 3:55 may sound strange. Such a claim about God sounds harsh. Yet let us not forget that this is exactly what God did. He killed Jesus for our sins. Isaiah said,

Yet it pleased the Lord to bruise Him; He has put Him to grief. When You make His soul an offering for sin, He shall see His seed, He shall prolong His days, and the pleasure of the Lord shall prosper in His hand (Isaiah 53:10).

To sacrifice is to kill. Isa was God's holy sacrifice for our sins.

A CAMEL CARAVAN

Kevin Greeson

Chapter Ten

Driven by a Dream

A caravan of the committed, driven by a dream.

AS NEWS OF THE CAMEL Method spreads, a growing number of Christians around the world are adopting and adapting its practical lessons to reach the Muslims in their own community. Whenever Muslims come to faith in Christ, the angels in heaven rejoice. But there is also rejoicing whenever a single Christian obeys the Great Commission to share the Good News with every man, woman and child – and that includes every Muslim!

Today, more Muslims than ever before are hearing the Gospel for the first time. Many of them are saying yes to Jesus and remaining faithful despite attacks, beatings and even death.

Let me invite you to join the growing Camel caravan of the committed pursuing the dream of all peoples everywhere bowing their knee to the One whose name is above all names. Here are a few of the emails, letters and comments regarding the Camel Method that we have received over the past couple of years.

After 15 years of ministry to Muslims, a mission leader in the Arab world learned the Camel Method and quickly shared it with the more than 400 missionaries serving in his region. After a year of watching the Camel Method being used in a variety of countries, he sent us this email:

> "We are finding the Camel approach to be very exciting and promising. We are beginning to think that the Camel may be a missing key to our strategy. It sure does open up doors. One of our workers in North Africa who had seen no fruit for ten years has seen six guys become followers of Isa in the last two month. Many others who are trying the Camel are also finding positive results."
>
> IMB Regional Leader
> North Africa and the Middle East

A pastor from a large suburban church in South Carolina visited South Asia in 2006. He was amazed as he entered mosques and *madrasas* in Bangladesh and India that he could use the Camel Method to boldly share with Muslims the uniqueness of Isa al-Masih, his holiness, power, and ability to take us to heaven.

> "Americans think of Muslims as terrorists, but I have just used the Camel Method to witness to Muslims in the mosque and this is amazing! This has had a great impact on my life. I believe that every pastor in America needs to know the Camel Method and use it to reach Muslims!"
>
> Pastor Mike H.

An American traveling in northern Iraq was excited at the way the Camel Method prepared him for what to say during a brief mission trip among the Kurdish people.

"The first time I used the Camel Method of al-Imran 42-55, the young man with whom I was sharing looked up in wonder and then tentatively asked, "So what do you think about Muhammed?" Fortunately I had read the chapter dealing with The Big Question the night before and was able to say, "I believe the same thing the Koran says about Muhammed," and let him read Sandhills 46:9. It was very powerful.

"My second experiment with the Camel Method was before a whole room full of people. As they read the text they shook their head profoundly saying, 'We have never heard this.'

Thanks to Kevin Greeson for his perseverance in getting in to witness the movement and subsequently write this book so that salvation may come to many."

BRL

෪෯෨෪

As the Camel Method spread into East Africa, a number of Christians commented that it eased their anxieties about sharing with Muslims. No longer were they left wondering how to begin a conversation or how to guide the conversation toward the Gospel.

One Christian serving the Lord in East Africa recounts his use of the Camel.

"I had read the Koran and used selected topical verses for years. However, after reading the Camel Manual, I was encouraged by its simplicity and straight forward approach. I never saw it as evangelism, but as a tool to build further dialogue and encourage my Muslim friends to a willingness to read and study the Bible with me.

"After reading the Camel Manual, I practiced the 'basic' presentation in my office for a day and then invited a fairly close Muslim friend over to the house. We had talked about spiritual things many times previously. On this occasion, however, when he arrived I placed a copy of the Koran (that he had given to me) and a copy of the Bible on the table.

"I began by reminding him that he had given me a present of the Koran some months before. I asked him if he ever read it much and he agreed that he did, but did not fully understand it…in Arabic or any language. (He normally read it in Arabic.) I asked him if he knew much about what the Koran said about Isa and he replied that he knew some, but not a lot. I then asked him to read Sura 3, The Family of Imran, but mainly the verses 42-55. He read it, not in the Arabic, but from the Koran he had given me, which was in his mother tongue. I asked if he understood what he had read and he said we should read and discuss it one verse at a time. Imagine that! So, we did!

"He did not have a difficult time with the dialogue of the angel with Marium. He accepted very quickly that the baby, Isa, was from Allah; actually his words were, 'Isa is the breath of Allah, His spirit, His essence. Just as I am the essence of my father and have his spirit, so Isa is the essence of Allah.' I felt comfortable with this, but did not push the overt issue looking for the word SON.

"We continued dialogue on the life of Isa and he allowed me to tell some Biblical stories relating to the power, miracles and life of Isa. Again I was very encouraged. He began to struggle a bit with the wording in his mother tongue in relation to Allah speaking with Isa and 'terminating' his life. (continued next page)

Kevin Greeson

(continued from previous page) He was dealing with the issue of a true prophet dying a violent death more than the fact that He died. He admitted he had never seen the verse that states that Isa would be raised again from death. He began to become talkative after reading that Allah was bringing Isa to paradise to sit beside Him and that Isa would know the true pathway to paradise. At this point, after a few questions...it became very quiet and I allowed him to just process.

"Suddenly he smiled and said, 'If this is true, then I must study and discover everything that Isa says about the pathway to paradise. If he knows, I must do whatever He says in order to walk that same pathway. I must read more in the Injils.' Well, I almost fell from my chair. I asked if he knew what to do and he said no, so I walked him into the Injils and then explained Rms. 10:9-10 to him. He asked a few questions about belief and faith. I quoted Jn. 3:16 and then asked if he wanted to pray and become a believer. He thought for a moment and decided not to at that time.

"He has been faithful each month in coming and studying...about Isa, but currently he has not accepted. He knows the truth, but finds it difficult to make a decision that goes against his family, his faith and his community. I pray and trust it will happen one day soon. The story continues."

    JB
    A missionary in Kenya

ᏣᏞᏬᏍᎡᏜ

One of the most touching stories about the Camel came from a Muslim-background believer in South Asia whose friend, Zulf Fakar, came to faith through the Camel Method, and then gave his life witnessing for Jesus Christ. Zulf Fakar was so exuberant about his new relationship with God that he immediately shared the Good News with all who would listen. Though he was able to win his family and three others to Christ, his bold witness soon earned him a martyr's crown. The following report came came from one of those who served with him in South Asia.

"Even if you kill me, I know that I will go to be with Jesus." How many of us can say that in the face of serious death threats or at work?

Zulf Fakar was handed a small green booklet by a stranger....The pamphlet had some Arabic writing on the front followed by another 20 pages telling who Jesus was in terms that a Muslim understands along with verses telling truth about Jesus from their Koran. This all happened 15 months ago. After reading the booklet, he began to read in his holy book, the Koran, that Jesus had a special birth, did miracles, was sinless, died on the cross, will come again to judge the world, and is a mighty prophet (all in the Koran!). His heart began to burn. Days later a believer who was a Muslim previously, shared with Zulf Fakar about the love of God in sending Jesus. His life was changed. He and his family took baptism in spite of troubles and their life took on new meaning. His wife and three daughters all embraced his new faith long with him.

Several months went by and different members in the community began to warn Zulf to be quiet and not to share this new faith that is against Islamic beliefs. But Zulf never stopped, in fact even last week some men came to his home and strongly threatened him that if he didn't stop, "serious consequences would follow". He responded by telling them, that "even if you kill me I know that I will go to be with Jesus". Two day ago in the market in a small remote village, 10-12 men gathered around Zulf and began to beat him with sticks, he died and the angels of heaven went wild rejoicing that one so precious would not bow his knee before the pressures in this world and renounce his new faith. Zulf is survived by his wife Zabia and three young daughters. There are now four other families that believe in the village but they are very afraid."

An Christian in South Asia

Kevin Greeson

☙❧☙❧

Among the Muslims of China, the Camel Method is beginning to bear fruit. A longtime missionary who had labored for years among China's Muslims peoples, sent the following email a few months after receiving Camel training.

> "The Camel just packages it in a nice neat clean cut way. The Camel also offers some guidance about how long to use the Koran and what to use the Koran for and what not to use it for. This is an advantage especially for those just beginning to share with Muslims as it is easy to try and do to much with the Koran and you end up getting "bogged" down in the Koran and you never get to who Jesus really is. Another thing that has been helpful to me from the Camel is the idea of giving the "seed" time (three months I think is what they say) to see if a POP (Person of Peace) is found. Before the thought seemed to be that you should be able to tell if a person is a POP pretty quickly. I have found that among Muslims this is not always the case - it may be but not always."
>
> A Missionary to China's Muslim Peoples

A short-term volunteer in China successfully used the Camel Method as a springboard into the *Korbani* Plan of Salvation.

> "I was in western China last week. We used CAMEL several times. We had a young man in whom the Spirit had already been working. As we shared, he agreed with everything we showed him. We began to talk about Korbani and quickly jumped to the Injil. Within 3 hours this young Hui man had joined the Kingdom! It was an incredible experience! He is living in Beijing and studying Arabic. He hopes to go back to (*****) to teach Arabic! Praise the Lord!"
>
> Eric G.

Even on the Saudi Arabian peninsula, the Camel Method is opening doors and leading Muslims to faith in Christ. This email was forwarded to us by some personnel who translated the Camel Method into Arabic and were amazed at how powerfully it spread through the Arab Muslim community.

> "We made the Camel Training Manual in Arabic available to them and they could not put it down! Within a few weeks they were not only using the Camel method (surat al Imran) but many other passages from the Koran to seek out other persons of peace. They trained their new convert who quickly led 3 members of her family to faith using the lessons learned from the Camel. FYI - we had heard of the Camel method before our training in **** but were hesitant to try using it for a variety of reasons…however, He changed our minds! The moral of this lesson is not "don't be afraid to try new things," the moral of this lesson is to "try new things.
>
> Second, teaching them the CAMEL method revealed and confirmed what God was already beginning to teach them as they began to reach others…in short, we believe the Camel was key in the growth we saw over the next few months. Understanding the Person of Peace (PoP) concept made a way for new believers to *fish* without putting all their cards on the table."
>
> A missionary to Arabs

As with most populations, there are probably more women Muslims than men. Fortunately, there are also more women missionaries to Muslim women than there are male missionaries to Muslim men. One missionary woman serving in Egypt had tried unsuccessfully to use the Evangecube to share the Gospel with Muslim women. She seemed to encounter a polite, but unyielding wall of resistance. After receiving Camel training, she blended the Camel Method into the Evangecube to produce what she called "the Koran-gecube."

> Mary (not her real name) learned the Arabic language well and developed many friendships as she lived with her family in a large Egyptian city. After trying many ways to share the Gospel with Muslim women, Mary enjoyed using the Evangecube, but was frustrated that, despite its clarity and simplicity, none of her Muslim friends came to faith in Christ through it.
>
> When Mary was introduced to the Camel Method, she found it easy to blend the two methods together. She used the graphic images of the Evangecube to illustrate the message in surah al-Imran, that Isa is holy, powerful and knows the way to heaven. Within a few months, Mary had led 12 of her Muslim women friends to faith in Isa al-Masih.
>
> A missionary to
> Muslim women in Egypt

CREAM

Driven By A Dream

In Habakkuk 2:14 (NIV), God shared with us His dream for a fallen world; it was a dream in which "the knowledge of the glory of God would cover the earth as the waters cover the sea." This knowledge is more than intellectual knowledge. It is a personal, intimate relationship with God. God desires to have a relationship with all mankind that is just as warm and personal as that which he had with Adam and Eve in the Garden before the fall--the same kind of intimate relationship with the Father that Jesus modeled for us.

God's dream, his vision, doesn't stop at the boundaries of the Muslim world. He so wants to see Muslims come to new life in

Him that He gave His only Son as a sacrifice for their sins, so that they, too, might have eternal and abundant life in Him,

Over the course of this book you have seen how God has used a simple tool like the Camel Method to penetrate the closed mind of Muslims, opening doors to the house of Islam and letting the glory of God's salvation in Jesus Christ pour in. What began in the humblest corners of the world, in the closing days of the 20th century, is now spreading across the nations of South Asia and into China, the Middle East, East Africa and North Africa. The Camel caravan is now poised to enter Europe, North America, South America and everywhere that Muslims are found.

It is true that more Muslims are coming to faith today than ever before in history. And yet, just as in the dream I had nearly a decade ago, countless Muslims are still falling every year into an eternity in hell without ever knowing the love of Jesus Christ.

What will it take to replace that nightmare with God's dream of a people who are truly submitted to His will and filled with His glory? What will it take for the Gospel to spread to the hundreds of millions of Muslims who have yet to see the holiness, power and gift of salvation that only Jesus can offer them?

For you and for me, it does not begin just because we have read a book. It doesn't begin through hearing stories of what someone else is doing somewhere on the far side of the world.

It begins with humble obedience, when we respond to the voice of God who says, "Do you see that young Muslim over there? Tell him about me." It begins with the words, "I've read something amazing in the Qur'an. Can I talk with you about it?"

It begins where it always begins, in a village, your village.

CAMEL ACCESSORIES

Kevin Greeson

Appendix One

Ask the Camel

NOW THAT YOU HAVE LEARNED to ride the Camel, you may still have some reservations. You are enthusiastic but still need to ask a few more questions before you are ready to climb aboard. This chapter is for you. Here are the questions we have heard over the past couple of years and a modest attempt at some answers.

1. Should Christians call God "Allah"?

Many devout Christians balk at using the name *Allah* for God. It seems to stick in their throat as they ask, "Isn't this a different god from the God of the Bible?" It may not be enough to respond to this question with another question: "Isn't there only *one* God?" Around the world, Bible translators have used thousands of local-language names for God, and then relied on the Bible to re-define those names with new content and meaning. The question is not, what do you call God, but what do you mean by that name?

If our doctrines and understanding of God come from the Qur'an, then we will certainly not end up with a Christian view of God. If, on the other hand, our authoritative source about God is the Bible, then our doctrine of God will remain true, regardless of which language we use to call His name.

Allah is simply the ancient Semitic name for the God of Creation, the God of Abraham, Isaac, Ishmael, and Israel. Arab

Christians were calling God *Allah* long before the Prophet Mohammed adopted it for his religion. Today, it remains the name for God not only among Arab Christians but among many non-Arab Christians from West Africa (Nigerian Hausa) to Indonesia (Bahasa Indonesia).

English-speaking Christians need to remember that our own name, "God", does not appear in the Bible, but was borrowed from the pre-Christian religions of northern Europe. It originally designated the divine spirit *Gott* and served as an alternative name for the Norse god Odin prior to the arrival of Christian missionaries who re-defined it with doctrinal content from the Bible.

Those looking for a biblical precedent to such a translation practice need search no further than the first chapter of John's gospel. John dared to call Jesus "Logos (the Word)," a term widely known throughout the first century world through the writings of Plato who associated it with the *Divine Plan* in his dialogues with Timaeus. Before Plato, the Greek Stoics used the term in their own philosophical speculations. Yet John saw in the term a perfect bridge for introducing Jesus to a Hellenized world as he filled the Greek concept with new meaning in the person and work of Jesus Christ.

The Camel Method is also a bridge. It bridges Muslims from their Qur'anic understanding of God into the biblical revelation of God. Once they accept the Bible as God's truth for them, it surpasses all previous conceptions with a new personal relationship to God as Father, Son and Holy Spirit.

2. Why not just preach the Bible to them?

This approach appeals to Christians because the Bible is how *we* came to know God, but it has little appeal to Muslims whose authority is the Qur'an. In fact, preaching the Bible to Muslims has been attempted for generations with very little fruit. This is due not to the inadequacy of the Bible, but because Muslims have been preconditioned not to hear it. For centuries they have been taught that the Bible has been corrupted and that the Qur'an has thoroughly replaced the Bible. When we can show them, from their own Qur'an, that the Bible *is* reliable, and that it has vital instructions for them about Isa that they desperately need, *then* they change their attitude toward the Bible and its message.

What this requires of us is to step into the Muslim worldview for a few minutes. Stepping into the shoes of Muslims helps us understand the reverence they have for the Qur'an and the power it holds over their lives. We don't have to accept the authority of the Qur'an to treat the Qur'an and the Muslims who adhere to it with respect. We are then able to use relevant passages from within the Qur'an to bridge Muslim persons of peace out of the stronghold of Islam and into the Bible where they can find God's revelation of Himself in Christ Jesus.

3. Is it right for a Christian to use the Qur'an to bridge Muslims to Christ?

This is the fundamental question of the Camel Method. Answer "no" and every other point is moot. Before you answer, though, picture a teenage Muslim boy who hears the Gospel for the first time. He runs to his father and says, "Father, I have decided to become a Christian!" Any one working with Muslims knows what will happen next. The father will incite relatives to beat his son, and possibly even kill him. If they do not kill him, he will be rejected by the family and kicked out of the house.

Now picture a different story. The teenage boy hears the Gospel from a person who calls himself an Isahi. The Isahi shared information about Isa from the Qur'an. Then he moved beyond the Qur'an to the Bible and shared the complete story of how God provided salvation through Isa to all mankind. With this exciting news, the boy runs home to his father and says, "Father, please take the family Qur'an from the shelf and read to us *surah al-Imran* 3:42-55." Together they uncover such truths as Isa is holy, He was given the power to raise the dead to life and Isa was killed and raised again to be with Allah. The son asks his father "Is it possible that Isa came from Allah and returned to Allah, and therefore knows the way to heaven?" The son evaluates the response of the father to determine the best time to share the rest of the Gospel story.

What can the father do? If he rejects his son, he is rejecting the Qur'an. He did not hear the word, "Christian" come from his son's mouth, so he cannot accuse his son of becoming one of "them." He read the Qur'an with his own eyes. His son did not preach to him; he only asked questions that led the father himself to admit the deity of Christ. In the end, the father may scold his son or direct him to talk to the Imam, but he cannot react the way he would if the son had come home and confessed that he had converted to Christianity.

Using the Qur'an as a bridge does not guarantee the safety of a Muslim who becomes a new follower of Jesus. Yet it communicates to family members the change in one's heart and belief that is easier for them to accept. Virtually every Muslim-background believer in the church-planting movements in South Asia has faced some measure of persecution. There is no escaping persecution, but the Camel Method does seem to diminish the incidence of martyrdom.

Using passages from the Qur'an as a bridge to share the Gospel has kept martyrdom relatively low while speeding the Gospel's spread throughout Muslim communities. In the West, evangelism programs have been developed such as Evangelism Explosion, FAITH, Roman Road, Steps to Peace with God, etc. These programs have been successful largely because they have taught Christians what to say when meeting a lost person. Most Christians do not share the Gospel with a lost person because they do not know what to say. Any time an evangelistic tool helps Christians share the Gospel, the tremendous power of the Gospel is released and a harvest follows. The Camel Method is no different.

Kevin Greeson

The Camel Method teaches Christians what to say as it bridges lost Muslims from the Qur'an to the Bible, from Islam to Christ. Once they have crossed the bridge, the Qur'an is no longer needed and is no longer the focal point.

4. How Christian are these Muslim-background believers?

Are the Muslim-background believers described in this book truly disciples of Christ or merely nominal Christians? This question has been at the forefront of two studies conducted over the past five years. Researchers wanted to know if these Muslim-background believers really believed in the deity of Christ and embraced the doctrine of the Trinity.

Broad samplings of testimonies conducted in 2002 found Muslim-background believers in widespread agreement as to the divinity of Christ. When asked, these Isahi and their leaders responded without hesitation that Jesus is fully God and fully man.

Regarding the Trinity, the researchers found that Muslim-background believers did not use that term. When asked more specifically, though, these MBBs were quick to acknowledge God as Father, Son and Holy Spirit. They recognized that this was a departure from their Islamic tradition, but found it to be central to their new faith as followers of Christ.

Further survey findings on this subject revealed three important conclusions:

a. Authority – Muslim-background believers associated with the Camel Method were solidly committed to the authority of Bible. When they had a question about the church or how to live their lives, they looked to the Bible for answers. With little access to other Christian books or outside teaching, the surveys revealed that they often found direction in the New Testament book of Acts.

b. Identity – The same surveys revealed that these Muslim-background believers had clearly shifted their allegiance from Islam to Christ. For this shift in devotion, virtually every one of them has faced severe persecution. Some had been tortured and even killed. There was no question among the Muslims around them that these Isahi have left Islam.

c. Culture – Nonetheless, most of these Muslim-background believers retained a cultural distance from traditional Christians or Christians from non-Islamic backgrounds. As such, they continued to relate to other Muslims in their community as much as possible, abstaining from pork and alcohol, and retaining their Arabic names and cultural forms.

5. How do we prevent reconversion?

If it were up to us, we probably could not prevent reconversions. Throughout the history of missionary outreach to Muslims, reconversion has been a persistent problem, with as many as 90 percent returning to Islam. This is in stark contrast to the movements in South Asia, where reconversion has been minimal. The 2002 study revealed few Muslim-background believers who even knew of anyone who had reconverted to Islam after baptism.

The reason for this may be found in the indigenous nature of the movement associated with the Camel Method. This is in sharp contrast to the history of Muslim conversions to Christianity which typically meant a conversion from Muslim culture into some form of Western Christian culture. That type of cultural conversion always has a very high rate of reconversion. In the kinds of churches associated with the Camel Method, there is much less cultural conversion and consequently much less foreignness in the resulting Isahi Muslim community.

6. Do Muslim-background believers still regard the Qur'an as authoritative?

If Muslim-background believers still held the Qur'an on the same level as the Bible, then the bridge would be incomplete. In

Kevin Greeson

all of our interviews with Isahi Muslims, we have found none who hold the Qur'an on the same level as the Bible. To probe this matter, we asked the question, "If the Qur'an told you to do something and the Bible told you to do the opposite, which would you follow?" The answer was always, "The Bible."

Do Muslim-background believers still use the Qur'an? Yes, but now they use it to win their family and friends to faith in Isa in much the same way that they themselves were reached. By starting with the Qur'an, they begin where their Muslim friends and family are. From this point, they are able to bring them into the light. Thousands upon thousands of Muslims who have become followers of Christ are grateful for that bridge.

7. **The Camel may have worked with Muslims in your country, but our country is different.**

Of course every country is different, just as every Muslim is different, but there are also things that all Muslims hold in common, and that is why the Camel Method has been so widely effective.

- Muslims everywhere revere the Qur'an. The Camel Method begins with the Qur'an.

- The Holy Spirit is already at work among Muslims, convicting of sin, judgment and righteousness. The Camel Method helps you find these spiritually hungry and responsive Muslims.

- Christians everywhere need a bridge to introduce the Gospel to Muslims. The Camel Method provides that bridge.

The growing body of testimonies concerning the Camel Method indicate that its value is not limited to one isolated corner of the Muslim world. The Camel Method is now being used effectively from Indonesia to North Africa. If you find that it does not work where you live, feel free to adapt it to the distinctives of your context and then try again.

8. Muslims in our country do not even read the Qur'an.

The truth is that *most* Muslims do not read the Qur'an, certainly not in the Arabic language. Even surveys of Arab Muslims reveal a paltry number of Qur'an readers. Neither do Muslims read the Qur'an in their colloquial language translations. Despite this lack of reading the Qur'an, it is often times these same Muslims who revere the Qur'an the most! For them, the Qur'an is a mysterious book of great power, holiness and authority. These non-reading Muslims are often amazed to find out what the Qur'an really says about Jesus, about Christians, about the Bible.

The Qur'an holds power over more than a billion Muslims, most of whom will never read its pages, but this does not diminish its role in their lives. They hear it, revere it and submit themselves to its authority. The Camel Method uses the Qur'an's authority in their lives to point them to Jesus and the Bible, even if the Qur'an itself is never opened or read. So don't let Qur'anic illiteracy prevent you from using the Camel Method to introduce Muslims to Isa.

9. Can Muslim-background believers who reject Christian culture really be Christians?

We first have to ask: "What is a Christian culture, and which cultures are truly Christian?" When Isahi Muslims reject the culture of the West, they are not rejecting the Gospel. Many elements from their traditional Muslim and Arabic culture have rich meanings that Muslim-background believers see little reason to reject. The name *Mohammed*, for example, means "one who praises (God)"; *Ahmed* means "the greatest praise"; *Abdullah* means "servant of God," and *Allahu Akbar* simply means "God is the greatest of all!"

Unlike Western Christians, Isahi Muslims follow the Muslim practice of holding their palms opened toward heaven when they pray to symbolically catch the blessings of God which they then wipe over their face after prayer. Most Muslim-background believers see little reason to abandon such practices as these.

Kevin Greeson

10. What are the greatest barriers preventing Muslims from coming to faith in Christ today?

The greatest barriers are found in two places: 1) in the minds of Muslims, and 2) in the minds of Christians.

Muslims have spent centuries building walls between themselves and the Gospel. Their leaders have taught them that the Qur'an forbids Muslims to read the Bible or accept the salvation offered by God in Christ Jesus. For too long these teachings have kept their minds closed to the Truth that God so passionately wants to offer them.

A second barrier in the Muslim mind is the deafening roar of his own culture. Muslims are proud of their Islamic heritage and consider it treasonous to abandon it for another culture. While Jesus might be Good News to them, they are less easily convinced that the West offers a superior civilization.

The Camel Method overcomes these two barriers by gently showing Muslims that the Qur'an does not forbid the reading of the Bible; in fact, it encourages it! It avoids the culture barrier between Islam and the West by using Islamic scripture and terminology to bridge the gap between the two.

Christians have their own sets of barriers. First, Christians do not know how to witness to Muslims. When Christians do share their faith they are stunned by the quick negative response Muslims give as they learn firsthand that Islam is the only world religion tailor-made to refute Christianity. Muslims have been taught to reject the Incarnation, the Trinity and the authority of the Bible. Once they have done this, most Evangelicals are left speechless and simply turn away.

Second, when Christians do witness they often fail because they ignore the culture of Muslims. Muslims do not separate culture from religion. When we share our faith with Muslims, we must do it in a way that speaks their cultural language. Attempts to force Muslims to reject their culture are doomed to failure, because most Muslims see too much good in their own culture and too much bad in what they perceive to be Christian culture.

The Camel Method teaches Christians how to speak to Muslims and what to say. It helps us know how to communicate within their culture while pointing them to the eternal truths that can only be found in the Bible. Even when our Muslim friend rejects or quickly dismisses us, the Camel Method encourages us not to give up. The object is not to win an argument, but to find the person of peace who will gladly receive the Good News and become a fruitful harvester within the Muslim community.

Kevin Greeson

Appendix Two

Your Church and a CPM

I F YOU WANT TO EXPAND your efforts from a lonely individual Camel rider to a Camel caravan, there is no better place to start than with your own church or small group.[1] As you gain confidence sharing with Muslims in your own community, allow God to stretch your vision by adopting a Muslim people group in their own homeland. That's right, missions is not just for missionaries anymore. More than ever before churches today are embracing the challenge of taking the Gospel to Muslims both at home and around the world.

A church in Naples, Florida recently answered the call and sent a team of church members to help a missionary working with a Muslim people group in Asia with a population of more than ten million. The team was given a specific assignment to conduct a sports camp that would help the missionary establish his platform and develop new relationships with athletes. The mission team was made up of eight men. The trip was successful; all goals were met.

Not long after the team returned to Naples, they began to sense an incompleteness to their work. Was there something more that God wanted them to do? They realized that the missionary was overwhelmed with the number of lost people in his people group. More importantly, they understood that if it were left to the missionary alone, millions in the people group would never hear the Gospel. The missionary was doing all he could, but even his best could not respond to the haunting cries of the millions of lost among his people.

It was around this same time that the church mission team first learned about church-planting movements (CPMs). They understood that CPMs were the fastest way to eradicate lostness, so they contacted the missionary and expressed their desire to be agents of establishing church-planting movements in areas of the people group that were beyond the reach of the missionary. The missionary agreed and identified segments of the people group that he would not likely engage for more than five years.

The team could see that if they were to adopt one of those population segments, they would need the continued help of the missionary. Yet they determined to do their best not to pull the missionary away from his current work. After a working agreement was arranged, the team sat with the missionary and together they developed a church-planting movement strategy.

It did not take the team long to realize that if they were going to pursue a church-planting movement strategy, they would have to change the way they did missions. In the past, they sent a large team to the mission field once each year. They could now see that this approach would not achieve their goal, because when large mission teams traveled together a significant amount of their time was spent on their own needs. Someone in the group would always get sick or would have special needs that would redirect the group's focus internally rather than maintain their focus on finding persons of peace and locating resources needed for starting the church-planting movement. In addition, there was too much gap time between trips to the field. Their strategies were not able to survive their absence.

To solve this problem, the team decided to divide into smaller units. They managed to have a single team member or a pair of team members on the ground in their adopted area four times a

Kevin Greeson

year. Each individual or pair had a specific assignment that came from their overall church-planting movement strategy.

Over a period of three years, the team acheived some remarkable accomplishments. They collected a portfolio of effective resources such as contextualized easy-to-read Bibles, tracts and media items and saturated their adopted area with these resources. They used the Camel Method to find persons of peace. The Camel Method increased their boldness and confidence. They also found committed national church planter partners to help them establish new churches. Along the way, they sought and received good counsel from missionaries on how to solve the problems that arose.

Today this Florida church is seeing the beginnings of a full-blown church-planting movement. In partnership with the field missionary and their national partners, they have seen 178 new Muslim-background *Isa jamaats* started. Emboldened by their success, they are now looking to adopt a Muslim population segment in another Asian country.

Church Adoption

You, too, can challenge and equip your church to be part of a church-planting movement among Muslims. You, too, can take a Camel ride on a long-distance journey. Individual Camel riders can accomplish much, but a Camel caravan church is supernaturally outfitted with gifts that can change the Muslim world.

We cannot rely on our missionaries alone to reach the 1.3 billion Muslims in the world with the Gospel. They will see much fruit, but to make a significant impact upon lostness in the Muslim world will take both missionaries *and* churches.

Have you been on mission trips where...

...you sensed more could have been done?

...you spent more time and energy dealing with internal team issues than cross-cultural obstacles of sharing the Gospel with the lost?

...you sensed that the answer to your prayer walking team's plea for God to send someone to share the Gospel *was you*?

...you realized that the missionary you were helping has not seen any lost people come to Christ in the last five years?

...you trained national Christians to reach the lost, only to find that, after you left, they stopped their outreach to the lost?

...you found where God was at work, but your team schedule kept you from joining God?

...you built a church building for local Christians, but year after year the church neither reproduced itself nor grew? Or the church asked you to come back again next year so that you could do repairs on *your* building?

If you have had any of these experiences, then you may be ready for a new mission strategy.

Before we look at specific strategies, we need to address some of the foundational issues that will help us be successful. Foundational issues include:

- Which Muslim population segment should we adopt?

- What can we expect from national Christians and churches?

- How do we best organize our church to give leadership for the adoption?

- What should the adoption agreement look like?

Kevin Greeson

- With whom should I partner?

- What should be our working relationship with a mission organization or individual missionary?

- God has blessed us with abundant financial resources, so how do we use them in ways that will not harm the emerging church-planting movement?

- What tools and resources are available?

- Is more than one church-planting movement necessary for our adopted area?

- How can we enlist our entire church to become involved in implementing our church-planting movement strategy?

Whom Should We Adopt?

Your first step in the adoption process is to pick a Muslim people group to adopt. Here are some of the broad families of Muslim peoples from which to choose a group for adoption.

a. Arab Muslims – are found in more than 20 countries across the Middle East and North Africa. While many of these countries are difficult to access, others welcome outsiders. Morocco, Tunisia, Egypt, Palestine, Jordan and Lebanon all welcome foreign visitors. Together these countries are home to more than 100 million Muslims.

b. Turkish Muslims – are found in Turkey, of course, but have Turkic cousins living across much of Central and South Asia's *stans* – Kazakhstan, Uzbekistan, Kyrgyzstan, Afghanistan and Pakistan. Turkey is particularly open to Western visitors and is home to more than 80 million Turkish Muslims.

c. South Asian Muslims - are found in India, Pakistan and Bangladesh. Not only are these three of the largest Islamic countries in the world, with a combined population of more than 400 million Muslims, they are also relatively open to outside visitors. India, with 130 million Muslims, has the second largest English speaking population in the world, making it a good candidate for adoption by an English-speaking church.

d. Indonesian and Malaysian Muslims – together Indonesia and Malaysia are home to more than 200 million Muslims. Both countries welcome tourists, and English is widely spoken in Malaysia.

With today's Internet access, you can find tremendous amounts of information about people groups without leaving your home or office. Ask God to guide you in the selection of a people group. Here are some tips:

- Don't hesitate to choose a Muslim people group that is already engaged by a missionary or mission organization. Most likely, there will already be numerous resources (tracts, Bibles, media, radio, etc.) in the local language for broadly spreading the Gospel and discipling new believers.

- Narrow your selection to a bite-sized segment of a people group. For example, rather than taking on all 100 million Urdu-speaking Muslims of India, zero in on the 100,000 Urdu-speaking Muslims in a district in western Uttar Pradesh state. This will keep your task manageable and your progress measurable.

- Do not be afraid to go for a rural people group. Most churches want to start with a city, where there are good airports and hotels, but church-planting movements among Muslims often begin in the rural areas before moving to the cities. So, you might find a city you like and then look a few miles away from it!

Kevin Greeson

- Look for places where God is already at work among Muslim people groups, and try to spread the fire from there into more unreached areas.

Local National Churches in Your Adopted Area

Starting a church-planting movement among Muslim people groups can get complicated. It is not always Muslim governments or Islamic extremists who are trying to stop the movement. Sometimes the hindrances to establishing a church-planting movement are within the local national church.

Missionaries who have tried working through local Christian churches have often become frustrated. Yet within the walls of these churches are evangelists and church planters who can be trained for church-planting movements.

In the same way, local churches might seem to be the best place to disciple new Muslim-background believers, but such is often not the case. Established national churches do not always share this vision. In fact, they will often try to stop all evangelism efforts, because when new evangelism efforts lead to persecution, the national churches are among the first to feel the heat.

This is where a missionary who understands the local situation can be of great service to you. He will understand how to balance the needs of open conventional churches with those of the newly formed *underground* church-planting movement churches.

If you want to have a successful partnership with a national church, avoid entering into a formal working relationship with the church as a whole. Instead, establish working relationships with like-minded individuals within the church.

Partners

Most mission agencies working among Muslims do not publicize where they work, so you will have to do a little research and networking. Here is a good place to start:

a.   **Frontiers** – a veteran agency with a passion for Muslims.

Frontiers ministries stretch across much of the Muslim world. www.frontiers.org

b.   Arab World Ministries – as their name suggests, AWM has dedicated its efforts to the world's 300 million Arab Muslims for more than a century. www.awm.Gospelcom.net

c.   Southern Baptist International Mission Board – the IMB is a denominational agency, but one with a growing track record of seeing Muslims come to faith in Christ. You will also find a commitment to church-planting movements and the Camel Method widely practiced here. www.imb.org

d.   Campus Crusade for Christ – is one of the largest mission agencies in the world. Their emphasis on evangelism, discipleship and training extends to Muslim and non-Muslim peoples all over the globe. www.ccci.org

e.   Operation Mobilization – began as a literature distribution to unreached people groups. Today, OM continues to take the Gospel to Muslim and other unreached people groups across the 10/40 Window. www.om.org

f.   Youth With A Mission – is not just for young people any more. YWAM has an enormous base of nearly 100,000 missionaries serving around the globe. www.ywam.org

g.   Other Agencies - there are a host of other agencies with ministries in the Muslim world including Pioneers, TEAM (The Evangelical Alliance Mission), SIM (Send International Mission), WEC (Worldwide Evangelization for Christ) and others.

Working with a Missionary or Mission Agency
   If your church has never been part of a church-planting movement overseas, it is best to work under the administrative

Kevin Greeson

umbrella of a mission agency or individual missionary. Tapping into their wealth of experience and knowledge of the Muslims in your adopted area will prove to be well worth the effort. They already know about best practice resources, local churches to partner with and not to partner with, and prospective national church planters you can mobilize into your adopted area.

Choose carefully, though. Many mission agencies and missionaries are doing good work but may not have a vision for a church-planting movement. Find a mission agency or missionary that understands the principles of what it takes to start church-planting movements.

Even when you find them, they may not be prepared to work with you. Many missionaries have served faithfully for years in difficult places and may find the thought of partnering with a church group from the West to be an unsettling prospect! They may feel intimidated if, after years of seeing little fruit, your church wants to see a church-planting movement.

More and more mission agencies, though, are realizing that a new day in missions is dawning with the possibility of churches from outside the Muslim world joining them in a great harvest.

Tips for working with an individual missionary (or mission agency) focusing on the same Muslim people group you have chosen:

- Ask if there is a population segment inside the people group such as a district or an area with boundaries that is on his schedule to reach but, because of the size of the people group, it will be another 5-10 years before he can engage that population segment. If he can give you this information, ask him if you may partner with him by adopting this area.

- Communicate with the missionary that you will need his help, but that your church's goal is not to pull him away from his current work.

- Learn from the missionary any information and best practices for reaching Muslims. Best practices are any highly effective means for achieving your desired results.

- Find out if there are any Christian groups in the area that might object to your work.

- Hire translators that the missionary recommends and avoid entering into any private agreements with translators.

Consider asking a member or members of your church to live in your adopted area to serve your church's strategy. Find a mission agency that agrees with your church-planting movement strategy for your adopted area and will allow you to send your church member(s) through their organization. If your church is not able to financially support them and take care of all their needs, then find a mission agency that will agree to support them and enter into an agreement that will allow your church member to execute a church-planting movement strategy focused on your adopted area.

Leadership for the Adoption

Church adoptions are most productive when a small committed group within the church gives primary attention to the adoption. We will refer to those who provide leadership for the adoption as the adoption team. The church members who catch the adoption team's vision can participate at several levels. Individual team members will be given specific assignments.

Adoption team members will bring a variety of talents and spiritual gifts that are needed for the following assignments:

Team Leader – calls team meetings, leads the team in strategy formation, tracks progress, holds team members accountable for their individual tasks, solves problems and serves as spokesman for the team.[2]

Prayer Mobilizer – creates a network of prayer warriors, gathers

Kevin Greeson

strategic prayer requests and leads the church to prayerfully support mission teams or individuals who travel to the adopted area. The prayer mobilizer can work with the research coordinator to collect pictures of Muslims from the adopted area, along with spiritual strongholds and maps to be used for prayer mobilization.

Research Coordinator – spends time collecting information about the adopted people group and the adopted area. The research coordinator can read online local or national newspapers from the adopted area and interview missionaries, mission agencies, or local national church planters working in and around the adopted area. He or she can identify needs, opportunities and insights that will help the team reach its goals.

Saturation Coordinator – develops a system that tracks Gospel saturation, including a map that charts Gospel distribution and areas that need more Gospel outreach.

Camel Riders – are those team members who have worked through the Camel Method and are prepared to go to the field to share the Good News with Muslims there. They should also prepare to train local Christian and Muslim-background believers to use the Camel Method to share the Gospel with the adopted Muslim people. These individuals should also be prepared to widely distribute Gospel literature, Muslim-friendly Scripture, and "JESUS" films among the target people.

The Adoption Agreement

Your adoption team should prepare a written adoption covenant. Set the period of time for the adoption at two years. Some may think that two years is not enough time for establishing a church-planting movement, but developing a two-year strategy will encourage urgency in implementing strategies. You can always extend the adoption by another year or two. Yet too much time working in one area can create unhealthy dependency of the new believers on the generosity and resources of your church.

Present the written adoption covenant to the pastor and then to the church body. The congregation should be made aware that they will be asked to involve themselves through prayer, contributing funds and actually traveling to the adopted area. Communicate that the adoption team will not be carrying out the strategies alone, but rather leading the church to be on mission in the adopted area.

Finances

Your church has been blessed financially. Using this blessing in your adopted area must be done wisely. Too easily, you can begin to use it like candy to gain the results you want.[3] Many emerging church-planting movements have been damaged by the unwise use of funds that come from foreign sources.

In order to minimize the negative effects of outside funds, try to follow these principles:

- Do not pay pastors of churches. Their income should come from their congregation.

- Do not build church buildings. These should be produced by the local church members.

- If you provide relief or financial assistance to new believers, be sure to provide it to neighboring Muslims as well. This will increase good will and help you avoid the charge of "buying" converts.

- You may choose to provide travel expenses for a national evangelist or person of peace who travels beyond his local setting to spread the movement far and wide, but you should avoid funding local persons of peace who do not have travel expenses.

Only those who function as missionaries should receive financial support. A missionary is an outsider (without a local base of financial support) who brings the Gospel into a new area. Local believers witnessing to Muslims in their own community do not function as missionaries.

Guidelines for mobilizing new national church planters into your adopted area include:

- Check to see if local churches already support evangelists in your adopted area. Try to encourage them toward this end.

- When giving support to a church planter, establish a clear beginning and ending date of any financial support.

- Do not give a church planter support above the level that he was receiving prior to his becoming a Christian.

- Consider setting aside some funds for the assistance of widows and orphans. A national church planter who serves on the front line is in a high risk situation. Be prepared to pay for his hospital bills when injured while working on the job or for his widow and family should circumstances require it.

- Before agreeing to the financial support of church planters, test their devotion, motives, character, and abilities with short term projects. Develop clear expectations of a church planter and maintain accountability.

Resources

By the end of your adoption your church should be able to say, "If any Muslim wanted to hear the Gospel, it was available" or "Muslim seekers of the Gospel did not have to look very far to find the Gospel."

One way to accomplish this is to saturate your adopted area with Gospel resources, not with just any resources, but resources that have a proven track record of clearly and effectively communicating the Gospel. Non-readers need the "JESUS" film or audio cassettes in their language.

Your adoption team will want to research and investigate the many best practice resources available for your Muslim people group. Develop a file with samples of individual resources including contextualized Bibles, tracts, videos, Bible correspondence programs, radio ministries and Gospel Web sites that are currently being used with your Muslim people group. Assign someone on your team for this challenge. Your goal is Gospel saturation within the time period of the adoption.

Attempt Multiple Church-planting Movements

Church-planting movements do not develop overnight. It may take years for a church-planting movement to emerge. Some grow rather slowly, while others unfold quickly. With this in mind, your church must work towards establishing multiple church-planting movements in the adopted area.

Attempting to establish multiple church-planting movements among your Muslim people group will pay off in ways that you may not imagine. Launching multiple CPM strategies in separate areas will allow you to test several methods and minimize the risks associated with putting all of your efforts into a single strategy.

Multiple attempts in establishing church-planting movements within the adopted area create a highly effective and productive research laboratory. If a strategy fails in one area it can be avoided elsewhere.

Enlisting Your Entire Church to Be Involved

Not everyone in your church will feel called to take on a leadership roll in the adoption, yet many may want to be a part by doing a limited strategic task. Some cannot travel to the adopted area for health reasons or because of their work schedule. The adoption team should spend time drafting creative assignments for individuals and groups in the church. Here are some activities for impacting your adopted area that will start the flow of ideas:

Kevin Greeson

1. **Mail the "JESUS" film to every politician and policeman.** The "JESUS" film is the most watched movie in history. Using address lists gathered by members of the church mission team, identify local community leaders who might watch the "JESUS" film in English or in the local language in the privacy of their home especially if they are encouraged to do so with a personal and motivating letter from you. You can order the "JESUS" film from Campus Crusade in Orlando, Florida (1-800-432-1997, e-mail: JesusFilmStore@Jesusfilm.org).

2. **After ordering your own copy of the "JESUS" film, gather a group from your church for a meal.** The meal should be a typical meal from your adopted people group. After the meal, spend time in prayer for political and law enforcement leaders of your adopted area. Write addresses of community leaders on envelopes. Place your hands on each "JESUS" film, pray for the recipient, place the "JESUS" film inside the envelope, insert a personal note, and mail the envelope.

3. **Mail a copy of the Bible and Christian literature to every library in your adopted area.** Be sure to include school and university libraries.

4. **Collect email addresses and send Camel portions or Bible messages via email.** Collect email addresses from phone books, advertisements and websites. Be sure to include a contact address and phone number. If any recipients are interested to know more, email the Gospel of Luke to them.

5. **Mail a copy of the "JESUS" film to all local video shops listed in your adopted area's phone book.** Mail also to cable TV companies, encouraging them to show the "JESUS" film for Christmas and Easter.

6. **Mail the Bible in the local language to each mosque and *madrasa*.** A *madrasa* is an Islamic school for children. Each one has a library which might add a Bible to their collection.

7. **Call churches in your adopted area.** If they have a telephone, most likely they have someone in the church who can speak English. Encourage them by asking what prayer requests they have. Pray over the phone. Ask them if they know of any Muslims in their community who are asking questions about Jesus or the Bible. If so, ask for the Muslim seekers' addresses so that a church planter can visit them or Gospel resources can be mailed to them.

8. **Chat online with Muslims from your adopted area.** Use the Camel Method as a format for discussion.

9. **Place a message or ad in newspapers that cover your adopted area.** Many newspapers can be found on the Internet. For Christmas and Easter seasons, explain the true meaning of these holidays. Wish Muslims a meaningful *Korbani Eid* and direct them to e-mail you about the true meaning and origin of the sacrificial system. Place an ad asking for pen pals or e-mail pen pals (e-pals). Make payment to the newspaper by wire transfer or money order.

10. **Write editorials in your adopted area newspapers promoting the greatness of Christ as discovered in *surah al-Imran* 3:42-55.** Use the Internet to research and contact newspapers from your adopted area.

11. **Find a pen pal from your adopted area through the Internet.** Write them and share your testimony.

12. **Organize a fundraiser for the purchase of Bibles and other evangelistic resources for your adopted area.** Set your goal to purchase one Bible for every village. The goal for individual cities should be no less than one hundred.

13. **Locate Muslims from your adopted area in your own country or community.** Research local universities. Invite international Muslim students to your home for Thanksgiving or Christmas dinner.

Kevin Greeson

14. **Ask a university in your adopted area if they have any students coming to your country for higher education.** Tell them that you would like to contact these students through e-mail or by phone. Even though the students may not live in your city, you can be an encouragement to them by phone. Help these students prepare for life in your country. Tell them that it would be good for them to understand Christianity since they will be living among Christians.

15. **Contact the English Department at a university in your adopted area.** Ask if any students want to practice their English writing. If so, then they can become your e-mail pen pal.

16. **Contact a businessman in your adopted area that has a similar business as yours.** Look in the Yellow Pages of your adopted area for businesses similar to yours. Start your relationship by talking on the phone about business related matters, then move into telling your testimony. Share the Gospel using the Camel Method.

17. **Pray for Muslims in your adopted area to be visited by Jesus in their dreams.** Start a *Dream Team* in your church that prays specifically for Muslims in your adopted area to experience Isa dreams.

18. **Equip your church's prayer ministry with news, pictures and specific requests related to your adopted area.** Read online English newspapers that cover your adopted area. Print and post in the prayer room articles about Muslims who are suffering or under bondage in your adopted area. Print pictures of strongholds.

Church-Planting Movement Strategy

Now that you are off to a good start, you are ready to lead your team in a church-planting movement strategy. Your strategy will have two parts. Part one is "Finding Where God Is at Work". This could also be called "Finding the Person of Peace". The second part is entitled, "Joining God at Work".

Your goal is not to start the church-planting movement; your goal is to find the people in your adopted area who will start the church-planting movements. This is why your adoption can be completed within two years. If church-planting movements are to emerge after you exit, it will all depend on you finding persons of peace and discipling them to become leaders of the movements. Use your first adoption as a learning experience. Capture what you learn and then apply those lessons to succeeding adoptions.

Part One: Finding Where God is at Work

Step One: Choosing Your Muslim People Group

Spend time researching and praying for several pockets of unreached and unevangelized Muslim people groups. When choosing a Muslim people group for adoption, it may be helpful to know that you will find God at work among the hardest to reach and most neglected fields. Beware of simply choosing a Muslim people group because your church as a relationship with a missionary living there. You are adopting a Muslim people group, not a missionary. To avoid getting bogged down in the selection process, leave the choice to either an individual or a small group in the church. Take into consideration if you have a particular Muslim people group that has migrated into your city.

Finally, consider choosing a Muslim people group that has either an existing church-planting movement or an emerging church-planting movement or is a people group located near a Muslim or non-Muslim church-planting movement. You will want to adopt a segment of this Muslim people group that is beyond the effects of the church-planting movement. Tapping into resources found in the nearby church-planting movement will serve your efforts well.

Step Two: Prepare a Profile

Use the Internet and other sources to build a profile of your adopted people group. Several mission agencies have already developed profiles on most Muslim people groups.

Kevin Greeson

Step Three: Organize a Caleb Team

Organize a team to travel to the mission field. Let's call this team the Caleb Team. They will serve in similar fashion to Joshua and Caleb the scouts that Moses sent into the Promised Land. Since many Christians already regard Muslim people groups as intimidating giants, a positive report from your Caleb Team is important.

The Caleb Team's work is critical. Based on their findings, the adoption team will be able to build a strategy. The more vague the information brought back from the Caleb Team, the more difficult it will be in building an aggressive strategy. Specific information better ensures that the goals of the adoption will be completed within the two year time period.

The team will need at least eight days on the ground. If the adoption area is determined before the team travels to the field, less time may be needed. Some information the team is looking for may be found through other sources like the Internet or from a nearby missionary. It is possible that the Caleb Team will need to make more than one trip to the adopted area to gain the information needed for an effective strategy.

Step Four: Strategy Preparation

Your plan is aimed at a vision. Your vision should include the following elements: 1) identifying where God is already at work among your adopted people group, 2) saturating your adopted area with prayer and the Gospel, and 3) finding God's person(s) of peace in your adopted area.

Your team should evaluate their progress on a monthly basis, modifying the plan as needed to fulfill the goal of Gospel saturation, finding a person of peace and launching a church-planting movement. At the end of two years, you can decide if you need to extend another year.

Do not be afraid to invite outside help. One church that needed funds for a distribution project in their adopted area called on a sister church to help fund the project. Without this help, the project would not have been possible.

Use the outline below as a guide for building your strategy:

I. Part One: Finding Where God Is At Work Among the (People Group) in (Location)

    A. Caleb Team Journey

    B. Saturation Strategy

    C. Prayer Strategy

    D. Identified Persons of Peace
        1) _____
        2) _____
        3) _____
        4) _____

II. Part Two: Joining God at His Work

The second part of the strategy is committing to God to join Him once you have found where He is at work. This part requires no instructions; it is simply up to you. Remember that if you find a person of peace, you have just found where God is at work. According to Jesus' instructions in Luke 10:7, you are to immediately drop what you are doing and invest your time encouraging and training the person of peace, sharing with him God's vision for multiplying new churches within his community.

Conclusion

Will your church rise to the challenge of reaching Muslims at home and around the world? Can a church function as a missionary, igniting church-planting movements among the world's unreached millions? For centuries, this was inconceivable. Yet today with new breakthroughs in communications, travel and information the world of Christian missions is radically changing. What was impossible only a decade ago is now not only possible, but long overdue. What is impossible for man is possible with God.

If local churches can stimulate new church-planting movements deep in the heart of the Muslim world, it will truly usher in a new era in missions. Soon churches in developed countries will not only support missionaries on the mission field, but they may also become the missionaries.

---

[1] An exciting new WIGTake resource is scheduled for release in early 2007 called *The Camel Workshop*. It will include an interactive workbook, instructional DVD and CD ROM resource kit. The *Camel Suite* is available from www.FreshWindDistributing.com.

[2] It is quite easy for well meaning churches to actually hinder the prospects for a church-planting movement. To help avoid this from occurring, the team leader should consult "Seven Deadly Sins" in Garrison's *Church Planting Movements, How God is Redeeming a Lost World*.

[3] *Church Planting Movements,* pp. 249-255. Injecting foreign funds into an emerging CPM can be harmful. Garrison calls the misuse of foreign money "the devil's candy". Not to totally discount the use of outside funds, he later states, "the lost will not pay for their own evangelization" (p. 267).

Kevin Greeson

Glossary

Al-Imran (al-ihm-RAHN) – The title of the third chapter or *surah* of the Qur'an. Sometimes translated "The Family of Imran" it refers to the family of Moses; in Exodus 6:20 Moses' father is identified as Amram.

Allah (ah-LLAH) – The Arabic name for the one God of creation and history. The name Allah precedes Islam and was found in Arabic Christian inscriptions from the 6th century (a century before Mohammed's birth). The name Allah is also used by Christians and Muslims for God in several other languages from the Hausa of West Africa to the inhabitants of Indonesia.

C1 to C6 – A simple system of classifying levels of contextualization in Muslim evangelism, developed by John Travis, a missionary to Muslims in Indonesia. C1 is the lowest level of contextualization and C6 the highest level. At C1 the Muslim background-believers are using traditional, foreign Christian language and forms of worship. At C6 the Muslim-background believers worship Christ only in secret, continuing to function within their communities as Muslims. The system is explained more fully in the *Evangelical Mission Quarterly*, Vol. 34, no. 4.

Contextualization – Attempting to adapt the style, form and language of the Christian faith and message to the culture of the people one is seeking to reach.

Contextualized Bible – See *Muslim-friendly Bible* below.

Eid (eed) – A recurring Muslim holy day or festival. In addition to the weekly Friday worship, there are two annual *Eids* celebrated by Muslims: the *Eid al-Fitr* [fast breaking] and the *Korbani Eid* (also called the *Eid al-Kabir, Eid al-Bakr* [first born] or *Eid al-Adha* [sacrifice]).

Eid al-Fitr (eed-al-FITR) – Literally *the festival of the breaking of the fast.* This holy day occurs at the end of the month-long fast of Ramadan.

Eid al-Kabir – (eed-al-ka-BEER) Literally *the big feast.* It is another name for the *Korbani Eid* or *Eid al-Adha* (feast of the sacrifice).

Imam (ee-MAHM) – Literally means *the one in front.* The term is used for leaders of the mosque or Islamic community. Many Muslim-background believers also use the term in reference to their Christian pastors.

Injil (ihn-JEEL) – Islamic name for the Gospel or the New Testament in general.

Indigenization – Literally means *generated from within* and refers to the local believers producing their own evangelism, new churches, leaders and theology rather than relying upon the work of foreigners.

Isa (EE-sah) – The Islamic name for Jesus as found in the Qur'an.

Isa al-Masih (EE-sah al-mah-SEE) – Literally *Jesus Christ.* The Islamic name for Jesus Christ as found in the Qur'an.

Kevin Greeson

Isahi (ee-SAH-hee) – Literally *one belonging to Jesus*. This is the self-designation of Muslim-background believers. They often accompany it with the term Muslim (i.e. Isahi Muslim) to mean one who submits to God's will by following Jesus.

Jamaat (juh-MAHT) – Literally *a gathering* or community. It is the term used by Isahi *and* Muslims for their religious communities, be they mosque or church.

Jibril (ji-BREEL) – The Arabic name for the angel Gabriel.

Jihad (ji-HAHD) – Literally *struggle*, the term can refer to Islamic holy war or the struggle to live a pure, God-pleasing life.

Kitab (kih-TAB) – Literally *book*, the term used in the Qur'an for the religious books used by people of the Christian, Jewish or Islamic faiths.

Kitab al-Moqaddis (kih-TAB al-mo-KAH-dihs) – literally *the Holy Book*, it refers to the holy books that preceded the Qur'an. These books are the Old and New Testaments. In Arabic, they are called the *Taurat*, the *Zabur* and the *Injil*.

Korban (kor-BAHN) – Literally *sacrifice*, it refers to the annual Islamic sacrifice offered to Allah for the forgiveness of sins.

L10 Evangelism – From Luke 10; refers to the quest to find a *man or peace* or a *person of peace*.

Man of Peace – Or person of peace, a term introduced by Jesus in Matthew 10:11-13 and Luke 10:5-6. It refers to individuals, men or women, who are preconditioned to be responsive to the Gospel message when it is proclaimed to them.

Madrasa (muh-DRAH-suh) – The Arabic word designating the Islamic schools of religious instruction, primarily for boys.

Maryam (MEH-ree-yam) – The Arabic name for Mary, mother of Jesus.

Masih (mah-SEEH) – The Arabic word for Messiah or Christ.

MBB – A common abbreviation for Muslim-background believer.

Muslim-friendly Bible – A version of the Bible that has been contextualized for Muslim readers by using familiar Arabic names and terms.

Qur'an (kur-AHN) – Literally *Recite!* The Muslim holy book consisting of 114 *surahs* or chapters purportedly received by Mohammed by revelation through the angel *Jibril* (or Gabriel).

Ramadan (rah-mah-DAHN) – The Muslim month of fasting, also pronounced Ramazan or Ramzan.

Taurat (taur-RAHT) – The Qur'anic name for the *Torah* or first five books of the Old Testament.

Zabur (zah-BUUR) – The Qur'anic name for the *Writings* or portions of the Old Testament beyond the first five books.

Kevin Greeson

Additional Resources

Books on Muslim Evangelism

Accad, Fouad Elias. *Building Bridges: Christianity and Islam,* Colorado Springs, Colo.: NavPress, 1997.

Adeney, Miriam. *Daughters of Islam: Building bridges with Muslim women,* Downers Grove, Ill.: InterVarsity Press, 2002.

Ankerberg, John and Weldon, John. *Fast Facts on Islam,* Eugene, OR: Harvest House Publishers, 2001.

Bilquis, Sheikh. *I Dared to Call Him Father,* Grand Rapids: Baker Book House, 2001.

Bramsen, P.D. *The Way of Righteousness: Good News for Muslims,* Spring Lake, NJ: CMML, 1998.

Braswell, George W. *Islam: Its prophet, peoples, politics, and power,* Nashville, Tenn.: Broadman & Holman, 1996.

Braswell, George W. *What You Need to Know About Islam and Muslims,* Nashville, Tenn.: Broadman & Holman Publishers, 2000.

Caner, Emir Fethi and Caner, Ergun Mehmet. *More Than a Prophet: An insider's response to Muslim beliefs about Jesus and Christianity,* Grand Rapids, Mich.: Kregel Publications, 2003.

————. *Out of the Crescent Shadows: Leading Muslim women into the light of Christ,* Birmingham, AL: New Hope Publishers, 2003.

————. *Unveiling Islam: an insider's look at Muslim life and beliefs,* Grand Rapids, MI: Kregel Publications, 2002.

Cate, Mary Ann and Downey, Karol. *From Fear to Faith : Muslim and Christian women,* Pasadena, Calif.: William Carey Library, 2002.

Cooper, Anne and Maxwell, Elsie A. *Ishmael My Brother: A Christian introduction to Islam,* Grand Rapids, Mich.: Monarch Books, 2003.

Cragg, Kenneth. *The Call of the Minaret,* Maryknoll, N.Y.: Orbis, 1985.

Crawford, Trudie. *Lifting the Veil: A handbook for building bridges across the cultural chasm,* Colorado Springs, Colo.: Apples of Gold, 1997.

Elass, Mateen. *Understanding the Koran: A quick Christian guide to the Muslim holy book.* Grand Rapids, Mich.: Zondervan, 2004.

Fleenor, Lester. *God Almighty!: His word for Christians, Jews, and Moslems,* Nappanee, Ind.: Evangel Publishing House, 2005.

Gabriel, Mark A. *Jesus and Muhammad,* Lake Mary, Fla.: Charisma House, 2004.

Kevin Greeson

Garrison, David ed. *Camel Workbook and DVD*, Richmond, VA: WIGTake Resources, 2007.

————. *Church Planting Movements: How God is redeeming a lost world, Midlothian:* WIGTake Resources, 2004.

Geisler, Norman L. and Saleeb, Abdul. *Answering Islam: the crescent in light of the cross,* Grand Rapids, Mich.: Baker Books, 2002.

George, Timothy. *Is the Father of Jesus the God of Muhammad?: Understanding the differences between Christianity and Islam,* Grand Rapids, Mich.: Zondervan, 2002.

Greenlee, David H. ed. *From the Straight Path to the Narrow Way: Journeys of faith,* Waynesboro, GA: Authentic Press, 2006.

Gulshan, Esther. *The Torn Veil,* Grand Rapids: Zondervan, 2001.

Hattaway, Paul. *The Heavenly Man*, London: Monarch Books, 2002.

Hoskins, Edward J. *A Muslim's Heart: What every Christian needs to know to share Christ with Muslims,* Colorado Springs, CO: DawsonMedia, 2003

Livingstone, Greg. *Planting Churches in Muslim Cities: A team approach,* Grand Rapids, Mich.: Baker Book House, 1993.

Love, Fran and Eckheart, Jeleta. *Ministry to Muslim Women: Longing to call them sisters,* Pasadena, Calif.: William Carey Library, 2000.

Love, Rick. *Muslims, Magic and the Kingdom of God: Church planting among folk Muslims,* Pasadena, CA: William Carey Library, 2000.

Madany, Bassam M. *The Bible and Islam : sharing God's word with a Muslim: a basic guide,* Palos Heights, Ill.: The Back to God Hour, 1987.

Muller, Roland. *Tools for Muslim Evangelism,* Belleville, Ont.: Essence Publishing, 2000.

Musk, Bill A. *Kissing Cousins : Christians and Muslims face to face in a world marred by religious conflict, can Christians and Muslims discover more positive views of one another?* Oxford: Monarch Books, 2005.

—————. *The Unseen Face of Islam: Sharing the gospel with ordinary Muslims at street level,* Grand Rapids, Mich.: Monarch Books, 2003.

—————. *Touching the Soul of Islam: Sharing the Gospel in Muslim Cultures,* Grand Rapids, Mich.: Monarch Books, 2004.

Parshall, Phil. *The Cross and the Crescent: Understanding the Muslim heart and mind,* Waynesboro, GA: Authentic Media, 2002.

—————. *The Last Great Frontier: Essays on Muslim evangelism,* Quezon City, Philippines: Open Doors with Brother Andrew, 2000.

Parshall, Phil and Julie. *Lifting the Veil: The world of Muslim women,* Waynesboro, GA : Gabriel Publishing, 2002.

Parshall, Phil. *Muslim Evangelism: Contemporary approaches to contextualization,* Waynesboro, Ga.: Gabriel Publishing, 2003.

—————. *New Paths in Muslim Evangelism: Evangelical approaches to contextualization,* Grand Rapids, Mich: Baker Book House, 1980.

Kevin Greeson

————. *Understanding Muslim Teachings and Traditions: a guide for Christians,* Grand Rapids, Mich.: Baker Books, 2002.

Swartley, Keith E. *Encountering the World of Islam,* Waynesboro, Ga.: Authentic Media, 2005.

Saal, William J. *Reaching Muslims for Christ,* Chicago: Moody Press, 1993.

The Challenge of the Scriptures: the Bible and the Quran, Maryknoll, NY : Orbis Books, 1989.

Woodberry, John Dudley. *Muslims and Christians on the Emmaus Road : Crucial issues in witness among Muslims,* Monrovia, Calif.: MARC, 1989.

Internet Resources

Christian Web Sites for Reaching Muslims:

About Islam http://www.aboutislam.com

Allah Assurance http://www.allahsassurance.com

Al-Injil: Good News For You http://www.injil.org/

Al Nour http://members.aol.com/alnour/

Answering Islam http:// www.answering-islam.org

Beyond the Wall http://btw.imb.org/default.asp

Bible and Quran http://bibleandquran.org/

Biblical Christianity Explained to Muslims http://www.
biblicalchristianity.freeserve.co.uk/muslims/index.htm

IsaalMasih.net http://isaalmasih.net/

Good News for the Crescent World http://www.gnfcw.com/

The Good Way http://the-good-way.com/

Gospel for Muslims http://gospelformuslims.org/

Path of Peace http://path-of-peace.org/

Spotlight on Muslim Misconceptions www.spotlights.org/

The Tandoor http://www.geocities.com/Athens/Academy/8559/

Waters of Life http://waters-of-life.org/

Bible Study Courses for Muslim-background Believers

Al-Kitab
http://www.answering-islam.org/Nehls/Alkitab/index.html

Word of Life http://www.word.org.uk/

Kevin Greeson

Index

A

Abdul 24, 25, 26, 27, 28, 29, 30, 33, 35, 36, 62
Acts 15, 16, 17
Adam 107, 108, 116, 117, 118, 133, 134
Arab 14, 19
Arabic 20

B

B2J. *See* Back to Jerusalem
Back to Jerusalem 49
Bangladesh 152
Baptist 23, 26, 32, 42, 44, 51
Bartimaeus 60
Bilal 26, 27, 28, 29, 30
bridge 12, 17, 19, 20
bridges 17

C

Camel Workbook 30
church-planting movement 23, 42, 49
Church Planting Movement. *See* church-planting movement
clandestine 73
contextualized 124, 128

D

dreams 38, 50, 51

Kevin Greeson

L

M

N

P

R

S

Acknowledgements

To Mukul, my brother
1961-2006

"Don't worry, brother. God is at work, and together we will find where He is at work, and we will join Him," were the words Mukul always gave me. He was there from the very beginning; for thirteen years we worked together, seeing more than two thousand Muslims in Mukul's area of work come to saving faith in Christ.

Six months before the printing of this book, Mukul found God at work among a Muslim Sufi sect estimated at 6 million. Several leaders were baptized and arranged to take Mukul and his message on a journey across the Indian-subcontinent with a mission of sharing Christ to the rest of their Sufi brothers. Mukul died yesterday (October 16, 2006). His last words to me:

> In this moment there are many matter[s] to tell [you] that I can't tell you for my sickness & weakness... but I trust in God 100%. Believe that He save[s] us from all trouble & problem[s]. When I get energy to move then I will go to India.

> Please pray for my healing. I believe that I will meet with you again ...I am very willing to see you.

In His name and Power
Mukul

To Samir, my mentor

"Send these two men to get their largest knives! Then position them on either side of me. If I say anything that is not in the Qur'an, tell these two men to kill me." In fullness of faith, Samir shares to large gatherings of Muslims starting with the Qur'an. He never fails to move beyond the Qur'an to the Gospel. His boldness is contagious, always inspiring, and lifts me to new levels of witnessing to Muslims in places deemed far too dangerous by most missionaries.

To my family who bless me every day

I am also indebted to Henry Blackaby for his significant work, *Experiencing God*, and to Randy, my fellow Camel practitioner. Special thanks to Lee and Leah, Steve and Carla, David, Mike, Duane and Kristy, Loretta and the International Mission Board, SBC.

Kevin Greeson
November 2006

Also from
WIGTake Resources

Bruce Wilkinson called it "The best book on church planting since the book of Acts."

$18.95
$11.40*

An international best-seller.

An interactive workbook and six-session instructional DVD takes you step-by-step into effective use of the Camel Method. Also includes a bonus Resource Kit on CD Rom

$39.95
$24.00*

"History has been waiting for a bridge to the Muslim world. The Camel Method appears to be that bridge."

$18.95
$11.40*

JERRY RANKIN, President
International Mission Board SBC

*40% Bookstore discount for purchase of 20 or more books. Plus shipping costs.

Order now from **www.FreshWindDistributing.com**

Fresh Wind Distributing
P.O. Box 560967
The Colony, Texas 75056

U.S. Toll-free 1 (866) 698-7564
Fax Orders to: 1 (806) 853-8076